Circus Bodies

Circus Bodies: Cultural identity in aerial performance is an extraordinary survey of 140 years of trapeze acts.

Flying trapeze acts transformed performance after 1859 with muscular male and female performers presenting artistically graceful but athletically strenuous flying action. In this pioneering study, Peta Tait investigates socially changing ideas of muscular action in relation to our understanding of gender and body shape. How do spectators see and enjoy aerial action? What cultural identities are presented by bodies in fast, physical aerial movement?

This is an untold cultural history of bodies, explored in a range of films, such as *Trapeze* (1956) and *Wings of Desire* (1987), and live performances, including:

- the first trapeze performers, Léotard and the Hanlon Brothers;
- female celebrities Azella, Sanyeah, black French aerialist Lala, the infamous Leona Dare, and the female human cannonballs;
- twentieth-century gender-benders Barbette and Luisita Leers;
- the extraordinary, record-breaking, high-flying Codonas, Concellos, Gaonas, Vazquez and Pages Troupes;
- imaginative aerial acts in Cirque du Soleil and Circus Oz productions.

'Tait's book brings feminist and performance theory to a popular cultural practice not yet investigated with such critical insight and verve. Tait captures the vitality and excitement of circus performance, while opening up its relationship to wider cultural meanings. A fascinating study of an overlooked form.'

Jill Dolan, *Zachary T. Scott Family Chair in Drama,*
University of Texas at Austin

Peta Tait is Professor of Theatre and Drama at La Trobe University, Australia. She is author of *Performing Emotions: Gender, Bodies, Spaces in Chekhov's Drama and Stanislavski's Theatre* (2002) as well as books on gender identity in Australian theatre, and editor of *Body Show/s* (2000).

Circus Bodies

Cultural identity in aerial
performance

Peta Tait

Routledge
Taylor & Francis Group

LONDON AND NEW YORK

First published 2005 by Routledge
2 Park Square, Milton Park, Abingdon, Oxon, OX14 4RN

Simultaneously published in the USA and Canada by Routledge
270 Madison Ave, New York NY 10016

Routledge is an imprint of the Taylor & Francis Group

Transferred to Digital Printing 2010

Typeset in Baskerville by The Running Head Limited, Cambridge

British Library Cataloguing in Publication Data
A catalogue record for this book is available from the British Library

Library of Congress Cataloging in Publication Data
Tait, Peta, 1953–
Circus bodies : Cultural identity in aerial performance / Peta Tait.
p. cm.
Includes bibliographical references and index.
1. Acrobatics—Social aspects. I. Title.
GV552.T34 2005
796.47—dc22   2004027371

ISBN 0–415–32937–X (hbk)
ISBN 0–415–32938–8 (pbk)

Contents

Illustrations

Acknowledgements

I am greatly appreciative of Steve Gossard's generous assistance and our invaluable exchanges. Thank you to circus historians George Speaight and John Turner in England; William Slout and Hovey Burgess in the USA; and Mark St Leon, Fred Braid and Jim Fogarty in Australia. Ongoing thanks to my theatre studies colleagues: Julie Holledge, Meredith Rogers, Geoffrey Milne and Ian Carruthers, and others who have looked out for relevant articles. Thank you to my aerialist collaborators in The Party Line, and all the aerialists that I have interviewed including the 13 Australian women in 2000. Thanks to the stimulating students in my subject at Melbourne's National Institute of Circus Arts.

I am grateful to the book's readers for their effort and astute suggestions knowing that they are under pressure of their own deadlines: Jane Goodall, Tracy Davis, Ramsay Burt, Philipa Rothfield and Peggy Phelan. Once again I am completely indebted to my longtime reader, Melissa Boyde, for her time and immeasurable support. Thanks to the librarians at the numerous archives listed below, CW's Erin Foley, and the long-suffering La Trobe University (LTU) interlibrary loans staff for their professionalism. A big thank you for research assistance to aerialist Jane Mullett for her thoughtful contribution, aerialist Kathryn Niesche for inspiration and information over the years, Sue Whyte, Stephanie Barnaud in France, Diane Carlyle, Jonathan Marshall, Megg Walstab, Eva Fisch, Annie McGuigan and Maria Brigida de Miranda. I received crucial assistance from LTU Central Grants in 2000 and 2002, and from the Australian Research Council with a Discovery Grant, 2003–5, which made this research possible, and support from the LTU's School of CACE and Faculty of HSS. My sincere thanks to Talia Rogers and her assistants for their support.

Measurement conversion table

(in feet and inches to accord with historical measurements)
1 inch = 2.54 centimetres
12 inches or 1 foot = 0.3048 metres
3 feet = 0.9144 metres

Archive collections and abbreviations

Citation refers to the first viewing of the material

BCML	Braathen Collection, Milner Library storage, Illinois State University, USA
BM	British Museum Newspaper Library, Colindale, London
BP	Bridgeport Public Library, USA
Clipper	*The New York Clipper*
CW	Circus World Museum, Robert Parkinson Library, Baraboo, USA
HC	Hippisley Coxe Collection, Theatre Museum Study Room, London
HFNF	Hal Fisher Collection, National Fairground Archive, University of Sheffield, England
HM	HorsLesMurs Archive, Paris
IL	Islington Library Reference, Local History Collection, London
JJBL	John Johnson Collection, Bodleian Library, Oxford University, England
MANF	Malcolm Airey Collection, National Fairground Archive, University of Sheffield, England
ML	Special Collections, Milner Library, Illinois State University, USA
MM	Mander and Mitchenson Collection, London
ES	Ecole supérieure des arts du cirque, châlons-sur-Marne, France
NF	National Fairground Archive, University of Sheffield
NYPL	Billy Rose Collection incorporating Townsend Walsh Collection, Performing Arts, New York Public Library, USA
NY	New York Historical Society
PAL	Performing Arts Library, Victorian Arts Centre, Melbourne
PC	Pansy Chinery Collection, Theatre Museum and Victoria and Albert Storage, London
TM	Theatre Museum Study Room, London
TS	Toole-Stott Collection, University of California Santa Barbara, USA
UA	K. D. Hartman's Collection, University of Amsterdam library

Circuses

RBBBC Ringling Bros, Barnum and Bailey Circus®, The Greatest Show on
      Earth®
BBC   Barnum and Bailey Circus
BMC   Bertram Mills Circus

Introduction
Aerial bodies

The applause becomes much louder as the petite, muscular Jill Pages turns herself slowly on a trapeze mounted on a passing truck. I am standing among the crowd in the street, sweltering in the summer morning heat, to watch the circus parade.[1] In intriguing mimicry of earlier action, Jill is on the same trapeze that film star Betty Hutton swung on fifty years earlier for the filming of the street parade in Cecil B. DeMille's *The Greatest Show on Earth* (1952). Hutton plays the character of Holly, who is a female aerialist and therefore emblematic of the circus spectacle, but her act is sidelined when a male aerialist is hired. In complete contrast to this story, Jill is a joint founder of one of the outstanding live aerial acts of the late twentieth century. Flying to her catcher and husband, Willie, she established important precedents in difficult mid-air turns that make her the successor to the record-breaking performers throughout aerial history. As this anecdote about Jill's street performance on a film prop preserved as a museum exhibit illustrates, however, public fascination with trapeze action has always been irrevocably bound up with other popular pastimes.

Aerial performance is a physical art created with the body, and although widely performed in theatres, is generally associated with circus. *Circus Bodies: Cultural Identity in Aerial Performance* describes aerial acts after the invention of trapeze in 1859 and explores social ideas of muscular action. What cultural identities are presented by bodies in physical and fast aerial movement?

Audiences everywhere appreciate aerialists. The suspension of a body seems to heighten its aesthetic qualities and beauty. I watch aerial acts, often tensely, with enjoyment and admiration, just like people of all ages and backgrounds in any number of countries. This is an international story: from its nineteenth-century beginnings with the graceful Frenchman, Léotard, leaping between trapeze bars, to the radical feats of his English female imitator, Azella, executing a somersault to a partner's grasp. In the twentieth century, the story spans North America's remarkable husband-and-wife flyers Arthur and Antoinette Concello, the unequalled Mexican family flying troupes and the striking, rapid action of Russian teams in Canada's Cirque du Soleil productions.

This is also an untold cultural history of bodies that encompasses the light gracefulness of males and the steely muscular strength of females. By 1880 female performers were the most highly paid aerialists. The earliest trapeze artists in particular exploded assumptions about innate physical gender difference. A decline in their status during the twentieth century coincided with the growth of feminine chorus spectacles.

My enjoyment of aerial performance of every kind makes me ask why it captivates. What is aerial action? How do spectators see it? Circus skills are physical actions performed to extremes of dexterity, velocity and height, and aerialists perform gymnastic action on and off apparatus suspended in the air. An aerial act is composed of a sequence of prescribed moves called 'tricks', which are linked together with freer choreography, in an interpretative artistic routine set to music that usually lasts about six to ten minutes. Most aerialists perform more than one act, distinguishable by its equipment. Innovation in tricks can often be traced back to a particular era and the invention of apparatus, and, with far less certainty, to individual performers. The aerialists discussed in *Circus Bodies* came to international prominence in the Euro-American history of aerial performance for their accomplished artistry, and/or exceptional mastery of difficult physical skills.

Crucially, then, aerial acts are created by trained, muscular bodies. These deliver a unique aesthetic that blends athleticism and artistic expression. As circus bodies, they are indicative of highly developed cultural behaviour. An aerialist is like an athlete who trains with exercises for upper-body strength, and often for competition. The ways in which spectators watch performers' bodies – broadly, socially, physically and erotically – come to the fore with the wordless performance of an aerial act. In their costumes called 'leotards', after Léotard, aerialists are generally perceived with either a male or female identity, even though all aerialists are muscular, if comparatively small-bodied. Regardless, the social perception of upper-body muscularity is not straightforward, because it is conventionally associated with masculine identity. Yet muscular female performers are equally central to the development of aerial performance.

Trapeze and other aerial acts are cultural inventions that have changed progressively over time. Accordingly, so has their staging in relation to varied political and social contexts that fostered spectacles of empire and colonialism as well as anti-establishment sentiments, and this makes aerial performance worthy of investigation. In circular responsiveness, reviews and publicity each inform the other, and journalism and subsequently cinema reflect social expectations of aerialists while also influencing public opinion. Aerial artistry inspires imaginative responses from artists working in other fields and from philosophers, and although mid-air aerial bodies are frequently described by them as leaving an impression of insubstantiality, the substance of aerial performance comes from intense physical training.

Circus Bodies investigates the performance identities of muscular aerialists and the social interpretation of them over 140 years. While the progression of aerial history has symmetry with the dominant western European and North American cultural histories, the identity of aerial bodies is not always similarly reconcilable. Aerialists deployed nationalistic symbolism but worked internationally. Early trapeze artists were entertainers and also competitive gymnasts, copying each other's feats at a time when athletic prowess acquired increasing importance within manly ideals. While aerial flight was poetically praised as god-like, from the 1870s the disciplined muscular (male) gymnast was understood to be demonstrating scientific progress and even notions of Darwinian evolution. At the same time, male bodies in graceful flight displayed qualities contradicting manliness and muscular females went completely against prevailing social patterns of bodily restraint. In defiance of public criticism, female aerialists trained for all aspects of aerial work up to the 1930s. By the 1950s, however, glittering female assistants working with star male flyers and heavier-bodied male catchers finally succumbed to fashions in cultural identity.

While the earliest flying action seemed to give female performers masculine qualities, by the twentieth century aerial performance had become associated with femininity in popular perception. The reception of performances by an elite of male flyers confirms a broad cultural shift from the nineteenth century's acknowledgement of femininity as a civilizing influence on manhood to anxiety about effeminacy by the mid-twentieth century. Admittedly, throughout this history cross-dressed male aerialists did opportunistically play to audience preferences for females. Most significantly, the developed muscular bodies and physical power of accomplished female aerialists was unprecedented elsewhere in society until the late twentieth century.

Circus Bodies presents a discursive history of representative aerial acts and spectators' commentaries. It brings together the recognized elements of aerial history and considers performers' identities within the cultural context. Chapter 1 describes how nineteenth-century male innovators from 1859, and females after 1868, as solo flyers and in flying troupes, were routinely accorded the attributes of both genders. While males retained an aura of manliness, females were seen as unfeminine. The physical action was termed 'flying', and it was spatially symbolic of birds yet metaphoric of gods. Females were outperforming males by 1880, and Chapter 2 describes the acts of influential leaders: the most (in)famous Leona Dare, black French strongwoman Lala, Lena Jordan doing the first triple somersault caught by a catcher, and aerialists famous for their controversial human-projectile feats. These innovative acts appeared extraordinary because of social beliefs that female bodies were physically inferior. But as this 'unnatural' physical action triumphed, butterfly acts evolved, evoking impressions of floating femininity.

Chapter 3 outlines examples of male cross-dressing and pronounced female muscularity in acts by gender-bending tricksters. It argues that gender identity in the aerial act was, and is, part of the physical action. In the 1920s female impersonator Barbette stripped off her elegant gown to reveal an androgynous look and ended the act with masculine gestures. In contrast, the developed muscularity of acclaimed female endurance aerialist Luisita Leers unsettled spectators with what seemed like a display of muscular drag. Chapter 4 reveals how live and cinematic aerial action became intertwined as attitudes to male aerialists oscillated between esteem for a muscular action hero and suspicions of effeminacy. The twentieth century's competitive gender hierarchy pushes a male elite of flyers to macho extremes and reduces expectations of female flyers to that of decorative presence. In the 1970s a world champion female flyer had to confront the prevailing values whereby only male flyers were expected to master the difficult triple and quadruple somersaults. Circus underwent major changes in the 1980s, and Chapter 5 describes innovations in aerial acts that are integral to theatrically unified, animal-free, new circuses of Archaos, Cirque du Soleil and Circus Oz. Queer identity became part of the aesthetic of this new circus, which by the 1990s was internationally controversial for its reinterpretations of sideshow freakery, anti-establishment politics and sexually explicit performance. But it was the transgressions of circus in cinema that often inspired this new circus to parody society's demarcations of identity based on gender, sexuality, race and disability differences. In a theoretical discussion of spectator thrills, delight and anxiety, Chapter 6 draws on Maurice Merleau-Ponty's concepts of reversible body phenomenology, in proposing that aerial motion is fleshed in ways that encompass cultural identity. Both the live muscular action of aerial bodies and the depiction of aerial action in cinema invite sensory visceral engagements and, although cinema also presents aerialists who display a range of emotions, fleshed live aerial motion can evoke ecstasy.

One book cannot encompass all the wonderful aerialists who inspire and impress audiences in numerous countries. Nor is it possible to cover the histories of the related older skills such as rope-walking, acrobatics, poles and horizontal bars. The premise for the selection of aerial acts in *Circus Bodies* is that the most adventurous, athletically skilled and artistically developed acts from around the world were eventually hired in suitable venues in London, Paris and New York, and by the largest circuses – most employment in theatres and circuses was seasonal on short-term contracts.

The speed of the flyer and the perilous balancing of a soloist inspire amazement, even awe. Accidents are an ever-present threat, but the performance of danger is illusional because spectators rarely perceive the actual risks. The entrepreneurial opportunism, risk-taking, disciplined athleticism and intentional artistry associated with circus are particularly pronounced in aerial history. Aerial performance remains unique as a demonstration of muscular power.

Discursive apparatus

The action of aerial performance was radically reinvented with the advent of trapeze around 1860. Previously, tight and slack, high and low, rope acts had raised everyday actions of walking, balancing, dancing, carrying and wheeling into the air. Undeniably, the progenitors of trapeze acts were somersaulting rope performers often working outdoors and acrobats working on the ground, both of whom go back millennia.[2] Trapeze-like devices were initially used for ground-based calisthenics and possibly to strengthen the trapezius muscles that raise the shoulders. Nineteenth-century flying trapeze acts initially involved the performers leaping between a row of single trapeze bars and ropes, mostly in theatre spaces. Acts in which the performer remained on a trapeze that was either static (fixed) or swinging came to prominence subsequently – and pre-existing apparatus such as a rope swing (cloud swing), and vertical hanging ropes (webs), some with loops for the hand or the foot, were improved and stan-dardized. Today, solo and duo acts on trapeze are ubiquitous in circus, while the inherent difficulty of mastering flying return tricks has made flyers an ath-letic elite.

Aerial acts became synonymous with circus during the twentieth century, in part because of the demise of variety show circuits in theatres. This modern circus, usually termed 'traditional', developed after 1768 in London when Astleys combined equestrian and pantomime shows, eventually in a standard-ized 42-foot ring that allowed a rider to utilize centrifugal and centripetal effects to stand on a fast-moving horse. Philip Astley toured his circus to Paris from 1772, and circus history has long-standing specialist scholarship (see Toole-Stott 1958–71: volumes I–IV (V); Wilmeth 1982), which invariably seeks to authenti-cate circus. Antony Hippisley Coxe succinctly defines traditional circus as 'horsemanship, zoology and gymnastics' (1980: 16), delivering a 'calculated' 'spectacle of actuality' (ibid.: 25). As Eric Hobsbawm (1983) points out, however, the practices that make up a tradition are invented, and as rituals with rules, they produce standards through repetition that become continuous with the past. The repetition of set formats over time has created the institutional form of circus which historians like John Culhane propose is the 'real circus', with horses, clowns, acrobats, animal acts in a ring and accompanied by a band (1990: 11). These days, the ritual produced by this formulaic circus becomes like visiting the past, and the idea that circus is unchanging has been furthered by acts that are family-operated economic groupings and therefore indicative of an earlier type of social organization (Carmeli 1991). While acknowledging circus as a live art form like dance or opera, Helen Stoddart recognizes its distinctive aesthetic centred on 'exceptional human physical achievement' (2000: 4–5).

In analysing the composition of separate acts within a circus programme, Paul Bouissac writes, 'A circus act is the performance of a set of rhetorically ordered "actions"' which like language, can be performative because 'they accomplish what they refer to' (1976b: 107 (Austin)). These actions predomi-nantly communicate as a visual language that encompasses balance and disturbance (ibid.: 116). Stoddart makes the point that the aerial body is a sign for the circus (2000: 7). Although Bouissac's definition is effective, there needs to be further qualification of how a language of action is realized through physical-ity that also communicates cultural identity, sometimes ambiguously. Moreover, an accompanying assumption that language structures meaning should not implicitly validate cognitive comprehension over other disorderly ways of ex-periencing circus.

Circus performance presents artistic and physical displays of skilful action by highly rehearsed bodies that also perform cultural ideas: of identity, spectacle, danger, transgression – in sum, of circus. Circus is performative, making and remaking itself as it happens. Its languages are imaginative, entertaining and inventive, like other art forms, but circus dominated by bodies in action can especially manipulate cultural beliefs about nature, physicality and freedom. At the same time, the overall effect of an act with rapid action may be viscerally thrilling rather than cognitively understood, especially if spectators do not knowingly see the calculated skill that went into creating its athleticism, artistry and cultural identity. Circus, as an institution, and through its separate skills, exemplifies cultural attunement to bodily display, and remains opportunistically responsive to social fashions, political events and shifts in cultural moods.

Circus had become a formative influence on ideas of cultural spectacle by the twentieth century. It excelled at promotion before early cinema did (Goodall 2002: 8; Stoddart 2000: 56) – in particular, the promotion of muscular bodies. Recent analysis of circus's class politics reveals contradictions in its status as working-class entertainment and its legitimization by the attendance of authoritative figures like royalty and presidents (Stoddart 2000: 71–3). A physical geography produced by touring tent circuses, often on the outskirts of towns, created a perception of separateness, but large-scale attendance at performances up until the 1960s reveals centrality within culture (Bouissac 1976a).

Aerial skills can be grouped artistically with the other dynamic circus skills steeped in acrobatic action, and aerial body identity can be considered indicative of human circus bodies more generally. Aerial arts remain distinctive from other circus arts – for example, clowning, tumbling, object manipulation, animal and equestrian – all of which at their best are highly specialized and technical. The fortunes of the American and Australian tent circuses, and both fixed-venue and tenting European circuses, fluctuated during the twentieth century, but circus as an institution has been reinvigorated by the post-1960s circus skills movement which produced animal-free new circuses. Distinctive circus skills have long histories, and they are now taught in professional training institutions from schools to universities and are manifest in community leisure pursuits everywhere, from holiday resorts to women-only circuses, undertaken for enjoyment and self-improvement. At the beginning of the twenty-first century aerial acts continue to gain prominence and popularity both as a leisure activity and as a professional art form.

I am not investigating 'the circus' as an institution, its economics and management or its national differences. Aerialists moved between organizations and countries. Moreover, I reject a conflation of circus performance with its offstage personal worlds, where performance analysis takes second place to journalistic and photographic accounts of lifestyle as subsidiary social performances of marginality. I am intrigued, however, by the importance of circus as a social idea, especially since aerialists became synonymous with circus, and subsequently with notions of desire and longing (Stoddart 2000). As an everyday expression, circus is deployed throughout cultural representation with meanings ranging from excitement and something out of the ordinary to extreme risk-taking or chaos. Social ideas of circus circulate everywhere, even though these days they are all too often severed from ongoing observations of its live performance, once omnipresent. Circus has become a potent idea in the cultural imaginary because of the artistry of its muscular performers.

Physical action is rarely faked, but not so cultural identity. While muscularity could bend gender identity, other aspects of identity were similarly adaptable, especially when acts had generic nationalities. Australian Aboriginal Con Colleano, considered the world's greatest low-wire performer for his feet-to-feet forward somersault, performed in the 1920s and 1930s utilizing this act's precedents of Spanish and Mexican costuming; he even performed for Hitler (St Leon 1993: 176). Artists and managers have always shown considerable creative license with performance identity. At the beginning of the twenty-first century no single nationality predominates in aerial work. Although black aerialists are under-represented, the Afro-American Universalsoul Circus in the USA is currently one of the most exciting experiences of circus.

The performance of cultural identity is part of aerial artistry. Dance theorist Susan Foster outlines the need to expand investigations of how the body is cultivated, 'molded, shaped, transformed' in all physical disciplines and social settings as 'the fabric of culture itself' (1997: 236 (Foucault)). In his analysis of the body in action in martial arts films, Aaron Anderson asserts 'the primacy of motion' over more passive musculature display for interpretation (1998: 2). Physical action can present visualizations of power that triumph over social structures, even class (ibid.: 6 (Connerton)). Moreover, aerial action even cuts across a presumption within gender politics that female bodies have things done to them for beautification and that bodily action brings about male muscles and thus masculine social power. Circus actions are performed by skilful bodies which also perform gender (Butler 1990), national, ethnic and sexual identities, and which replicate but also challenge social power relations.

An aerial performer is not separate from his or her mechanical equipment; a body is a 'body-tool', part of a 'body-machine complex' (Foucault 1979: 153). Michel Foucault discerns how power relations produce, and are produced by, technologies of the body, and that these forces manifest through 'types of knowledge' and create '*discursive* apparatus' (1980: 197, italics in original). Aerial performance became a type of knowledge generating a distinctive discursive history. Performing bodies are culturally marked and manifest a politics of visibility in relation to their (unmarked) viewing (Phelan 1993). Therefore physical action can also be understood to contribute to the politics of visibility and, importantly, to the body as an apparatus of identity. An understanding of bodies communicating with and as sensory entities conditioned and disciplined by ideology (Foucault 1979; Crossley 1994) reveals convergences in perception and viscerality.

Circus Bodies explores cultural paradoxes in perceptions of bodies in leading aerial acts after the invention of trapeze. Performers in this popular performance directly challenged ideas of social power based on difference, and yet remained widely celebrated for their feats. In arousing visceral thrills, the artistic actions of aerial bodies are repeatedly acknowledged as compelling, dazzling and unmatched.

Chapter 1

Graceful manliness, unfeminine maidens and erotic gods

Male aerial gymnasts were doing flying acts by 1860 and several female performers are identifiable by 1868, imitating the flying action of males. As early as 1862, 10-year-old Natalie Foucart on fixed trapeze, with muscles like 'a big boy's', aspired to copy and outdo Léotard, the first flyer (Munby 1972: 122). The aerialists performing on the new trapeze apparatus were quick to explore the greater possibility of appearing to fly by executing strenuous physical leaps, dives and turns between combinations of trapeze bars and hanging ropes from suspended platforms. They embodied long-standing cultural aspirations for flight.

Aerialists in the nineteenth century were attributed physical qualities that mixed up their gender identity. The aerial action of males was praised for manly daring and for graceful lightness and poise, qualities of movement that were more conventionally the preserve of femininity. Similarly, female aerialists were described as beautiful, and as adventurous and courageous, traits considered manly. Male and female aerialists alike were admired for their muscular development.

In becoming airborne and overcoming the existing limits to physical action, aerialists exemplified later nineteenth-century scientific advancement and pronouncements about evolutionary theory. Paradoxically, wingless flying invited poetic responses of wonder and astonishment that elevated it beyond humanness, as if performers were superhuman and god-like. Flying acts evoked ideas of freedom from the constraints of everyday movement, reinforced by the defiance of gravity, of natural laws.

Muscular flying action

Jules Léotard is widely recognized as the inventor of flying trapeze action. His action involved leaving one swinging trapeze and leaping forward to grab hold of a second, and then a third (see Figure 1.1). While a number of male performers quickly copied Léotard's act – some easily surpassing its athletic achievement – no one equalled his legendary status. Not only was Léotard an inventive athlete but, according to the accounts of audience members, he also moved with exceptional grace. It was the lightness and ease of Léotard's muscular action as

Figure 1.1 Léotard poster, courtesy of Dr Alain Frere's private collection.

much as his physical skill, daring and creative inventiveness that contributed to his reputation. Performance on trapeze has parallels with dance because it expresses an artistic sensibility through the quality of a body's movement.

The year 1859 is of major significance in aerial history for two events: Léotard debuted in Paris, and French rope-walker Blondin (Jean François Gravelet) crossed Niagara Falls, both greatly surpassing the existing limits of physical action. Steve Gossard's (1994) research locates trapeze-like apparatus in earlier performance as well as leaps to ropes and between ladders, which confirms an intriguing and unstable history of equipment invention and technique innovation.[1] The basic trapeze had a horizontal wooden (later metal) bar wrapped with fabric, suspended between two hanging, vertical ropes, also covered near the bar. The Siegrist Brothers are credited with introducing the trapeze to North America, although it was the Hanlon-Lees Brothers and their Zampillaerostation (trapezes in a line) that became star attractions in New York in 1861 (McKinven 1998: 15). Trapeze had reached Australia by 1863 with Charles Perry (St Leon 1983: 123). Aerial performance history is one of exceptional athletic feats, and although it is a contested account of who came first, Léotard established the performance precedent for the action of unencumbered leaps and somersaults between trapezes termed 'flying'.

While the term 'Bird-man' was used for traditional rope-dancers, and some were even called *voleur* (flyer) (Russell and Depping 1871: 172), the action of flying unaided through the air away from the apparatus made the trapezist more like a bird in flight than simply elevated up with the birds on a rope. Social ideas were changing and after 1798 the flight of birds, long associated with divinity and the soul, was explained by the action of bird 'muscles' (Hart 1985: 28–9, 56 (Paul-Joseph Barthez)). Hot-air balloons facilitated becoming airborne through mechanical means, but human bodies that flew unaided were irresistible attractions drawing large audiences. As theatre attests, with mechanical apparatus for staging flying traceable back to classical Greece (McKinven 2000: 1), mastery of the air was both an imagined ideal and a practical pursuit. Apparatus for suspending bodies, adapted from Europe's fairgrounds, was used within nineteenth-century ballets, and rope-dancing positions corresponded with ballet positions (Winter 1964: 103, 108). Léotard was developing his aerial skills in France at a time when French ballet, rope-dancing spectacles and 'wordless theatre' were widely emulated (ibid.: 18), and French aviation experiments became central to progress in mechanical flight invention during the 1850s and 1860s (Gibbs-Smith 1985: 31–41). In theatres and circuses after 1860, aerialists on trapeze, often with assumed French names, evoked long-held artistic, cultural and scientific ambitions.

Léotard may have performed in the provinces before his famous debut, on 12 November 1859, with Franconi's at Cirque Napoléon, Paris, later to become the important fixed venue Cirque d'Hiver.[2] His Austrian father, Jean, ran a gymnastic school in Toulouse, and Léotard reportedly practised over the swimming baths into which he could fall if he missed the bar. The conventional account is that he invented the trapeze himself after noticing nearby hanging ropes. But a triangular type of apparatus had been available to men and women for calisthenics from the 1820s; equipment in gymnasiums resembled an aerial rig, and the label 'gymnast' was used interchangeably with 'trapezian'. The presence of Léotard's father on a narrow platform swinging his trapezes towards him, and his mother as his offstage dresser with chalk to dry his hands, confirms that this was certainly a family act, and the likelihood is that he was physically trained from childhood (Hollingshead 1895: 212; Léotard 1860: 24). In 1860 Léotard leapt across 27 feet, at a height of 15 feet.[3] He was 'modest' in his lavender leggings, black velvet shorts and black leather boots, working with 'unerring certainty' while his graceful 'movements were more like those of a bird than of a man' (Hollingshead 1895: 213–14). Like acrobats, Léotard wore knitted leg hose – stockings were a male fashion from the fourteenth to eighteenth centuries. But his unique design of a neck-to-fitted-crotch singlet facilitated easier movement and it also displayed his body to advantage (Léotard 1860: 187–8). Léotard set the precedent for aerial flying, and gave his name to the costume subsequently worn with flesh-coloured tights called 'fleshings', so that legs seemed bare.

Swinging across an auditorium holding (or standing on) a trapeze bar, Léotard let go and executed a single somersault before grabbing a second swinging trapeze bar. Accounts vary and in some venues there was an iron frame and later up to five trapezes (Rendle 1919: 205). Léotard may have let go from the downward swing to maintain his momentum.

Nineteenth-century observers were attentive to muscular appearance. Englishman Arthur Munby writes, 'The man himself, Léotard, was beautiful to look upon; being admirably made and proportioned; muscular arms shoulders and thighs; and calf ankle and foot as elegantly turned as a lady's' (1972: 97). Englishman Thomas Frost confirms the grace of Léotard's action (1881: 153). A muscular small body suited aerial performance, but such observations about the relative proportions of male and female bodies also indicate the scientific propensity to objectify and describe nature and allocate set measurements, as well as the influence of idealized bodies from Graeco-Roman art. A premise of scientific enquiry, however, scarcely masked the underlying erotic allure of some bodies.

Written in the style of diaries of the day, Léotard's memoirs recount his unassailable popularity with women and hint at sexual liaisons, but claim that the male body is more beautiful than the female (1860: 188). He verifies his manliness with claims about his large audience of women from all classes, some of whom fought to get better seats and sent him adoring letters. A newspaper satire suggests some veracity to these claims.[4] Léotard implies that women attend to admire his body as much as his act.

Is it surprising, then, that other aerialists immediately imitated Léotard's physical action even from hearsay, and appropriated his trademark name? Within months his act was reproduced by Richard Beri and James Leach in London, who performed before him at the Alhambra music hall. Victor Julien, 'the only gentlemanly artiste',[5] copied Léotard's single somersault between bars, and there were appearances by Verrecke and Bonnaire (Frost 1881: 153). The risks of the action increased as the tricks became more arduous under pressure to outdo other performers. After the addition of extra trapeze bars, and after one somersault between two bars had been mastered, the somersault was doubled, and the distances between the trapezes increased. From 1868 performers doing double somersaults between bars included Niblo (Thomas Clarke), who probably set the precedent (Speaight 1980: 74). If Niblo's graceful feats as Flying Man surpassed what was imagined for 'human effort',[6] close behind were other performers. Onra was soon advertising a 150-foot leap,[7] and double somersaults (ibid.: 74), and there was also Avolo, whose 'motive power' to spring from one bar to another was mystifying.[8] Dressed as a female, Lulu did three somersaults down to a mattress (see Chapter 3), thereafter bettered by Cleo doing four somersaults to his net, and reassuring the audience that 'all idea of danger is banished'.[9] Despite this proliferation of acts, by the 1870s aerial gymnasts in England were probably less than a third of the 120 to 150 acrobats and gymnasts listed annually in *The Era Almanac*.

Aerial performance suited a growing public penchant for spectacle. The competitive pressures from other aerialists and the need to improve on tricks in order to maintain audience interest were accompanied by competition from exciting new visual technologies. On his return to the Alhambra in 1861 with 'feats hitherto unattempted', Léotard performed in a programme that included a painted scene, a diorama, of political events in England's colony, India.[10] Circus was becoming known for spectacles of nationalities, albeit with creative license, and Frost notes that Andrew Ducrow staged his first 'gorgeous Eastern Spectacle' in 1830 at Astleys (1881: 61). Helen Stoddart recognizes the complicity of circus in representing public events (2000: 86). If the orientalism and imperialism of circus spectacles is unmistakable (ibid.: 102–3; Davis 2002: 199–206), a glorification of violence also became part of their depiction of military engagements. Even though it did not in itself present an imperialist narrative, aerial performance could not be considered innocuous within the sequential programming of a range of acts in variety shows. There was a meta-cultural significance in the juxtaposition of flying acts demonstrating bodily mastery of air space and spectacles presenting expansionist stories of conquered geographical space. Prior to this, the German gymnastic movement promoted patriotic virtue and xenophobia through the development of superior physicality but, as it spread throughout Europe, by the 1880s it would contradictorily also become associated with cultural tolerance (Ueberhorst 1979). A demonstration of the capacity to overcome the known limits of mobility in space existed in an ideological continuum. Aerial performance confirmed a belief that European culture was headed towards an unstoppable domination of the natural world and non-European societies. Abstract aerial performance did not replay political events, but it fitted alongside spectacles that validated nineteenth-century ideas of empire and spatial domination.

When the now-famous Léotard performed his twelve-minute act across the Atlantic in New York on 29 and 30 October 1868, competitive standards within aerial performance meant that he was no longer the leading sensation. His imitators had pre-empted him. Léotard performed after ten in the evening, following a comic pantomime and with six to eight attendants securing the guy ropes for his apparatus. The reviewer writes,

> Grasping two handles attached to long ropes hanging from the dome, he started on his aerial journey swaying through the air backwards and forwards alighting each time on the iron frame as lightly as a bird. This he repeated several times. The next feat was swinging from this frame and catching a second trapeze midway between the frame and the back of the stage . . . and with his head downwards turns a half somersault and catches the second bar – while it is swinging – with his hands, and alights on the frame at the back of the stage.[11]

The reviewer is unimpressed with Léotard's somersault, wanting to be 'electrified' rather than 'simply pleased', and explains that the Russian Pfau performing with the Hanlon-Lees Brothers is just as daring.

What motivated these performers to undertake aerial work and risk injury? Most started performing as children or adolescents, but a few were adults seeking a challenge or seizing an opportunity for work that was often scarce. Frost recounts how two males imitated a trapeze duo in which one dropped head-first down the body of the other, who caught him with his feet, and although they initially earned £5, they became disappointed with the unpredictability of their weekly earning capacity (1881: 255–60). Crowd-pleasing celebrity performers who were well managed, however, earned big incomes. Léotard earned £100 a week in London in 1860, and subsequently earned £30 a night (Hollingshead 1895: 213). An innovative aerial act could earn in a week the equivalent of half a year's pay for an ordinary worker. By the mid-1870s in North American circus, acrobats and gymnasts were paid between $25 and $100 weekly – one refused $125 – and females could receive 'fancy' amounts.[12] One reason that aerialists were condemned in some newspapers was that they were perceived to take risks for money.[13] Although public efforts to ban aerial acts intensified – fuelled by literary depictions of adult cruelty to child acrobats (Steedman 1995: 100–2) – these were not successful even in England.

The appeal of aerial performance was not simply its sensationalism, but also its artistry of abstract movement delivered seemingly effortlessly. This evolved from unsupported leaps through the air to turns and twists metaphoric of playfulness – the performance of exuberance. Perceptions of aerialists as bird-like were compounded by their abstract physicality. The execution of somersaults curled up, ball-like, as well as complex pirouettes and twists, in which the performer turns his or her full-length body, would become the mark of great flyers. By the late nineteenth century flyers sought to master a mid-air triple backward somersault to the hands of a catcher – following the earlier often injurious efforts of ground-based acrobats called 'leapers' or 'vaulters' (Gossard 1990).

Importantly, aerial performance became a muscular contest that repeatedly pushed beyond its existing limits. Performers promoted themselves as muscular athletes: Adair's 'muscular strength is something out of the common order of things'.[14] New inventions and modifications of aerial apparatus extended the capacity to contort in precarious mid-air balances. In 1867 C. S. Burrows was balancing on ladders and chairs on a trapeze.[15] Two performers could balance and do handstands at either end of a ladder horizontally across a suspended platform. Novelty acts developed; for example, the Alfredo family suspended a trapeze under a bicycle on a wire in the 1870s (Slout 1998a: 4). By 1870 American Keyes Washington had a small metal saucer screwed into the centre of the trapeze bar to allow a head balance with the upside-down body inclined (Speaight 1980: 72–3). (In the mid-twentieth century, female aerialists Pinito Del Oro from Spain and Russian Elly Ardelty, with a one-leg stand, were the leading artists of the spectacular trapeze Washington balancing act.)

Aerial performance was popular if not quite respectable, and perhaps it became less acceptable once women began performing in the late 1860s. Charles Russell, translating and enlarging on Guillaume Depping's *Wonders of Bodily Strength and Skill* . . ., dismisses Léotard's trapeze act as short-lived, low-class entertainment that appeared to be 'dying out' (1871: 185). Rope performance, however, was acceptable because of its illustrious heritage and royal patronage on ceremonial occasions. Adherence to the 'cultural developmentalism' of humans advancing from biblical peoples meant that nineteenth-century industrial society was considered a triumph of mental abilities denied to so-called savage peoples (Stocking 1987: 183–5). Earlier cultures, including Greek and Roman, depended on physical strength, and were therefore more primitive. This made nineteenth-century physical displays anomalous within linear creationist ideas of social development. Thus during the 1860s Russell and Depping and others would condemn trapeze performance as primitive and degenerate because it involved physical display. It might be new action but it denoted the past, when 'adoration was paid to physical beauty' and strength and sporting contests happened between nations (Russell 1871: 12).

Prejudices against gymnasts, however, underwent a transformation during the 1870s when socio-cultural evolutionism came more fully under the sway of Darwin's *On the Origin of Species* (1859), with its controversial ideas of natural selection and human descent from apes (Stocking 1987: 147), in combination with Herbert Spencer's ideas of self-improvement and aggression in survival (ibid.: 217). The human body's physical improvement became an unavoidable feature of these new ideas. By the 1880s beliefs about successful physical adaptation within societies and between races had become politicized in the loosely termed social Darwinism (Gay 1993: 39). The reconciliation of ideas of (male) mental and muscular development coincided with increasing numbers of trapeze acts. During the 1870s a male aerialist's effort to competitively perfect his physique had become indicative of scientific principles and was loosely accommodated within notions of social advancement and species progression. In popular perception, gymnasts came to exemplify the promise of human physicality, its future.

Aerial gymnasts were particularly esteemed because their flying action demonstrated the impressive potential of muscular power. The body's muscles were not on display per se as they were with ground-based acrobatic and weightlifting acts, but nor were they remote like the grandeur of adolescent bodies in romanticized, neo-classical paintings and sculpture since the Renaissance. Although aerialists developed upper-body muscle, thick necks and strong muscular legs, they often had a comparatively small stature. Therefore their aerial action displayed a surprising muscular capacity for velocity and force. Early trapezists soared and swooped as if moving with an ease that seemed involuntary, like birds. At the same time they presented trained, disciplined physiques working with precision that promised to fulfil a long-imagined human potential for flight. While their purpose was theatrical, aerialists flew between scientific precepts and poetic accolades.

Dangerous women

The first adult female aerialists on trapeze became celebrities in 1868. Perhaps this is not surprising because flying by male performers was no longer a novelty in itself. Instead of trapeze disappearing, female trapezists became the popular new attractions. No doubt moral condemnation, and newspaper warnings against people with weak nerves attending, helped increase audiences.[16] The promotion of the aerial act as an attraction to managers and to audiences was enhanced if the aerialist could claim to be the first to do a feat, reflecting the cultural celebration of pioneer inventors and explorers. Like most other aerial firsts, claims to be the first woman aerialist are contestable. Aerialists as professionals did not have organized competitions until 1974 (except in Russia), whereas amateur male athletes had records set from the revived Olympics after 1896 and females from the 1920s. Geographical dispersal meant that the initial accomplishment of a new trick could be overlooked.

The prominence of Madame Sanyeah is due not only to challenges to her status as the first woman aerial flyer, but to the existence of two main Sanyeah partners, Ada and Maud(e). The act debuted with a Madame Sanyeah (Ada) working with Samuel Sanyeah in England after 1867, and a Sanyeah duo performed for the next decade in North America. In one early trick, Madame Sanyeah leapt forward to Samuel who was hanging upside down with his knees hooked over a trapeze. Although she was imitating the long leaps of Jean Price in London, who worked from hand-held rings to a trapeze bar (Frost 1881: 163, 180), drawings suggest Madame Sanyeah caught a trapeze bar held by Samuel in an early example of a partnership. He may have caught her body too. In a revealing description arising out of newly industrialized Euro-American society, Samuel was the man of 'Iron Muscle', and she was promoted with the title of the 'Most Daring Woman in the World', and acclaimed for her 100-foot flight and her handsome face and form.[17]

There were aesthetic and practical reasons for working with partners. It turned out to be easier for a flyer to be caught by a catcher making minor adjustments during the flight than it was for a soloist to catch a trapeze bar swinging with a nonadjustable momentum, although the catcher does risk being hurt by the impact of a flyer's body. Additionally, two performers made a more exciting act. Among the significant male duos at that time were the Spanish Rizareli Brothers, Francisco and Domingo, who debuted to a standing-room-only crowd in 1871 at London's Metropolitan, following their New York appearances in 1869. Each performer swung out on a trapeze over a safety net, let go, grabbed a second swinging trapeze before turning back to catch the first and returning to the starting position; then beginning together from opposite ends of the venue, they exchanged trapezes midway.[18] They are widely attributed with the invention of a special board on an aerial platform, which gives the flyer more lift into the air.

Observers responded to the novelty of the Sanyeah partnership with a female performer in notably visceral language, as if accounting for a physical shock. The Sanyeahs' feats are 'so daring and so apparently dangerous as to be really unpleasant to those of a more sensitive nature . . . beyond all computation of human strength as to be truly marvellous', causing 'a suspension of breath and a painful sensation on the part of the beholders'.[19] Samuel, 'although small in stature, has a development of muscle few men can attain', and Madame Sanyeah's actions are done to 'chill one's blood with fears for her safety, as calmly and self-possessed as if being rocked to sleep'.[20] Her nonchalance would have been important to the act's impressive theatricality.

As Kerry Powell has pointed out about attitudes to nineteenth-century actresses, they were received by critics with a rhetoric of both admiration and anxiety which, while socially controlling, also allowed female performers to exceed 'the limits of what was thought proper to woman's nature' (1997: 13). Powell notes that the dislike of qualities in women that were appreciated in men produced comparisons with animals and monstrous behaviour. The mix of admiration and disgust towards very good performances was described through bodily reactions like those of a shock or an assault (ibid.: 16–17). While it was almost a convention to describe exaggerated bodily reactions in the reception of nineteenth-century performance, reports about female trapezists were graphically visceral.

In rivalry that caused the Sanyeahs to assert Madame Sanyeah's status as the first woman to do leaps,[21] English performer Zuleila (also Zullela) claimed that she was the first female to work with a partner and do the leap for life from a rope or a trapeze, although this is unlikely. Instead Zuleila appears to have broken the record for the distance covered across the length of a New York theatre auditorium.[22] Zuleila leapt from the upper circle to the back of the stage in a transept flight, or a 'Niagara leap' as it was called in North America, 'causing a thrill of terror among the audience', who wondered how a female could do this feat.[23] Like the Sanyeahs, Zuleila flew to catch a trapeze or her partner, Ventini. In 1869 Rose Lucelle was also performing a leap in an act that included an iron jaw trick held by M. Coutellier, who had a 'wonderful amount of muscle', and was programmed alongside the adolescent Albert Gregory turning a somersault between his brothers with Arthur throwing him to Jean's catch, leaving the audience 'screaming' enthusiastically.[24] Zuleila is praised for obedience and for replacing an ill Zoe in the adolescent De Lave Sisters' act.[25] The latter surpassed the Rizareli Brothers' somersault to a rope, because Lila travelled twice the distance and turned a somersault first to a bar and then to grab hold of Zuleila's body. Although the gender identities of the De Laves are questionable (see Chapter 3), increasing numbers of female aerialists were doing the same tricks as male aerialists and setting new records.

The confusion over who was the first female flyer increased because of a public dispute between the Sanyeahs.[26] A Madame Sanyeah left Yankee Robinson's circus around July 1869, but there was a Madame Sanyeah performing there in late August.[27] Samuel was advertising by mid-October 1870 against his first partner, Ada (Mrs George Holland), who billed herself solo as the original Madame Sanyeah who debuted with the leap.[28] Samuel writes, in dispute with Ada, that a number of men and half a dozen women could do the Sanyeah leap, and '[s]he forgets that we copied it from "Perrier," the Spanish lady' performing in Manchester in December 1867.[29] Although Samuel performed with Geraldine (possibly a Leopold) in competition with another duo in March, and then by himself (Odell 1936–8: volume VIII, 674), his aerial partnership with Maude existed from late 1870 through to 1873 (see Figure 1.2). By 1876–7 they were attracting notice with an acrobatic balance act on four revolving globes (Odell 1936–8: volume X). Recognition for the Sanyeah act might be shared between Ada and Maude even if they could not share the title of female first. It was probably Ada who was first 'clad in maidenly innocence breeched with the American flag, and strong alike in modesty and muscle', and described as so irresistible that even the gods should see her.[30] In co-opting the symbol of American patriotic virtue perhaps the Sanyeahs hoped to allay the blatant gender irregularity of female muscularity.

In London, Frost accords Mademoiselle Azella with the title of the first female trapezist (1881: 179), and by the mid-1870s she had certainly become one of the very first performers somersaulting to a catcher and, crucially, one of the first performers flying out to a catcher and then returning to her starting point. Azella first appeared on 15 February 1868 with Hengler's Circus, imitating the action of males, and was called 'the female Léotard' (Turner 1995–2000: volume I, 8). Her solo act initially involved a flight across the 100-foot arena and a single somersault down 30 feet to a mattress. When Azella appeared at the Holborn Amphitheatre, extra seating had to be provided for the predominantly male crowd; one reviewer writes that she 'excited much astonishment; but we are doubtful if such an exhibition can be in good taste'.[31] Until inventors made seating improvements in the 1870s, audience seating was far more comfortable in the theatre than in the circus tent, where feet did not reach the ground and shoes accidentally soiled other people's clothing.[32]

Figure 1.2 Madame Sanyeah (possibly Maude), courtesy of the Mitchell Library, State Library of NSW.

Interestingly, Frost writes as if the audience expected Azella to equal the gymnastic feats of males and was disappointed because she did a somersault to the ground. He writes that this feat 'caused some disappointment to those who have witnessed the performances of those renowned gymnasts at the Alhambra' (1881: 179–80). Once an aerial trick was mastered there were expectations, and therefore competitive pressures, for other performers to achieve the same level of skill regardless of gender.

Munby describes '"the wondrous Azella" in pink tights, leaping from bar to bar like a man' (1972: 252), although Frost confirms that a female should adhere to society's precepts of attractiveness. He writes about the famous French rope-walker, Madame Saqui, who was appearing in London in 1816: 'her masculine cast of countenance and development of muscle giving her the appearance of a little man, rather than of the attractive young woman' (1881: 53). About Azella he writes, 'The grace with which all her evolutions were performed combined, however, with the beauty of the person and the novelty of seeing such feats performed by a woman, to secure her an enthusiastic reception whenever she appeared' (ibid.: 180). Azella's muscularity may not have been fully developed when she first started performing.

Such references to beauty were no doubt also covertly praising the exposure of a female body shape in a closely fitting costume. The contrast between acrobatic or aerial costuming, and women's fashions in full-length dresses, could not have been greater. The bustle, popular after 1870, protruded backwards supported by a hoop of whalebone, and encased the body and limited mobility. Aerial costumes were bloomer suits with gathered fabric and/or elastic to allow expansion with movement, and were completely unlike underwear, which was still worn in loose layers. Costumes were unbelievably short for the time, either flared or contoured at the top of the thighs, and often had frills and ribbons. In studio photographs, costumes can be pulled in around the chest like corsets, and/or bound in at the waistline, but this varies and costumes may not have been worn tightly during performance. Some photographs of performers like Azella depict looser costumes (Munby 1972: plate 22; Thétard 1947: volume II, 136), and paintings with very corseted figures (Garb 1998: 93) seem idealized. Certainly, the legs were visible in woollen tights and short soft leather boots, and cotton and the more expensive raw silk threads meant that by the late 1870s performers had considerable choice of fabrics and colour.[33]

Aerial acts can be grouped with other titillating entertainments such as ballet and burlesque. Popular burlesque shows from the 1850s to the 1870s with singing and dancing involved females in revealing leg tights, cross-dressed as fairy kings or noblemen. England's Lydia Thompson and the troupe known as the Blondes took burlesque to New York in 1868 and created a sensation (Allen 1991; Gänzl 2002). By that time there were also variety acts in major cities that simulated nudity. Women in body-fitting fleshings, sometimes wearing short tunics, posed as classical sculptures called 'living statuary' (*tableaux vivants*). Robert Toll cites a New York advertisement for a woman of 'faultless form' dressed as a nude sculpture in 1848 (1976: 210), and the English regulated against these acts in 1849 (Banner 1983: 120). By comparison, the sexual allure of aerial acts may have been substantially enhanced by the novelty of the action. This was suggested in the early 1860s by the energetic horse-riding act of the controversial American poet performer Adah Isaacs Menken as the mythic male hero 'Mazeppa', and in posters she was costumed naked in flesh-coloured hose complete with a moustache (Mankowitz 1982: 129–30; Barnes-McLain 1998).[34]

Female aerialists might have been admired for their shapely dimensions like burlesque performers, but the appeal of the act also came from its athleticism. Visible from all angles to those watching below, female aerialists attracted attention and caused consternation with muscular action that could also be very fast. Although imitating male flying, female aerialists were perceived to be at greater risk. Observers seemed to conflate the dangers of physical risk-taking with those of a seductive sexual identity that was considered socially dangerous. The female aerialist performed an idea of heightened danger.

In England, as elsewhere, attitudes to female aerialists ranged from admiration to conservative moralizing that manifested in ongoing campaigns to prevent child and adolescent gymnasts performing. These campaigns also expressed concerns about safety; Azella had missed her trapeze turning a somersault in early April 1868, falling onto the platform, and was replaced by Mlle Pereia (Pereira) and the Spanish troupe.[35] (Could Pereia be Samuel Sanyeah's Perrier?) Pereia's flight was 'not to be surpassed for elegance and agility' and was 'recklessly daring'.[36] She was one of an estimated 16 female acrobats in London, although how many were aerialists is unclear (Munby 1972: 252–3). Munby describes Pereia's 'undressed' solo act on static trapeze as 'unfeminine feats done in a simple maidenly fashion: hanging head downwards, and by one leg' (ibid.). The immodest muscular action made the female body seem unfeminine, as did its recklessness. It is therefore not surprising to find that in 1870 London's licensing magistrates refused to grant a spirit license to the proprietors of the Pavilion music hall until they promised to exclude female acrobats, a policy that received incredulous comments.[37]

Despite magistrates and social campaigns, Azella was still appearing at the Holborn Amphitheatre in 1873, as their 'greatest card', doing 'astonishing feats' and working with Mademoiselle Rosita.[38] By then Azella had her own imitators (Munby 1972: 255). She was working in a trio with a leading male aerialist, Gonza, by 1877 and somersaulting to him as the catcher hanging from foot stirrups.[39] Gossard's research into the origins of the flying return act finds that as one of its pioneers, Azella left Gonza's grasp and returned across the space to the swinging trapeze and then to her starting point, executing a flying return (1994: 114). There were also double somersaults to a catcher in this act. The return action would subsequently become the basis of all flying trapeze routines.

Females in aerial work were exposed to sexual inferences and no doubt middle-class men's perceptions were that performers were of a lower class, and that they were not only sexually available but were also temptresses (Dijkstra

1986: 356–8). Munby's description of Lolo de Glorion's performance provides rare detail of the full repertoire of an act's aerial positioning, which is still in use a hundred years later (Speaight 1980: 75). To Munby, Lolo's sexually objectified body seemed undressed working pressed against the two males, the Glorion Brothers, in public (Davis 1991: 123; Day 1992: 146–7). Dressed like the men, Lolo did not look or move like a woman to Munby, especially upside down, and yet he reveals embodied sexualized but protective responses. He has to stop himself from rushing forward to save her, and he seems uneasy about female perspiration and body heat. Munby responds habitually to a female body regardless of the way that he sees it as masculinized by its action. He does not doubt that Lolo, being female, must be feeling vulnerable and scared – there is no comparable comment about the male performers. Munby is unable to see Lolo as the confident athlete he describes as casually brushing down her costume:

> Her arms were all bare; her legs, cased in fleshings, were as good as bare, up to the hip; the only sign of woman about her was that she had a rose in her bosom, and another in her short curly hair.
>
> (Munby 1972: 286)

By implication, the social category of Woman was manifest through clothing. Lolo elevated herself to a trapeze, 20 feet above, by pulling her body up in a neck hold on a rope threaded through a pulley. The brothers and Lolo sat, side by side, on the trapeze bar, before doing a series of hanging movements. Munby writes that Lolo slides down the body of a male, head first:

> catching her feet under his armpits, and coming up again by grasping his body between her knees and his leg with her hands, whilst she brought her head and shoulders up by a strong muscular effort; and lastly, balancing herself on the small of her back upon the trapéze, till at a given signal the two men, who were hanging head downward on either side of her, each seized one of her ankles, and pulling her so by main force from her perch, flung her bodily forward and downward, and so held her upside down in the air, her limbs all sprawling apart.
>
> (ibid.)

Next Lolo climbs up above the crowd to do the leap for life, 80 feet across the auditorium, breaking through two paper-covered hoops, to be caught by a male partner unable to see her. The ending, 'grasping his body, her face against his breast', seemed to mimic the sex act, and had she not been a professional aerialist, 'every man present would have rushed to rescue or assist her' (ibid.: 287). Munby's embodied reactions arise from a male physicality conditioned to respond to female physicality in set ways, and specifically to perceived helplessness, and these are attributed to the spectators around him. Not surprisingly, the Glorions' act was very successful, and was in New York in 1874, and on tour in Australia as 'the greatest sensation of the age' in 1877.[40]

How did female spectators perceive aerialists? Although the cost of attendance would have been an inhibiting factor as working women earned less than men, women of all classes attended theatre matinées and, accompanied by males, also went to night-time performances. There was 'little distinction' between London audiences attending conventional theatre and music hall for variety shows (Davis and Emeljanow 2001: 211). Variety and shows in which aerial acts appeared had a lower status than dramatic theatre but provided daytime entertainments at crowded venues like the Crystal Palace and the Royal Aquarium in the 1870s, with easily 6,000 spectators on a holiday. Tony Pastor's Hall, a major venue in New York, instigated afternoon and evening performances for women as early as the 1860s and 1870s to change its image from saloon bar to variety venue (Peiss 1986: 142). Alison Kibler writes that while North America's legitimate theatre audiences were divided by 'class, ethnicity, race, and gender', variety audiences spanned these categories (1999: 5).

Women's watching habits are difficult to substantiate. In the context of 1890s English circus, and admiring of males himself, John O'Shea reiterates Léotard's claims, saying that women watch male bodies. O'Shea writes,

> Even among the fair sex I fear there is more admiration for a man who is a splendid animal than for a weak-eyed puny poet how sweetly soever he may sing . . . I could look for hours at the supple exercises of a well-graced athlete . . . the well-developed calves of his legs are things of beauty. That foible is shared by hundreds of thousands.
>
> (1892: 281)

O'Shea assumes that women, in line with convoluted social Darwinism, were ruled by evolutionary instincts, and could not help but look at the most well-developed male bodies. The foreground of James Tissot's painting *The Sporting Ladies* (1883–5) (Speaight 1980: 160) has two female spectators and other women in the background crowd, and above them are two male aerialists sitting on trapeze bars in an overtly sexualized manner, with muscular chests and spread thighs. As O'Shea indicates, men freely expressed admiration for other male bodies, which may or may not have had homoerotic significance; the lack of comparable comments from women reflects public culture's silencing of female inclinations and desire.

The impact of young women's romantic tastes on North American theatre from the 1870s becomes more evident in the era of the 'notorious matinee girls' who mobbed male performers (Studlar 1996: 7, 103–7). They had an impact on theatre everywhere including Australia (Kelly 1996: 117). Yet Elaine Aston argues that women in English audiences followed male impersonators because they presented a mythic ideal of male beauty (1988: 255), and it seems likely that the graceful muscularity of male aerialists had a similar appeal. Some

women attending American vaudeville were rowdy like men in their appreciation of muscular males, although male managers expected women to enforce
social propriety, and associated women's tastes with those of children (Kibler
1999: 46, 51). Women were invariably stereotyped as more impressionable,
gasping at aerial acts (Moffett 1901b: 257).

If women spectators admired demonstrations of physicality, by the mid-1870s
young women were copying acts by other women aerialists. Female trapeze
artists doing new tricks multiplied rapidly after 1868. In New York, Millie
Turnour (Tournour) balanced on a swinging trapeze without holding the side
ropes 'with perfect freedom and [she] goes through many daring feats that
are seldom attempted by the most daring male gymnasts'.[41] A Señorita Sagrino,
advertised as a Cuban circus performer, was also drawn in this balancing act.[42]
Turnour's appearance was as tempting as Eve in the Garden of Eden: 'Mlle
Tournaire-turn-in-the-air, we presume . . . will make the spectator's blood run
cold'.[43] She had a long career working in a range of aerial acts in circuses,
including Ringling Brothers, until 1904 (Slout 1998a: 307).

Female partnerships improved the respectability of aerial acts by removing
the suggestive male–female body contact, although performers billed in sister or
brother acts were not necessarily related. The Lawrence Sisters, Hattie and
Jennie, were one early female duo to do leaps between ropes and bars, working
in America and then Europe; Jennie also worked solo like Maggie Clare, the
Venus of the Flying Rings, managed by entrepreneur P. T. Barnum.[44]

The increasing centrality of women to aerial performance after 1868 is a fascinating social phenomenon. Performances executed by males and females on a
single trapeze without leaps or dives increased during the 1870s, possibly to
offset the controversy about the safety risks of flying between bars, but equally
because performers remaining on a trapeze could work in a bigger range of
venues. Solo acts would evolve into a generic act for females in the twentieth
century. The first part comprised ballet-like poses, twists and stretches holding
and hanging from a static trapeze with hands, feet or knees, and the second
part involved swinging out on the trapeze and releasing backwards or forwards
from a sitting or standing position, and catching the bar. Despite the comparative physical restraint of acts on single trapeze compared to flying acts, female
performers in solo and duo acts continued to far exceed expectations of female
physicality.

Aerial performance arose in European, North American and Australian societies that vigorously enforced the rules of gender separation for dress codes,
social behaviour and comparative mobility. Aerialists contravened these rules
and accompanying beliefs that females were naturally weaker and dependent on
males. It becomes evident that with females imitating the flying action of males,
gender nonconformity prevailed in aerial performance.

A gothic science

The Hanlon-Lees Brothers became well recognized for their scientific approach to aerial work, but they became notorious for comic pantomimes about macabre deaths. Flight in aerial acts required a performer to fall, and a performing body leaping between trapeze bars could appear to be moving out of control despite advertised claims of safety. Léotard had to demonstrate that he could fall off his trapeze onto mattresses and stand up unscathed before Franconi's would hire him (Hollingshead 1895: 212). Leaping and diving actions no doubt induced psychic fears of maimed if not fatally injured bodies, in accord with what Freud (1986) outlines in his 1919 essay 'The Uncanny', as a darkly disturbing psychic underside to what is outwardly cheerful and reassuring. The Hanlon-Lees were among the first groups to use safety lines and nets (Hanlon-Lees 1879: 71) but, despite their careful efforts, William fell in 1860, and Thomas in 1865, and pain possibly led Thomas to commit suicide three years later. Nevertheless the group went on making successful comedy about disturbing fears. Circuses and theatres routinely mounted fantasy and dream-like pantomimes with dance and acrobatics, but it was the brilliantly inventive Hanlon-Lees who conceived of combining nightmarish scenarios and comic pantomimes, initially alongside their aerial work. After 1872 they substituted ground-based acrobatics for aerial routines.

Even though acrobatic contortionists like Eugenie Petrescue and the Rowe Brothers were praised as 'science contributing to art' (Stokes 1989: 86–7), such acts were also condemned by others as vulgar entertainment. Contortion-posing in particular could make the body seem bizarre with positions that induced fascination and fear. Hugues Le Roux describes English acrobat J. H. Walter, Serpent-man, 'in an alarming pose, which recalls the monstrous gargoyles of Gothic sculpture; for the acrobat drops his feet, knots them under his head, and in this attitude, with starting eyes, and rigid, open lips, he resembles a skull supported by cross-bones' (1890: 250). Le Roux questions Walter about the attentions of women, and he replies, 'the chastity which monks do not always observe is forced upon an artist of my class' (ibid.).

The Hanlon-Lees Brothers' pantomimes, however, did not withstand moral scrutiny. Initially an acrobatic troupe, the brothers became one of the greatest nineteenth-century aerial troupes during the 1860s. Thomas, George, William, Alfred, Edward and (adopted) Frederick came from a theatrical family and debuted as children in athletic competition in Manchester, as performers in London in 1846–7, and as aerialists in New York and at London's Alhambra.[45] Prior to 1858 Thomas worked separately from three younger brothers who toured as far as Australasia with their teacher gymnast, Professor Lees, in the Hanlon-Lees' Risley act – in a Risley act, children work in acrobatic balances and throws from the hands and feet of adults commonly lying on their backs. Thomas joined his brothers in New York after Lees died, and they returned to

England, and subsequently developed an aerial act incorporating suspended horizontal ladders, ropes and then trapezes.

Aerial performance acquired scientific significance between the 1860s and the late 1870s with the Hanlon-Lees among its leading exponents. Newly invented equipment was indicative of how mental application facilitated technological progress that could also encompass the human body. The Hanlon-Lees' flying trapeze act debuted on 12 December 1861 in New York. It was reported as having a full audience of 'highly respectable' males for a display of 'fine physique', and was subsequently recalled in 1881 to have attracted most of the city's gymnasts to 'witness a great trial of muscular power' and to have been a 'scientific' performance since the Hanlon-Lees were known for their careful calculation and training based on constant exercise with light apparatus instead of heavier weightlifting equipment.[46]

By the mid-1860s the Hanlon-Lees were presenting short, comic mimes depicting violence, dismemberment and beheading (Towsen 1976: 178), a reputation enhanced by the import into the USA in 1865 of a decapitation Sphinx trick using mirrors. They collaborated on pantomimes with French juggler Henri Agoust, although eventually he would be in dispute with them (McKinven 1998: 81–7) – the brothers seemed prone to such disputes. Their earliest scenarios of violent death, which apparently also drew on the Hanlon-Lees' dreams included *Pierrot Carpenter*, about a coffin seller; *The Village Barber*, which involves Columbine's lover beheading her parents; and *Pierrot the Terrible*, about two tailors undressing a customer before going to a butcher's shop that has sheep heads which wink and calf tongues that lick, followed by night-time escapades, one of which is in Columbine's bed (Hanlon-Lees 1879; Towsen 1976: 178–81; McKinven 1998).

A macabre sense of humour probably also reflects the tastes of the predominantly male crowds at the English music halls and early American variety theatres, the main venues for the young Hanlon-Lees' aerial act. Prohibited from staging drama, London's music halls evolved out of saloon theatres and clubs, coincidentally with the advent of trapeze performance. The Hanlon-Lees' methodical preparation contrasts with the out-of-control, nightmarish, grotesque physicality of their pantomimes, that had some precedents in French ballet influenced by fairground entertainments (Winter 1964: 41, 46–7). In Paris, after 1872, the Hanlon-Lees concentrated on acrobatic pantomimes to create a new type of night-time show that combined music hall tastes for sexual innuendo with newly invented mechanical devices for theatrical staging, and this gave them considerable success over the next three decades in conventional theatre. The Hanlon-Lees pioneered flying trapeze performance and inventive stage mechanics, and provided an early forerunner to the adults-only 1980s sexualized new circus (see Chapter 5).

The Hanlon name and scientific reputation continued in aerial acts for two decades after the Hanlon-Lees Brothers stopped performing aerial work. Once a family act attracted work and audiences, its durability was assured, with unrelated apprentices often adopting the family name. In the 1860s the troupe acquired several child apprentices, including Patrick Carmody, who became known as Little Bob or Robert Hanlon (Gossard 1994: 61). In New York in 1869 the Hanlon-Lees' equipment included a new rectangular frame consisting of 'two long horizontal bars with cross pieces at and near the ends' from which the catcher caught child flyer Bob as he descended.[47] By 1870 Little Bob was doing a double somersault (McKinven 1998: 29). In the mid-1870s three apprentices would form the Hanlon-Volta Troupe with Volta Brothers (Ted and Taff Sharpe) (Le Roux 1890: 260–3, 273), exchanging hostilities with the Hanlon-Lees in English newspapers. As an adult performer, Bob Hanlon with the Hanlon-Voltas claimed that his regime of eating what he liked but abstaining from alcohol during the day, together with care of the apparatus, made aerial work relatively safe (Low 1895: 735). In apprentice training practices probably initially acquired from the Hanlon-Lees, the Hanlon-Voltas trained with preparatory flip-flaps, handstands and splits, lessons on safety lines and falling, and gradual increases in the height of the trapeze (ibid.: 730–5). The training of acrobats requires different physical outcomes to those of contortionists or 'human snakes', because 'undue slackness in the muscles of the back unfits a man for the performance of many acrobatic feats' (ibid.: 730).

An impression that an aerialist was moving out of control may be most evident in casting techniques whereby a flyer's body is thrown through space to be caught. The Hanlon-Lees with Little Bob probably invented this trick,[48] and young Alfred Silbon was also being cast by the 1870s. Casting is considered less accomplished in the hierarchy of aerial flying, because it requires less muscular control by the flyer even though it requires strength and skill from a caster and a catcher. Casting with somersaults was made famous by the Potters, spectacularly so as the Peerless Potters in the 1930s. The Nelsons, another of the great nineteenth-century English family troupes, had a flying return act which involved casting at London's Aquarium, possibly by 1877 and certainly by 1881.

A small number of aerial acts followed the Hanlon-Lees' example of imaginative grotesqueness instead of the common bird and angel motifs. The Costello Brothers were costumed as demons for an act in which they dropped between higher and lower suspended bars (Gilbert 1968: 51–2). The association of aerial work with winged flying also delivered macabre amalgams of species such as human-fly acts; for example, human fly Aimee walked upside down on footholds on the roof in the 1880s.[49] Most aerial acts, however, stirred romantic sentiments rather than pandering to gothic perversity.

Aerial flying and catching in particular were received by spectators as demonstrating scientific principles and efficiency – circus had long appropriated scientific labelling in its promotion. Performers acknowledged the importance of fractions of a second, also saying that trapeze tricks depend on 'feeling the time they take' (Moffett 1901a: 213). The speed of a flyer in a somersault becomes rapidly greater with height, and is increased by throwing up the knees and slowed down by opening out the body, and the head must be in the right position because the body follows the head.

Flying tricks reflect the physics of weight moving at speed and at angles. As well, there are meteorological considerations because hot weather makes the aerialist perspire and affects the body's action, as does cooler weather. In tent venues, the ropes and apparatus are affected by rain and fog, and by hot air rising off the audience. Applying Foucault's (1979) ideas about the social ordering of bodies, the rigour of aerial training and discipline produced scientific discourse although the performance effect was contradictory. It invited admiration because it appeared effortless, an effect that required considerable practice. Bodily 'feeling' of the timing might seem to be imprecise science, but it was only achieved through the body's machine-like repetition.

Ambidextrous sexing

A nineteenth-century performer was gendered by costume and name, so a popular cross-dressed female burlesque performer who confused gender coding was described as having the 'horrible' attractiveness of an 'alien sex' (Allen 1991: 25 (Howells)). As a scientific display of muscular power, aerial performance was masculine, but this became confused by its bird-like defiance of gravity. Ballet and later nineteenth-century visual art pervasively depicted lightweight feminine bodies rising upwards to represent nature as a universalized and submissive domain (Goodall 2002: 190–3; Dijkstra 1986: 87). In its resonances, aerial performance presented doubly gendered action that could seem forceful and masculine and yet involuntary and feminine, and this fusion would have seemed alien to some. Such an impression was furthered by troupe performances in which female and male bodies were demonstrably interchangeable.

The Siegrist and the Silbon Troupes were headline aerial acts internationally for over 50 years. The rise and prominence of such families reflected the increasing specialization of flying action and the rising prominence of group acts. Leading troupes were loosely arranged family businesses, and children with an aptitude for aerial performance were taught by older, more experienced relatives and/or a manager. Tricks and acts acquired embodied genealogies, and aerial lineages multiplied as individual aerialists married – or quarrelled with their families – and moved between groups, and other non-related performers joined. As the Hanlon-Lees, Siegrist and Silbon families show, difficult skills were and are learnt from accomplished performers; aerial arts are passed on body to body.

A profusion of moving aerial bodies had greater visual impact. By the late 1880s competition between the Hanlon-Voltas, Silbons, Siegrists, Dillons, Rolandos and Eugenes was apparent in London, and between the Fishers and LaVans in the USA.[50] The larger American circuses began programming more than one aerial troupe. A poster from the 1890s advertised the Five Phenomenal Silbons (Walter Silbon's troupe), doing head-first dives from perch to perch, on flying rings, and with double somersaults from the tent's top in 'Great Displays of Muscular Strength'.[51] On the same bill, the Siegrist Troupe was described as doing 'single and double somersaults in mid-air, while rapidly flying from one trapeze bar to another, with heads covered with sacks, and securely blindfolded'. From the 1890s the Silbons and Siegrists worked as separate family acts and together. A review of the combined families' act at London's Aquarium describes dives and catches, and states, 'They are a handsome and well-proportioned group, men and girls alike.'[52]

Theatrical shows of muscular display increased in number and importance as greater social value was accorded muscular training. Social attitudes were somewhat polarized between prudery about covering up vulgar bodily displays and unabashed praise for muscularity. For example, muscle showman Eugen Sandow is described as 'the marvel of muscle . . . every muscle standing like mountains on arms, legs, shoulders and neck' of 'his wonderful body'.[53] After Florenz Ziegfeld became Sandow's manager, his shows focused on displaying his muscular physique in neo-classical poses, an adaptation of living statuary, and he was admired for the even roundness of muscles over his body. Although Sandow rejected his past doing circus acts and competing against other strongmen, the circulation of photographs of his near-naked poses was a key to his theatrical success (Boscagli 1996: 109), as photographs became for Professor Desbonnet and other exponents of the body-development movement (Garb 1998: 56–61). In her exploration of the impact of Sandow in New Zealand after 1902–3, Caroline Daley (2003) provides substantial evidence of how male and female spectators imitated the muscularity that was seen in his live performance, and which was widely promoted in magazines.

Gymnastic exercise was being championed in accordance with nineteenth-century Euro-American beliefs that discerned moral superiority from physical appearance. Middle-class male identity was undergoing a transformation. As Gaylyn Studlar explains, 'For character-builders the physically developed male body in motion was not only a sign of physical perfection but the primary vehicle for the expression of character as a process' (1996: 31). In subscribing to a belief that a body had a finite amount of dynamism, social reformers championed productive physical activity over energy-wasting pursuits. Its proponents, like American Bernarr Macfadden, sought to change society through physically perfecting bodies. While some specialists criticized too much focus on one athletic activity because it produced unbalanced muscularity (Mrozek 1983: 71 (Sargent)), overall, muscular activity exemplified masculine virtue. The physical dynamism of the European body was being championed as reflecting the progress of humanity.

Interestingly, some commentators used the example of both male and female gymnasts to expound theories of a future higher order of physical agility. Responses to playwright and novelist Charles Reade's ideas of 'The Coming Man' also envisaged an ambidextrous body, and one journalist explains that male and female gymnasts, including those on trapeze, demonstrated greater muscular ambidexterity. The journalist writes, 'they are all more either-handed than the world . . . when the male and female athlete puts up the agile, and holds him or her in the air with straightened arms, the outburst of muscle seems equal in both arms'.[54] In this account of the ambidextrous right and left muscularity of the gymnast and aerialist, female bodies are also interchangeable with male bodies. Ambidexterity is extended to gender. Certainly males and females in nineteenth-century and early twentieth-century aerial troupes did demonstrate similar muscular actions working as flyers and catchers. Gender identity was functionally ambidextrous in the act's physicality.

The ambidextrous Silbons and Siegrists would continue working with RBBBC until the 1930s. The Siegrist Brothers, Auguste, François, Andre and Louis were an acrobatic, aerialist and clown group from Germany (Slout 1998a: 276). They performed in many leading European and American venues prior to 1870 on tight-rope and trapeze, in a balancing act on four globes, and doing a flying routine. The family name was maintained by the next generation, Blanche, Louis, William and Toto – who may not have been related – and through marriage, with the Zanfretta Troupe (ibid.). The intergenerational English Silbon family of Cornelius, George, Walter, Alfred, Ida, Minnie, Eddie and Kate were working in the major circuses throughout Europe and North America after 1875 as flyers and catchers (Turner 1995–2000, volume I: 121; Slout 1998a: 277), and subsequently as early performers of double somersaults to catchers. The group and its year-by-year international touring schedule are detailed in Eugenie (Jennie) Silbon's unpublished recollections.[55]

The rival families merged as early as 1892 when Toto Siegrist formed a partnership with Eddie Silbon, who could do a flying return trick. Eddie would later pioneer a double-and-a-half somersault, and established the double cut-away in which a weight-bearer hanging from one trapeze holds a second bar by the cables to which a second aerialist drops. Confusingly, performers who left one troupe created similarly named groups. After 1903 Toto Siegrist and Eddie Silbon's troupe with BBC was renamed the Imperial Viennese Troupe and had nine or ten performers with two catchers, one male and one female, placed centre, back to back, and facing flyers who came towards them from opposite directions of the enlarged rectangular rigging.[56] By 1916 the troupe had a record-breaking 14 performers including the Codonas, and flyers crossed each other mid-air at right angles from a four-cornered rig shaped like a cross.

Contrary to widespread misconceptions, women traditionally worked as catchers in these troupes. The work of females – between a third and a half of the performers – helped make these groups internationally successful. Their inclusion was unquestioned at a time when paid work was allocated according to gender identity. Conveniently, husband-and-wife aerial combinations shared incomes. Eugenie Silbon, who married Eddie, was an aerial catcher, as was Edythe Siegrist, married to Charles, who was considered one of the greatest flyers. Catching a flyer is arduous work. Edythe recalls that she never overcame the pain but 'learnt to endure it', and 'gained the distinction of being the only woman ever to catch an entire act, including heavy men performers' (see Figure 1.3).[57] A number of women were gifted athletes, but others pointed out that they did not start out with muscular strength. Aeleen Siegrist, performing in the 1920s, explains, 'Exercise for women seems to have been lost sight of to a great extent.'[58] Aeleen claims that while she was not strong when she first started exercising with her father, she gradually developed her muscular strength.

The discipline of flying was sustained within, and passed on between, nominal family groupings. Thomas Herbert took over as catcher in Walter Silbon's group in Australia and worked with BBC in the USA and Europe, sometimes to daily crowds of 30,000 until, with his wife, aerialist Kate Silbon, they formed the Great Herbert Trapeze Troupe. Back in Australia in 1905 the Herbert troupe included Australian Steve Outch, who later joined the Codonas, and Englishman Alec Todd, who taught flying to the Wards, a pivotal aerial troupe (Chapter 4). A journalist writes of the Herberts,

> Ariel herself could not have excelled their daring, bird-like flights. They are momentarily achieving the apparently impossible, and doing it with a grace and 'finish' which make it appear easy. Yet it is all a matter of unremitting practice, constant thought, the most scientific accuracy of adjustment in bar and line and trapeze, intense nervous and physical exertion – and heredi- tary tendency and training. For these people represent the artist 'born' as well as bred.[59]

The evidence of eponymous family acts implied that an individual aerialist's mental and physical capacity could be attributed to inheriting improved body development. In actuality, this capacity came from access to methodical training from an early age for those with aptitude, and aerialists were more likely to be 'bred'. Young female performers in particular benefited from a proximity to regimes of physical training, and from the social protection of family troupes that suggested more respectability. In the meantime, ambidextrous flying action promoted the interchangeable muscularity of both males and females.

Cultural paradox

Aerial action was considered flying after 1860 as trapeze acts revolutionized aerial artistry and spatially expanded the resonances of human body identity. While aerial performance generally conveyed masculine attributes of strength and courage, at the same time it was feminized by comparisons with birds; that is, by an association with weightlessness and daintiness. Nevertheless manliness could be confirmed by muscular power even though flying was graceful, and a paradoxical double gendering for male aerialists was further offset by the increasing appreciation of their scientific approach and technological inventive- ness. The double gendering of females was much harder to reconcile with the predominant identity.

Figure 1.3 Edythe Siegrist Troupe, Milner Library.

By the 1880s aerial gymnastics represented progress within human physicality, and were an early example of body technologies in industrial society (Balsamo 1996). But the social implications of females imitating males were accommodated uneasily within scientific and technical frameworks. Paradox in evolutionary ideas became particularly apparent with regard to gender identity. As Rosemary Jann discusses, in relation to the influence of Victorian gender norms and modes of sexual conduct on Darwin's ideas of species continuity, Darwin worked hard to account for female inferiority and yet retain Victorian ideas of female choice over male force in natural selection, and he assumed that women could be strong without being intelligent (1996: 85–7). Where female aerialists were singled out, they were ambivalently accorded alternative cultural associations by promoters and spectators. They remained more commonly framed by poetic, emotive references, and mythic or historic identities, rather than by science's imprimatur within the nineteenth century's progressive present. As George Stocking explains, paradox could be accommodated because the culture perceived itself in transition: 'If paradox is the intellectual side of the coin of cultural ambiguity, ambivalence is its emotional obverse' (1987: 230).

Manliness in European-derived societies had undergone a transition in the nineteenth century, from aristocratic anarchic indulgence and spiritual morality to a more middle-class group-orientated physicality seeking moral improvement through embodied self-restraint (Mangan 1996: 30). Anthony Rotundo identifies an individualism in the USA turning into a manhood obsessed with 'physical aggression, bodily strength, primitive virtues, manly passions' (1993: 253). In England Charles Kingsley had distinguished muscularity from Greek paganism and he became known as the leading figure of 'muscular Christianity'; Thomas Wentworth Higginson became its exponent in the USA. Later Kingsley joined those attempting to reconcile Darwinism and Christianity. The middle-class preoccupation in the 1880s and 1890s with the revitalization of true manhood meant building character and self-control through building muscle. This movement championed gymnastics and sports, and had become particularly influential on the upbringing and education of boys by the late nineteenth century. In US cities the YMCA gradually built gymnasiums, although they often had to hire less religiously inclined, retired circus performers and fighters as instructors (Mrozek 1983: 203). Stocking suggests, however, that the sublimation of aggressive male sexuality within muscular Christianity was more rhetoric than social practice (1987: 200). The adoption of the term 'physical culture' would help remove the Christian imperative and values and secularize the moral value of exercise, and this increasingly assumed racial importance (Bederman 1995: 20). The arguments of the era about a return to a (white) masculine primitive had come about because of its restorative potential to counteract a perceived weakening of the species – this came to mean race – due to female influences and a sedentary life of mental focus within industrial society.

While physical discipline was upheld as a manly virtue, women's nature was essentialized as morally virtuous. The wild and base male appetites and drives needed for the public world and for building the nation state were also under-stood to be civilized under feminine (domestic) moral guardianship (Stocking 1987: 198–9; Mosse 1985: 17). This meant that feminized manliness was some-what more acceptable than masculinized womanliness, which was feared (Gay 1984: 192–3). Women's moral virtue was accordingly reinforced by popular culture, but the fostering of male physical self-control lessened the need for female moral guardianship.

The espousal of masculine identity through muscular display and action made female aerialists anomalous – 'masculinity' was more widely used as a term after 1890 (Bederman 1995: 6). Muscular womanliness had to be framed in ways that acknowledged impressive physiques while avoiding any obvious implication for transforming everyday relationships. Middle-class women who followed exercise regimes were believed to be more attractive to men, and to be improving their health for motherhood, and family life. The recognized social benefits of women's body development were those that emphasized emotional dependency. In line with the social order, female aerialists were also framed within correspondingly more emotive language.

The nineteenth-century aerialist was surrounded by an aura of cultural grandeur – in contradiction to the low social status of performers offstage. Promotional advertising frequently ascribed nineteenth-century celebrity per-formers, inclusive of rope-walkers, the mantle of circus royalty; males were kings and females queens. Identity from the top of the social hierarchy was transferred to bodies physically performing at height in a literal deployment of the symbolic ordering in society. While aerialists on elevated perches are spatially symbolic of birds, flying action also became culturally metaphoric in its elision of actual and symbolic spaces.

The use of classical mythology and generic names like Venus for female per-formers was a long-standing and widespread practice in conventional theatre and ballet. Similar naming made female aerialists in particular seem more mythic than sporting and athletic (see further examples in Chapter 2). Interest-ingly, elevation to a god-like status also served to circumvent an inference of a retrogressive feminine primitivism through overly developed physicality.

In layered artistic exchanges and borrowings, aerial action resonates through culture's visualization of imaginary bodies, of Venus, of angels. Spectators responded with language that included classical allusions and confirmed a Ruskinesque ideal of an aesthetic experience of personal uplift as an end in itself. This emotive evocation in promotion and reception subsumed the materiality of bodies. As Peggy Phelan writes, 'In moving from the grammar of words to the grammar of the body, one moves from the realm of metaphor to the realm of metonymy' (1993: 150). Emotional metonymy was evident in the responses to muscular bodies in aerial action.

The reception of aerial performance reflected both scientific aspirations and exaggerated romantic sensibilities.[60] For example, Kingsley's claim that the soul in flight from its proper body was feminine is reiterated by descriptions in poetry of its torment and ecstasy, and violent tearing from the body (Tucker 1996: 170). The soul's transcendence was a poetic preoccupation so physical acts of transcendence by aerialists also appealed to poetic sensibilities. Aerialists became poetically metonymic of the sublimation of nature as well as of its excessive passions.

Performers on trapeze acquired prestige despite the comparisons with birds (thought brainless). With a couple of exceptions like Munby, writers did not compare performers in trapeze action with monkeys in the same way that they did performers working with rope. In 1862 Blondin, by then world-famous, acted as an ape rescuing a Brazilian plantation owner's child in a pantomime (Blondin 1862: 104–10; Shapiro 1989). Significantly, Blondin's action was reframed as ape-like within the pantomime story. But Blondin performed an unparalleled feat of geographical conquest crossing Niagara Falls, and was so celebrated that England was flooded with Blondin merchandise that included neckties, lace, stationery and confectionery by the time he arrived on 1 May 1861. Léotard had the only comparable souvenir industry for a flyer (Verney 1978: 210). Aerialists embodied a scientific future in demonstrating superior mind and body control, and in the wider context of ethnographic shows they were inadvertently (or otherwise) staged within late nineteenth-century efforts to present the evolutionary chain, including missing links (Goodall 2002: 97).

Aerial flying evoked spiritual ideals of wonder in a mechanistic industrial age (and continues to do so in a technological one), with its implied bird-like naturalness that was seemingly open to chance, an effect that was mysterious. Jane Goodall (2002) finds continuities between dancers, aerialists and more eccentric scientific theories of energy loss and rising vapours. Nineteenth-century ballet productions integrated performers on vertical ropes and suspension devices, to highlight lightness and femininity and to suggest mysticism.[61] Yet aerial muscularity was still distinguished from a dancer's fragile femininity of 'tottering' on points after 1830 (de Marly 1982: 93), even in ballet with its fantastic and ethereal narratives. Suspension required athletic effort. As one female French dancer explains in 1844, to be suspended on wire lines, sit on pasteboard clouds, disappear through traps, ascend chimneys and exit through windows involved physically arduous training and dangers, comparable to the way 'a soldier in war-time accustoms himself to pillage'.[62] Male spectators often preferred newer chorus members over the tautly muscular, experienced dancers (Banner 1983: 60). In contrast to story-based ballets, the trapeze act without scenery remained unfixed in social place. It was a short, self-contained performance with no dramatic context. Its cultural meanings arose in relation to paradoxical ideas of body identity and metaphoric spatial associations with angels and gods. Thus dislocation from a particularized and dramatized context made aerial performance very suited to the romantic imagination seeking to personify abstract ideals.

Artistic depictions of physical performance ranged from imputing demeaning degradation to suggesting uplifting freedom by the late nineteenth century. At one extreme was Goethe's influential fictional child rope-dancer, Mignon, who appeared to his late eighteenth-century character, Wilhelm, as genderless in a strange, dislocated, trapped physicality (Steedman 1995: 23–4). At the other extreme, Naomi Ritter (1989a; 1989b) details how nineteenth-century writers, artists and philosophers like Friedrich Nietzsche, with *Thus Spake Zarathustra* (1884), looked to rope-walkers and vaulters and then to trapezists to represent the human spirit transcending the restrictions of ordinary experience and exemplifying political and spiritual freedoms. Aerialists were used to embody the metaphysical, 'the question of human freedom' and art (Faber 1979: 1). Nietzsche upheld a dualism of spirit and matter and perceived degeneracy as a problem in his age, which needed to be countered by a superhuman exponent of vitalism. For Nietzsche, the tight-rope walker is literally above animals if not yet superhuman, in dynamic ongoing displays of conscious action. The male rope-walker is Apollonian in a higher order of being, but he ultimately falls after his release from the hell of false beliefs (ibid.: 6–7, 23, 25). This is a cultural fantasy of freedom from the mind as well as its attached (body) materiality. In contrast, writer Franz Kafka uses trapezists to mean feminized unconscious action in life, and the mechanical enactment of a 'deceptive illusion of freedom' (ibid.: 62–3, 71). An alignment of metacultural binaries of culture/nature, mind/body and masculine/feminine is replicated within Nietzsche's consciously thought superhuman action and Kafka's free action as unthinking. For both, transcendence is a body in silent mid-air action. Paradoxically, then, these notions of a transcendent spirit arise from muscular power and control. Spatial transcendence as an 'aerial sublime' became a modernist ideal of freedom by distorting and discarding material bodies (Russo 1994: 11).

A body's spatial suspension seemed to facilitate cultural suspension of identity. Ritter proposes that part of the aerialist's appeal was the arousal of 'fantasies of sex change in the male spectator' in the 'double illusion of the spectacle itself and ambivalent sex' (1989a: 177). This suggests an imagined gender substitution, since nineteenth-century androgyny was a male or a female that perversely had the qualities of the other sex; gender indeterminacy denotes twentieth-century androgyny. Muscular flying action was received as symbolic of birds, metaphoric of supernatural fantasy figures, and metonymic within abstract idealism, as it also demonstrated the possibility of ambidextrous gender.

Chapter 2

Unnatural acts, female strongmen

Aerial acts of strength, daring and speed by females were out-performing male acts by 1880, and female identity was central to the impact of these major attractions. Adolescents potentially excel in aerial athleticism as they do in sport, and young female performers in particular were trained to do spectacular performances because they also made the action seem more remarkable to nineteenth-century audiences. Their performance identities utilized descriptive and visual symbols from history and mythology, and of nationality, to garner public affection.

Leading female aerialists set records; their rivals were each other. Leona Dare, Lala, Emma Jutau and the aerialists doing human-projectile tricks were leaders in a performance history forged by specific bodies. It was Lena Jordan who first performed the sought-after mid-air triple backward somersault to the hands of a catcher. Trained female aerialists demonstrated physical mastery and daring on a scale not previously known, and they were seen by tens of thousands of people. During this era, spectators attending daytime and night-time popular entertainments in major cities would have found it difficult to avoid seeing one of these performances.

Such popular acts were esteemed in a category of their own although they invariably also aroused cultural anxieties. Given the wider context, female identity itself became a balancing act. A feat was additionally enhanced to seem marvellous in its contravention of a female performer's aura of softness and docility conveyed with advertising images and promotional rhetoric. The performance of femininity became a precarious domain of duplicity by the 1890s and with the advent of human butterfly acts, but not before female aerialists had widely revealed the full extent of their muscular power.

Arrogant Amazons?

The nineteenth-century music hall song *The Flying Trapeze*, by George Leybourne, describes 'a daring young man' on the trapeze, who could 'fly through the air with the greatest of ease'. The lyrics explain that he was attractive to women, and forms a duo with a female admirer, who then does most of the work and seems like a man:

He taught her gymnastics and dressed her in tights
To help him live at his ease,
And made her assume a masculine name
And now she goes on the trapeze.

(Mander and Mitchenson 1974: 44)

This popular song describes what happened in trapeze history as females copied males and then became more successful. It also reflects popular prejudices that young women trained for such extreme physical acts out of love and/or familial obedience. Whatever the assumptions about performers' offstage motivations, the performances themselves generated female physicality that was fearless, brazen, even outrageous, and which broke social taboos.

The performers discussed here gained widespread attention and, perhaps not surprisingly, stimulated controversy. While censorious judgements detracted from an act's impact, equally important were its enthusiastic defenders. Nonetheless the message about female muscular power may have been offset by assumptions about the offstage control of male managers. Only young Zaeo claimed to supervise the invention of her apparatus (S. R. 1891: 17). Solo acts required teamwork so that male managers, often father-figures or husbands, were influential in their success. Adolescent performers did not generally have the independence to initiate their own work, but instances of independent behaviour by Dare and Zaeo suggest that professional success brought financial rewards, artistic choices and independence.

In 1848 Reverend James Smith succinctly summarizes, 'Woman is the Image of Nature, as man is the image of God; and nature is an objective, as God is a subjective being'.[1] Thus man with God-given agency is able to command, and woman has to be managed. As Carroll Smith-Rosenberg argues, gender difference itself was considered natural and women who contravened its constrictions were 'physiologically "unnatural"' (1985: 245–6). They required rational male authority because they could become uncontrollable. Males were more likely to be attributed full command over their bodily action, and social beliefs about women led to some anxiety about whether female aerialists were in full control of their physicality. Aerial acts theatrically played with, but ultimately questioned, social beliefs in the natural fragility and inferiority of female physicality. In presenting a strong muscular athletic physique, aerialists seemed to defy nature.

Circus presented muscular women in acrobatic and equestrian acts well before the advent of trapeze acts, and weightlifting acts by men and women pre-date eighteenth-century circus. Weightlifting acts came to include gimmicks; for example, small cannons were shoulder-held and fired. The less common, but equally impressive, equivalent strongman acts by females deliberately invoked the precedent of mythic women through costuming and nomenclature. Antony Hippisley Coxe describes how Katie Sandwina (after Sandow) as a 'magnificent flaxen Juno made her appearance in a Roman chariot', for an act in which cars were driven across her body and a granite block was sledge-hammered as she lay on nails; she supported the weight of four men and she caught a cannonball with the back of her neck (1980: 62–3). She was also billed as the Russian ruler, Catherine the Great. Coxe points out that the use of other acrobat bodies in these acts avoided the implication of faking weights; for example, one woman lifted a baby elephant (Frega 2001: 51). The existence of a number of strongwomen, often in acts with their husbands, provided ample evidence that female physicality encompassed a range of body types (Desbonnet 1911).[2] With these performances, nineteenth-century society had indisputable evidence of women's strength potential.

A florid neo-classical stylistic mix typified the aesthetics of popular spectacles. Public taste was indirectly influenced by drawings and museum collections, and later photographs, of recovered Roman and Greek sculpture and art that displayed well-developed, semi-dressed female and male athletes, often with missing limbs, and censored for propriety. This art was legitimized by rhetoric about classical (naked) beauty, and male examples were co-opted within national identity movements; female equivalents were also commonly repre-sented through medieval and other romanticized symbolism especially as personifications of death (Mosse 1985: 15–16, 148). More than one observer may have wished that the strongly built Graeco-Roman female statue bodies were still intact: 'one has only to endeavour, by the aid of imagination, to supply the missing portions of the broken statues in order to become deeply interested in the objects exhibited'.[3] Live entertainment pandered to this nine-teenth-century inclination to view exposed female limbs, scarcely camouflaging its sexual purpose with mythic identity symbolism.

An aerial act was much more than a burlesque limb display by a strong-woman. The lightness of aerial action offset the look of solid roundness of developed limbs, and it was distinguished from weightlifting by the space, suspension apparatus and movement technique. Displays of female strength might have provoked anxiety, but aerialists were mostly praised, and the label 'Amazon' appears to be complimentary (e.g. S. R. 1891: 53). Amazons abounded in nineteenth-century ballet, often with accompanying warlike associ-ations. Chiarini's Circus even promoted the negative connotations of warlike behaviour: 'These arrogant Amazons, with antiquated Roman armours, mounted on superb steeds, disputing the palm of superiority with spears, swords, pistols and darts.'[4] Clearly females with symbols of aggression remained a novel attraction, but did the abstraction of aerial action allow it to evade the judgemental effects of the literalism of mythic happenings and fictionalized stories? By the late nineteenth century, adventure narratives that had fictional female villains behaving like men, shooting people and escaping to become outlaws, were common in penny-dreadful novels. Popular culture served the social fascination with fallen women who invariably faced retribution by the story's end (Staiger 1995). Female aerial acts, however, were not particularized with stories of immorality, badness or social rebellion.

Aerial action seemed to allow aerialists to 'rise above' social regulation, even with public campaigns about age, sexual propriety and safety. Female aerialists were publicly praised, even adored and called exemplars of womanhood as they demonstrated bodily control that defied all precepts of gender submissiveness. Even the addition of warlike symbolism to an act could be excused since it remained somewhat ambiguous. One feature of the action by female aerialists, however, could not be overlooked. The performance of physical dominance over a male body detracted from her mystique and aroused suspicions of arrogant calculation.

Perfected womanhood and iron jaws

Lala, Leona Dare and Emma Jutau were at the peak of their careers for their London debuts. Lala performed at the central hall in the Royal Aquarium in 1879 (replacing Zaeo) and in 1880. The Oxford theatre billed Dare performing in 1878 and 1879, and Jutau in 1879. All three worked with iron jaw apparatus as well as with trapeze. Remarkably, given social values in Victorian England, the muscular physiques of these performers were described as exemplifying admirable womanhood. Lala rose to prominence in Paris in 1879 and was probably still performing in 1887.[5] Dare was definitely working solo by 1871, making headlines in 1872 and still performing around 1890. Jutau is billed in circuses by 1874, and was still advertising her availability in 1890.[6]

Courtney Cooper asks, somewhat facetiously, why are most iron jaw artists women (1931: 165)? Certainly, women were among the first performers on this apparatus to become celebrities. By the early twentieth century, iron jaw or dental or teeth apparatus consisted of a thick double-sided, two-inch-wide leather and metal strap or tongue about a foot in length with a leather mouthpiece at one end, gripped by a performer's teeth. At the opposite end there might be an extension or a metal hook. A solo performer could grip the mouthpiece end, with head and body facing upwards, and hang the hook end from a trapeze bar or rope. A swivel below the hook allowed the apparatus to turn and spin the performer. With a duo, one performer hung upside down, legs around a trapeze, and gripped the iron jaw mouthpiece with an extension attached at the waist or neck of a second performer suspended below.

These strong muscular women doing iron jaw acts were advertised with maximum hyperbole. Lala was billed as La Vénus noire (black Venus) in Paris, and an African Queen in London with a story about how she had been deposed when her chiefs gave allegiance to Queen Victoria, was sold into slavery and ended up in a southern French circus (Gossard 1994: 15). Dare was the 'Queen of the Antilles' and 'The Pride of America!'; Jutau was 'Engaged at an enormous salary. The most Wonderful Performance ever seen in England.'[7]

Reviews of this aerial royalty were correspondingly elaborate and enthusiastic. While Lala's iron jaw work appears to have followed Dare's 1877 appearances in Paris, Lala demonstrated greater strength.[8] A reviewer writes, 'Dare is quite eclipsed by La-La, a lusty African lady' noting the 'sheer power of her ivories'.[9] Lala was Olga Kaira or Kaire, born 21 April 1858 in Stettin, who debuted at nine years of age (Desbonnet 1911: 351). Lala's tricks in London are reconstructed here from a compilation of the 1879 newspaper reports and poster drawings.[10] She hung upside down with her knees bent over at least one trapeze, suspending a second trapeze below her from an iron jaw. In the first part of the act, a boy, a woman and a man took it in turns to do acrobatic poses on the second trapeze below her. Then two worked together on it. One drawing shows a smaller woman upside down in a foot hold from the second trapeze bar holding a third woman by the arms. At some point in her act, Lala hauled herself up to the roof with a rope, probably attached to an iron jaw threaded through a pulley. (This process may have been used to reach the trapeze from the ground in the three-storey-high Cirque Fernando.) Lala may have copied Dare's trick of suspending an adult male body with an iron jaw apparatus, which was connected to a swivel at the front and centre of a belt worn around his waist. This allowed his body to spin horizontally. Following this trick, Lala lifted three men. A drawing of the trick has two upright men hanging on to Lala's arms, and another off an iron jaw, while Lala is hanging upside down from the trapeze with one leg over the bar. For the finale, Lala hung upside down again, while a small brass cannon was manoeuvred into place from its wheeled carriage by three men (some commentaries cite four or five or six men to embellish its heaviness), and, using a pulley and iron jaw, Lala lifted it up into the air with a chain. The cannon was then fired, which echoed loudly in London's Aquarium, and the shock of the blast caused Lala to recoil involuntarily.

In her studio photographs, which were used by nineteenth-century performers to promote their acts, Lala has curly hair and stands simply (Thétard 1947: volume II, 137). Photographs show her with a troupe or another performer, Kaira Le Blanc (Desbonnet 1911: 351–2) or alone beside a cannon.[11] In equivalent photographs, Dare and Jutau have an expressly feminine look in the enticing pose for trapezists: they are dressed in low-cut, frilled one-piece costumes with long, flowing curly hair, and they stand on one leg, bend the other behind and stretch one arm up to a low trapeze bar (Odell 1936–8: volume IX; Gossard 1994: 17). Performers' photographs were also collectable *cartes de visite*, and were currency for erotic fantasies (Davis 1991: 131–3). In another studio photograph from New York, Dare reclines on a couch, head turned slightly away, with the trapeze lying at the back of the couch, her prone body seemingly tamed and inviting to a (male) viewer.[12] While an offstage demeanour of seductively alluring acquiescence in photographs suggested a compliant body, this also usefully exaggerated the act's converse presentation of athletic force.

Lala avoids the sexualized conformity evident in the poses of her peers. In 1879 she was described as an Amazon and admired for her physical attributes. She was 'dusky', 'extraordinary', 'strong above the average of womankind in the jaw, or perhaps, as we should say, in the teeth'.[13] A second reviewer writes of her as 'mulatto', 'about 30' and a 'tawny Amazon'.[14] She is 'marvellous', compared to 'Sampson' and with fellow performers, the Kaira Troupe, described as 'more or less coloured'.[15] Her body was described as very strong and was observed in detail, and racial difference was specified.

Astonishing Paris, Lala was said to 'eclipse' all previous acts including those by males. One female predecessor (from circa 1873) was P. T. Barnum's Mademoiselle Angela, sketched lifting a cannon with a man (Monsieur D'Atalie) on top, carrying weights in either hand, and described as 'The Female Sampson', 'artillerist heroine', and 'beautifully formed woman'.[16] In 1870 a wave of all-female minstrel troupes in North America impersonated black men and women, and some, like Mademoiselle de Granville, did feats of strength (Toll 1976: 221).

One commentator describes Lala's feats as forestalling views about the inferiority of black people:

> She does all that her muscular rivals have done, and a great deal more . . . Lala, as we have hinted, is a representative of a dark-skinned race, but in the matter of strength she is prepared to assert her superiority of the boastful people who will have it that all the virtues are associated with a light complexion.[17]

Her act is reported as refuting a race hierarchy. George Stocking explains that racial separation was not yet absolute and 'Celtic Irish, black savage' was a grouping in the same way that woman and child were subordinated within the economic order (1987: 229–30). In the 1870s identity was not thoroughly subordinate to hereditary determination, even though studies that measured heads and weighed brains and other physical differences were influential (Gay 1993: 73–4). As Peter Gay explains, 'If Social Darwinism embodied a largely illegitimate set of inferences from a legitimate scientific theory, racism embodied a wholly illegitimate set of inferences from illegitimate pseudoscientific assertions' (ibid.: 75). Ideas of socio-cultural evolution dealt inconsistently with the way the contrasting cultures of indigenous peoples fitted into a Eurocentric linear sequencing of human development, and so did social attitudes.

Admiration for Lala suggests a complicated response to her identity. Lala is racially marked as 'mulatto' within the dominant (white) European culture, alongside acknowledgements of her superior physique. Perhaps Lala was caught up in a European fascination with performances of an imaginary Africa. Astley's had billed an African equestrian by 1793 in its Ethiopian spectacle (Greenwood 1898: 101–9). Attitudes to Lala's act probably reflected the widespread discussion of the competition between nations and races as European nations amassed empires and resources, in the 'frantic colonization' of conquered peoples (Gay 1993: 85). Despite French nationality, a black woman was still associated with a nonspecific colonized people, which, in social Darwinistic approaches, made her closer to animals, and therefore accorded her a primitive natural strength. Yet, as indicated in Chapter 1, athletic strength was becoming significantly implicated in social progress. By the 1890s some black Americans expressed the view that strength could assist with 'racial progress' for both men and women who had been so subjugated by white racist practices, even though for men, sporting prowess contained a contradictory identity encompassing brute nature and manly control (Captain 1991: 86, 95–6). Similarly, Max Nordau argued for Jewish racial regeneration with the development of 'new muscle' modelled on Jewish circus performers (Presner 2003: 283).

Lala may have been an early forerunner of what Ramsay Burt discerns are the lived contradictions of black dancer Josephine Baker's Parisian identity in the 1920s that ranged across both essentialized racial and 'multiple' identities (1998: 70 (hooks)). While Lala's appearance was accorded a formulaic cultural identity, her physical feats were celebrated and revered, in ways that intruded on a race hierarchy.

The act's challenge to male physical superiority seems less acceptable. A reviewer writes,

> The man of the party is presently hauled aloft, and being taken by the teeth of the Amazon, is turned into a kind of human teetotum, to be whirled round with an amount of rapidity which, we should say, was conducive to a shocking attack of giddiness. Then LaLa, still hanging by her legs, supports three men – three hulking fellows, as Mr Charles Reade would call them – one by her teeth and the other two by her hands and arms.[18]

Lala's action was taken as befuddling male bodies and treating them like objects, in what seems like male spectator identification with, and diffidence about, what was done.

Edgar Degas painted *Miss La La at the Cirque Fernando* in 1879 (see Figure 2.1), and her beautiful, realistic image has been preserved in art history. She is performing dressed in a white, short-sleeved tunic with gold trim, as she moves up towards a muted orange roof. Her legs, lower body and chest are clearly visible viewed from below, while her face is obscured. Roy McMullen writes that it is considered 'among the artist's most striking and complex achievements' (1985: 318). Degas watched the act for four nights but had problems, identified by Italian masters as painting 'from below upward' and adhering to 1870s theory on colour choices. More particularly, Degas had difficulty capturing 'the pose that would convey her soaring movement and the strain on her jaws' (ibid.). For Degas, Lala's act presented the problem of drawing live action rather than a static pose. Her aerial body could not be easily objectified.

Anthea Callen summarizes how the female body was described and visualized in late nineteenth-century thinking, and in Degas's art, in ways that contained women within notions of femininity, and within scientific objectification and physiognomy that measured physical difference. Degas has been shown drafting physiognomies with his images of dancers by 1878–80 (Callen 1995: 22–5). When a woman socially transgressed as a sexual deviant and/or hysteric, she was considered to be a 'throw-back to primitive woman',

Figure 2.1 Miss Lala at the Cirque Fernando by Hilaire-Germain-Edgar Degas, courtesy of ©The National Gallery, London.

manifesting qualities that were naturally inherent, and with masculine propensities (ibid.: 20). Callen explains that 'robust or powerful physique (i.e. generally working class) was considered degenerate', and associated with primitivism, due to European culture's elevation of inactive middle-class women (ibid.: 21). An alignment of female robust labour that was socially pathologized as inferior and the female body capable of a hysterical involuntary loss of self-control does not quite accord with the way female aerial acts were received, even with acknowledgement of the action's masculinizing effect.

Lala and other females were widely promoted with mythic identities that helped distance them from the everyday and aerial action clearly surpassed mundane activity. Any taint of primitivism was avoided by pronouncements that feats were inspirational and wondrous, and Lala's capacity to lift three men must have underscored her distinctiveness. If manual labour was degenerate, in comparison, muscular aerial displays seemed superhuman. Certainly, female bodies displaying strength mimicked masculine control, as they demonstrated superior bodily self-control, challenging a schema that required control over female bodies. A black female body in exceptional action at height momentarily outmanoeuvred its low social positioning. At least during aerial performance, Lala's black womanhood could be esteemed.

To avoid obvious conclusions that challenged male superiority, Hugues Le Roux (1890) and others located female athletes in a parallel realm of perfected womankind, one that idealized and idolized them, but kept them subordinate to a statuesque, perfected manhood. There was some misapprehension repeated by Le Roux that female aerialists could not sustain the physical strength needed for the duration of the act. A converse corollary that female physical progress might outpace male body development remained a deeper underlying anxiety.

Leona Dare (probably Susan Adeline Stewart or Stuart), associated with the Antilles Islands, was the leading aerialist of her era, but her performances were often received warily. As well as solo and duo trapeze acts in theatres and circuses, Dare performed outdoors under a hot-air balloon, both with a partner and solo. Dare's balloon acts caused a sensation. Importantly, her theatre audiences clearly included a sizeable number of 'well-to-do', 'thoroughly respectable-looking women'.[19] She showed artistic versatility and invented new aerial action; she was probably the first woman to hang from a trapeze supporting and spinning the weight of a man from iron jaw apparatus. Dare came from a family of acrobats (Turner 1995–2000: volume II, 31), and was performing in New York between October 1871 and March 1872 (Odell 1936–8: volume IX, 225, 197, 325). She worked with Warner's Circus in 1872, and as 'The Comet of 1873'.[20] (Emma Jutau was with Warner, Henderson and Company in 1874.) On Dare's return seasons to New York in 1873–4, and in 1875, her rivals included Water-Queen Lurline (Sarah Swift) holding her breath for over two minutes in a water tank (Odell 1936–8: volume X, 73, 75).

Working on trapeze under a hot-air balloon basket in the USA in 1872, Dare did more than lift her partner, husband Thomas Hall, off the ground and spin him with an iron jaw; she appeared to carry him away beneath her. Hall, who performed as Thomas Dare, was doubly helpless under Dare's iron jaw hold and the balloon's drift; the female aerialist was doubly defiant of the perceived natural order with her strength and her sustained power over a male body. Accompanying its sexual innuendo of male surrender was an impression of predatory abduction and disappearance fuelled by masculine fears of being overpowered by increasing female strength. The male partner in an 1878 theatre version of this iron jaw act without the balloon played a surprised spectator, and he was tellingly and sympathetically identified as an unsuspecting victim to Dare's cruelty when she made him 'giddy' and turned him into a crab, a 'shapeless dummy'.[21]

A poster image of Dare at the Folies Bergère in Paris in 1877 represents her upright on a descent rope, waving two American flags, wearing stars and stripes on her body-fitting costume, and also hanging from the trapeze by her feet, head downwards, supporting a horizontal male body (see Figure 2.2).[22] As a successor to Madame Sanyeah, Dare's costuming suggests a predecessor to the cartoon heroine Wonder Woman. Helen Day points out that Dare's American identity meant being 'modern, brash, outrageous, and independent' in Europe at that time (1992: 153).

The stories of Dare's offstage life and rumours of an aristocratic lover reinforced the idea of an uncontrollable woman. She left her marriage and professional partnership with Hall in 1878 and, as the maker of Dare's equipment, he sued and won £100 from the Oxford when she appeared there in 1879.[23] Hall had actually encouraged the Oxford to hire her, but Dare was supposedly frightened by Hall's arrival and left her equipment behind, which did not satisfy Hall and he sought financial compensation. In a court action in the Court of Common Pleas, Justice Denman made a widely appreciated joke about the consequences of teaching a wife to fly.

Dare's reputation was unparalleled even though she may have later borrowed tricks from her rivals. In a description of Dare's solo act, she is 'very strongly built'; using an iron jaw, she lifts herself 40 feet up from the stage to a trapeze where she is 'hanging head downwards by her feet', holding on by a leg and hand (quoted in Turner 1995–2000: volume II, 31. Dare was probably the highest-paid aerialist of her day. She worked with the Renz Circus in Berlin in 1883 and one anecdotal report claims that she was paid as much as US$1,000 a week at that time.[24]

In Madrid in 1884 there was a tragic fatal accident when M. George dropped from a trapeze held with an iron jaw by Dare.[25] The crowd stampeded in panic and, not surprisingly, Dare was extremely upset, screaming, and may have retreated from performance for a while. In 1890 she was working solo under a balloon in Paris when she had to induce a fall:

> She went up at the Porte Maillot attached, as usual, by her teeth to a trapeze hung below a balloon. The wind was strong, and seeing that the

Figure 2.2 Folies Bergère Leona Dare, 1877, Paris by Jules Chéret, courtesy of the
Musée de la publicité, Paris, tous droits réservés.

balloon ran a danger of being carried away, Dare let go her hold and fell to the ground. Her leg was broken above the ankle by the fall. She was immediately removed to the hospital.[26]

Dare may have continued performing after this fall, and she lived until 1922.

Aerial action was also fostering impressions of a female body that could move very fast. Emma Jutau sped down a 200-foot or longer sloping wire suspended from an iron jaw, with claims of reaching 65 miles an hour (see Figure 2.3). She was an experienced trapezist, touring with American circuses after 1874 and probably under pressure to invent tricks that would outdo rivals and outlast bankrupted circuses.[27] She worked in a trapeze duo with George Brown, and leapt between trapezes, but it was her solo speeding trick that made her internationally famous (Thétard 1947: volume II, 161 (photograph)). An illustration of Jutau at London's crowded Oxford has her suspended below a sloping cable, long-haired, wearing a frilled costume, her feet crossed and her arms held out.[28] She is 'the Venus of the High Trapeze', who stands out from other women for her 'shapely' 'loveliness', suspended by her 'pearly teeth', in a unique act which earns her five times the income of any other aerial gymnast.[29]

If Lala was exceptionally strong, and Dare was particularly adventurous, Jutau moved very fast, her speed increasing during the trick. Whereas lifting and holding bodies mid-air emphasized the female body's muscular strength, speed masked it. Jutau's promotional images in 1879 conveyed an impression of feminine softness. Yet Jutau was strong, and an 1886 drawing depicts a well-built upper-body physique and an aerialist's thick neck, evidence of her years of trapeze work.[30] The speeding trick suggested a passive body that lost its self-control once it was moving down the trajectory of the wire. But this was an ambiguous theatrical illusion. Fast acts also represented an evasive female body, one speeding away from a masculine (strangle)hold.

Deadly damsels

By the late 1870s projectile tricks in which a body was propelled into the air established speed as the new frontier of aerial performance. While Jutau's fast action down a wire remained largely under her control, this was not so for the finale tricks of aerialists Zazel, Zaeo and Alar. Most popular projectile spectacles presented female bodies moving unaided at considerable speed, and metaphorically as deadly weapons. An aerial body as part of a war-machine supplanted its dainty bird-like associations.

The first Zazel, English-born Rosa Richter, was 15 when she debuted at London's Aquarium, on 2 April 1877, with a spectacular finale to her aerial act in which she was propelled by the release of elasticized strings and sprang 70 feet out of a cannon. Shane Peacock gives an extended description of this act and those of the other Zazels because Zazel was the protégée of entrepreneur–manager Farini, who patented the act (1996: 229–39).[31] Canadian rope-walker

BEAUTIFUL JUTAU

THE VENUS OF THE HIGH TRAPEZE,

And **TRIUMPHANT HEBE OF HEROINES,** all fresh and fragrant from innumerable public and highest social conquests across the sea. At once, a rarely accomplished and high-bred Lady and a Reigning Toast. **In Society a Queen. In the Arena a Living Meteor.** Professional Beauties pale to common-place plainness in the bright presence of her **Shapely and Bewitching Loveliness,** and her exquisite Grace, Miraculous Skill, Charming Courage, Delicious Ease and Smiling Confidence, lend irresistible and incomparable fascination to

ORIGINAL, TREMENDOUS MID-AIR FEATS

Which no other performer, male or female, can, or dares to imitate. In **Lofty Single and Double Acts** and **Appalling Long Leaps** from the **Dizzy, Slender, Treacherous, Swaying Bar,** she is incredibly great, and indescribably all-surpassing and astounding, while her

LAST CULMINATING ACHIEVEMENT

In the fabulous accomplishment of which

SUSPENDED BY HER PEARLY TEETH ALONE

She flashes down 200 Feet of Wire, from the lofty Apex of the Stupendous Hippodrome, is

AN EFFORT BEYOND ALL DESCRIPTION

Figure 2.3 Emma Jutau, *Courier Barnum and London,* 1883, courtesy of Circus World Museum, Robert Parkinson Library, Baraboo.

Farini had been Blondin's challenger, also walking across Niagara Falls, and Farini went on to invent aerial apparatus and to manage celebrity aerial acts including the cross-dressed Lulu (see Chapter 3). Peacock effectively describes how Zazel was Farini's Zazel, and the act, but not Zazel, earned from £120 to £200 a week playing to crowds of 20,000 a day in England and the USA (ibid.: 234).[32] Her launch was theatrically enhanced with an explosion, and the performer was instructed to keep her body rigid at the launch and go limp before she landed in the net. One writer proposes that men and women should not miss Zazel's act, which produces 'pleasurable but strongly excited sensations', but while for women she demonstrates the benefits of an athletic education, for men her 'most perfect' figure warrants repeated viewing.[33]

Projectile action is distinctive from other aerial work, and remains especially dangerous because the performer has far less control over the trajectory of movement. Projectile tricks belong to a category of circus act developed in the latter part of the nineteenth century that demonstrated unstoppable machine power rather than muscular power, and were exemplified by the double somersaulting automobile act of La Belle Roche.[34] Coxe claims that, by the 1950s, 'Out of some fifty human projectiles more than thirty have lost their lives, mostly by falling outside the net' (1980: 108). During the mid-twentieth century male and female members of the Zacchini family working with RBBBC were propelled with compressed air out of a cannon, and they practised for eight hours daily with their expensive equipment.[35]

Why did these projectile feats become so popular? They certainly provoked more cultural anxiety than other aerial acts, not least because of their theatricality with the use of cannon symbolism that heightened an impression of danger and death. At a time when plots in melodrama routinely featured a helpless damsel in distress needing to be rescued, projectile action presented females who willingly endangered themselves.

The rival act in North America was that of Australian high-wire-walker Ella Zuila and her husband and partner George Loyal. Both Richter and Zuila were primarily wire-walkers and trapezists, but by the late 1870s female aerialists needed gimmicks to stand out, with Maria Spelterini crossing Niagara Falls in 1876 (Shapiro 1989: 83). Richter walked a tight-rope without a balance pole, lay down and stood up on one leg, turned repeatedly around a trapeze bar, and caught herself by her knees before flying with a single somersault down 97 feet to a safety net. Zuila had gained international prominence in 1876, riding a velocipede on a wire across the Magani Falls in Natal, and for her outstanding solo high-wire act 90 feet up (Tait 2003a: 80–92; Durant and Durant 1957: 172 (poster drawing)). Wire had mostly replaced rope by the mid-1870s. Nonetheless, Zuila was not Zazel's rival for her exceptional wire-walking but because she did an act in which she hung upside down from a trapeze as catcher to Loyal, who was a human cannonball. The Zuila–Loyal partnership was engaged as a star attraction in North America's largest circus of the time, Adam Forepaugh's

Aggregation, to outdo Barnum, rumoured as being about to tour Zazel in 1880.[36]

Zuila emulated Dare as one of the first females holding a male performer's body weight; in addition, Zuila was catching Loyal as he moved towards her at speed. This was one of the first instances of a female catcher and a male flyer in action.

The projectile action was imposed on Zazel. Richter's self-controlled physical mastery in her wire-walking and trapeze display was followed by comparatively inactive propulsion. This reinstated an impression of femininity at the end of the act, and corresponded with female imagery in visual art that beautified death as sleep-like and passively seductive (Dijkstra 1986: 61). As a symbol, a cannon conjured up helplessness for those facing its forceful destruction. The female body in its aerial trajectory, however, sped away from the cannon and in this action triumphed over sleep-like stillness, over deadness. Contradictorily, the female projectile remained deadly within the resonances of a body technology of death.

By the late 1870s some spectators had become less believing that this was the action of female physicality. A journalist satirizes another journalist writing for the *Living Age* who mistakes Zazel's gender:

> 'Zazel appears to be a muscular young man made up to slightly resemble a young woman, but not so nice a performer as Lulu.' Appears to be a muscular young man. It is clear that the muscular young man who wrote that paragraph saw Zazel – after dinner.[37]

The *Living Age* writer refuses to accept that a female body could be so muscular.

Regardless of whether female muscles were credible to everyone, there would seem to be a discrepancy between the widespread acknowledgement of the muscularity of female aerialists and admiring statements about their perfected figures at a time when even exercising in private was controversial for women. These performers were unquestionably admired for their fuller figures, their exposed rounded muscularity. In her exploration of shifts in the fashions of nineteenth-century American female body shapes influenced by European trends, Lois Banner finds that, by the 1870s, a voluptuous look was being favoured in opposition to a pallid feminine waif, and became a forerunner and eventual sexual competitor of the statuesque woman of the 1890s (1983: 127, 151). The well-rounded physicality of aerialists coincided with a changing public predilection for voluptuousness while remaining an anathema to the sedate inactivity of a morally virtuous domesticated woman. Symbols of death in the aerial act added to the excitement surrounding the shapely aerialist, but also implied that her physique was actively perfected at its social peril.

The popularity of projectile tricks brought further imitation. It also intensified the efforts of campaigns hostile to such entertainments. An ex-acrobat's crusade in England tried to suppress all female aerial performances including those of Dare, Jutau, Zazel and Zaeo, with the intention of improving 'respect for a woman's jaw'. Tracy Davis (1991) argues convincingly that nineteenth-century performing female bodies were perceived as sexualized and mouth apparatus may have delivered a more focused oral eroticism, making for a moral crusade against the innuendo of such displays. It was well established by 1883 when one Zazel in Boston, USA, had a serious accident.[38]

Zaeo (Adelaide Wieland) did a catapult trick at the finale of her aerial act, projected by springs out of a ballista. When Zaeo slipped off the net in 1880 in London, her doctor's statement that she was not seriously hurt was published.[39] But it was not until 1890, when she returned after a decade-long continental tour, that Zaeo really polarized English public opinion. A poster-making innovation led to the pasting around the streets of an image of her mature, full-length body in a costume that was particularly fitting across the tops of her well-rounded thighs. The National Vigilance Association, campaigning against prostitutes at London's Aquarium, effectively banned boxing and eventually also Zaeo's posters, which showed her with developed triceps and her arms raised revealing her armpits, which Tracy Davis points out had erotic significance (1990: 4, 9). Benefiting from the publicity, Zaeo remained the star attraction at the Aquarium for over a year, and Zaeo's supporters created a satirical musical about these events. Born on 31 January 1866, Zaeo became an equestrienne and trapezist working in her manager–teacher H. W. Wieland's circus by 1878 – she later married Wieland. Her biography contains first-person statements and claims that she wanted 'excitement and activity', and after seeing Zazel and other trapezists, she imitated their action (S. R. 1891: 10–12).

Zaeo precedes her description of her 1879 London debut by acknowledging how the music affects her performance, and continues,

> I looked down from a platform which was fixed fifty feet from the ground, and when I took my first two steps on the wire it really seemed that I was walking on the air, which was filled with the dazzle of the lamps; but I felt no fear, only a joyous exultation, and walked straight on, till I arrived on the pedestal at the other side of the vast building.
>
> Then I heard for the first time in my life the applause of 12,000 people who had been watching me from below. The blood turned cold in my veins, for it rolled up with a sound like thunder, and I was filled with a dazed wonder as to what it might be or mean . . . I realised that it was applause . . . But all this time no fear, no sense of being in a dangerous position.
>
> It was when I ascended to the roof for the great dive and looked down upon the people below, that I first remembered where I was.
>
> (ibid.: 14–15)

The biographer comments that the young performer did not yet have 'magnificent proportions, and indeed gave no promise of becoming such a splendid specimen of womanhood' (ibid.). There was clearly a distinction between the bodily charms of adolescence and those of an adult.

Although Zaeo's wire-walking was done on a thin wire, the demand for a more sensational trick led to Zaeo's being catapulted from a ballista up in a half-circle and down. Cannon projection was done from a raised position with the performer fired out and downwards. Zaeo became celebrated in Europe, her earnings exceeding those of other gymnastic acts (ibid.: 31, 33). In a Spanish poem Zaeo is elevated to the status of a Greek goddess:

> Poor man before you on the ground do creep,
> While so high you on angel's wing do leap.

> (Munro 1971: 28)

Zaeo had at least two further accidents, in 1881 and 1883, but she had a long career, eventually managing other performers. In 1898 she was still advertising demonstrations of physical culture and calisthenics, fire dances, and an act with 500 yards of 'Lurid Lingerie' fabric, possibly involving the illumination of veiled body shapes.[40]

From 1894 the English Alar (Pansy Murphy), the Human Arrow, working with the Flying Zedoras, did a projectile trick in which she was propelled from a large crossbow and through a bull's-eye target, and was sometimes caught by her sister Adele (Adelaide Murphy) (Tait 2005). The bow and arrow apparatus was original and patented by Adele's husband, Tony Zedora, and as Farini had established, female performers attracted more attention for new inventions. In another precedent, the twin Vaidis Sisters promoted Edward Leamy's new revolving apparatus with two trapezes on a rotational axis, and went on to acclaim in North America forming their own company without naming Leamy.[41] He subsequently toured the apparatus in Europe in the 1890s with the Leamy Troupe that included Lillian Leitzel's aunt and mother and eventually Lillian herself.

By 1896 Alar and the Zedoras were star attractions with BBC in North America and then on tour in Europe. Alar was propelled by a spring mechanism off a platform shaped like a bow, through a paper hoop to a catcher hanging upside down on trapeze (see Figure 2.4). A BBC bill (circa 1896) proclaims, 'upon its massive and mighty string the dainty feet of the Bravest of all Living Artists take the place of insensate wood and stone'. Although this act's weapon seems gentler than a cannon, social ideas of deadliness were deployed through the additional symbolism of past (dead) cultures and their weaponry. The female body's mimicry of an inert deadly object fired into space remained blatantly warlike imagery.

Predictably Alar's act was controversial in England, and may have hastened the English Parliament's passing of The Dangerous Performances Act, 1897, which raised the age limit to 18 for female acrobats and 16 for males, previously set at 14 in 1879 (Strong 1898: 95–7). These efforts to regulate aerial performance in response to outrage at the inherent dangers and the occasional serious

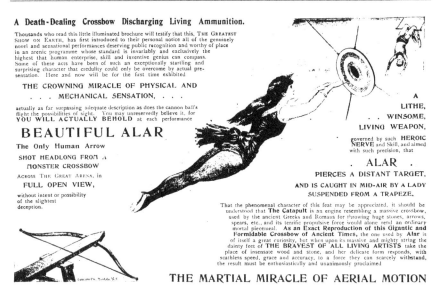

A Death-Dealing Crossbow Discharging Living Ammunition.

Thousands who read this little illuminated brochure will testify that this, THE GREATEST SHOW ON EARTH, has first introduced to their personal notice all of the genuinely novel and sensational performances deserving public recognition and worthy of place in an arenic programme whose standard is invariably and exclusively the highest that human enterprise, skill and inventive genius can compass. Some of these acts have been of such an exceptionally startling and surprising character that credulity could only be overcome by actual presentation. Here and now will be for the first time exhibited

THE CROWNING MIRACLE OF PHYSICAL AND
. . . MECHANICAL SENSATION, . . .

actually as far surpassing adequate description as does the cannon ball's flight the possibilities of sight. You may unreservedly believe it, for YOU WILL ACTUALLY BEHOLD at each performance

BEAUTIFUL ALAR

The Only Human Arrow

SHOT HEADLONG FROM A
MONSTER CROSSBOW

Across THE GREAT ARENA, in
FULL OPEN VIEW,

without intent or possibility of the slightest deception.

A
LITHE,
. . WINSOME,
LIVING WEAPON,

governed by such HEROIC NERVE and Skill, and aimed with such precision, that

. ALAR .

PIERCES A DISTANT TARGET, AND IS CAUGHT IN MID-AIR BY A LADY SUSPENDED FROM A TRAPEZE,

That the phenomenal character of this feat may be appreciated, it should be understood that **The Catapult** is an engine resembling a massive crossbow, used by the ancient Greeks and Romans for throwing huge stones, arrows, spears, etc., and its terrific propulsive force would alone rend an ordinary mortal piecemeal. **As an Exact Reproduction of this Gigantic and Formidable Crossbow of Ancient Times,** the one used by **Alar** is of itself a great curiosity, but when upon its massive and mighty string the dainty feet of **THE BRAVEST OF ALL LIVING ARTISTS** take the place of insensate wood and stone, and her delicate form responds, with scathless speed, grace and accuracy, to a force they can scarcely withstand, the result must be enthusiastically and unanimously proclaimed

THE MARTIAL MIRACLE OF AERIAL MOTION

Figure 2.4 Alar, *Barnum and Bailey Herald*, 1896, Circus World Museum.

accident must also have been due to expanded numbers of adolescent female aerialists. Pansy remembers,

> I am 88 and from the age of 16 was shot from a giant bow. I was billed as Alar, The Human Arrow in music halls and circuses and in many countries. I know the Sensation of being shot, . . . Well it is so quick that you hardly realize it.[42]

Alar probably had three accidents, one of them certainly due to apparatus failure. The Zedoras' act also included a male performer walking on the ceiling, his feet in rings, a female flying to a female catcher wearing a blindfold, and iron jaw work. The troupe's membership had expanded to six in 1900, and Tony claimed the invention of passing leaps in which two performers pass mid-air.[43] This flying troupe broke up in 1902 after Adele died, but Pansy worked in iron jaw, acrobatic and dance acts in theatres for another two decades.

Death was depicted in nineteenth-century paintings and literature by beautiful, inert young women as ideals of heroic sacrifice (Dijkstra 1986: 50). Young female projectiles might be emblematic of romanticized death but they were not floating or lying inert. They were propelled with force. Alar is drawn mid-air on posters with feminine frills and flowing curls, rapidly moving upwards. The female aerialist was celebrated and yet the theatricality of the projectile act was 'loaded' with disturbing cultural significance. Propelled from a lethal weapon, the body was literally in an action that might kill the performer, as it metaphorically mimicked the action of powerful deadly objects. Such tricks also suggested an aggressive female body-machine eluding social control. Technological motion further propelled the female aerialist into an unnatural identity.

Balancing butterflies

In 1881 at Cirque d'Hiver in Paris, Henry Whiteley saw Mouche d'or (Golden Fly) flying up and down on pianoforte wire in a programme that included Zaeo (1981: 18). Iron jaw apparatus attached to wire allowed individual female performers to be suspended mid-air on equipment that was not easily discernible at a distance. They could appear to balance and float. The subsequent proliferation of the more delicately named 'human butterfly' acts in circuses over decades produced a socially conformist female aerial identity. Muscular aerial action during performance effectively countered superficial impositions of femininity, including that of its own advertising and costuming, until the development of butterfly apparatus. The impression of muscularity during aerial performance was undercut by an expansion in butterfly display from the 1890s and an accompanying perception of feminine naturalness.

In the late 1880s the adolescent Venetian Erminia Chelli climbed 50 feet up a ladder to stand on a trapeze and bend down to pick up a handkerchief on the bar with her teeth. Holding the side ropes, she balanced on a globe, itself balancing on the trapeze bar, and stabilizing herself, let go her hold. Her act finished with a fall to a net, and kisses blown to the audience. Le Roux describes the scantily dressed Erminia as a beautiful 'natural somnambulist' who exemplified his observations of the hypnotic focus of aerialists (1890: 232). His argument, however, that female performers were better at balance (equilibrist) acts, while men make better acrobats because they cannot suppress their strength, would seem to be based on his beliefs about bodies (1890: 209–10). Regardless of the muscular control taught by her father, Erminia's capacity for balancing was perceived by Le Roux as arising naturally in females. Furthermore an association with male tutelage alleviated a logical conclusion of female self-control and therefore unnaturalness. Socially obedient female bodies could still be physically trained to do exceptional feats. This convoluted gender logic doubles back on body identity, because the female performers of unseen, off-stage, social acts of feminine submission showed spectators their muscles as they did tricks of strength.

Once again addressing the perception that most whirling and spinning iron jaw artists were female, this apparatus became widely used with all-female choruses known as 'aerial ballets'. Banner claims that from the 1890s female choruses made American stage shows successful (1983: 180). Vertical suspension from an iron jaw maximizes the visibility of a female body as it minimizes its muscle flexing, and draws attention to the mouth cavity. The plentiful, but anonymous, aerial ballets receive only a passing mention in commentaries, but their erotic appeal is obvious in poster imagery.

A butterfly's wing-span is large in proportion to its smaller body, and fabric wings could almost hide the torso. Energetic leaping, flying and diving could be replaced with hovering, flapping, floating and gliding. Human butterfly acts multiplied, initially as a second act by proficient aerialists, for example the Curzon, Tybell and Silbon Sisters.[44] Butterflies were especially feminine in their seemingly weightless action that did not appear to imitate masculine strength and power, and could even be disassociated from iron jaw technology. Angela Dalle Vacche finds that the aeroplane, butterfly and circus aerials of early action in Italian cinema expressed anti-technological fantasies of flying upwards out of femininity, and female body movement was polarized between an airborne arabesque and a ground-based grotesque (2002: 459, 465 (Russo)). Of course this is not an ethereal experience for the female performers who risk teeth extraction or worse (Beal 1938: 73–6). The sexual allure of bodies in vertical suspension acts persisted well into the mid-twentieth century. Aerial ballets would expand from performers waving body-length fabric wings attached to their arms, to sexy bikini-clad, showgirl dancers removing their ostrich feathers to spin from web hand and foot loops. In North America at Coles in 1949, under the artistic direction of Barbette, a master of feminine disguise (see Chapter 3 and Figure 2.5), the chorus on iron jaw were billed as 'A Nostalgic Walk Up Memory Lane with the Granddaughters of the Spangled Queens who Made Grandpappy's Blood Bubble . . . with Reckless Reliance on Dental Tenacity'.[45] The humorous tone suggests that these feminine displays were cynically staged for male tastes, and did not have the respect accorded other aerial artistry.

By the early twentieth century, aerial acts with dance-like body positioning were common and the scientific explanations of aerial action were reserved for flying return tricks. Therefore with the exception of flying troupes, aerial performance became feminized because of the apparatus, movement and increased numbers of female aerialists. Amy Koritz describes how female performers so dominated ballet by the second half of the nineteenth century that male parts were danced by cross-dressed females in substitutions that were non-threatening for the male spectators, but also because males were poorly trained (1995: 23–4). Dance-trained female performers and later gymnasts with a basic introduction to aerial apparatus would be employed extensively in aerial spectacles during the twentieth century. Because aerial ballets became a standard act in most large circus programmes, they became associated with general perceptions of aerialists. If a spectator so chose, showpiece acts of sexually titillating display could offset the impact of female muscular power.

As such acts increased in number, social perceptions of radical physicality in aerial performance – epitomized by soloists Dare and Zaeo – could be supplanted. The femininity of aerial ballets with and without difficult tricks made them more socially acceptable, but this had other consequences. During the twentieth century female performers had to work against expectations that the floating, decorative acts were their allocated, (naturally) easier mode of performance.

Figure 2.5 Butterfly Act, directed by Barbette, Circus World Museum.

As well as the aerial ballet, the generic solo act that requires considerable skill and muscular effort also came to be allocated to female performers, especially after the 1930s as numbers of male soloists, still often the stars, proportionally declined. This feminization undercut perceptions of aerial athleticism at a time when the aerialist came to represent circus itself. Although aerial soloists and duos are photographed everywhere for publicity, their carefully practised, strenuous routines are often given cursory attention. As a consequence the individuals who had, and have, the athletic disposition, discipline and bravery, the choreographic flair and showmanship, who made and make aerial acts so captivating, often remain anonymous to audiences and known only to other specialists. This anonymity followed similar processes in ballet (Koritz 1995: 28). The nameless aerialist became absorbed into the cultural imaginary as emblematic of insubstantial femininity although ambiguously also of danger.

Triple somersaults backwards

Until several circus historians rediscovered her 1897 precedent, Lena Jordan's backward triple somersault was omitted from circus histories for 60 years

(Couderc 1965: 26). Instead the first execution of a triple was widely attributed to Ernie Clarke in 1909, who performed as a celebrated flyer for nearly four decades (see Chapter 4). Yet Lena's feat was still known by some, as Bernard Mills acknowledges without naming Lena in 1933 (1933: 8). Interestingly, the Jordans and Clarkes were performing together by 1907 (see Figure 2.6), but to date there is little trace of Lena's name with the troupe after 1898 or mention of her triple. Her 60-year omission from circus histories reflects a wider pattern in twentieth-century attitudes to female aerial athleticism.

The Jordans' triple, in which Lena was said to 'leap from the dome' to Lew Jordan as catcher in the Flying Jordans' act, was described in newspaper reviews in Sydney in 1897.[46] According to the Jordans' trade advertisement, it may have happened as early as 1896 in New York.[47] The unpredictability of the trick's execution probably meant the troupe could not promote it. Lena's status as first to do a mid-air triple somersault has been unjustifiably qualified as cast; Lena was supposedly thrown by Mamie but Lena also leapt and/or swung out holding a trapeze fly bar.

There was a decline in female participation in difficult flying tricks in the ensuing decades and especially after the 1930s. Had Lena's feat been more widely recognized in circus annals prior to the 1960s, would female performers throughout the twentieth century have been expected to routinely train for the most difficult flying tricks, and would the few that did seem less anomalous? Lena's omission is significant since it coincided with the stalled recognition of the remarkable achievements of nineteenth-century female aerialists.

Lew and Mamie were doing a flying return act with BBC by 1891, and significantly Mamie had mastered a double somersault to a catcher by 1892. Over 25 years, the Flying Jordans with Russian-born apprentices Lena and Oscar, would become a major family-based troupe touring to Europe, Australia, South Africa, north Asia, and North and South America. An unnamed young woman 'is a perfect type of muscular development'.[48] Lew admitted choosing the light-weight Lena in order to train her for casting and catching. At 18 she was 4 foot 10 inches, her 'extraordinary biceps' felt by journalists, with back 'muscle lying like knotted rope under the skin, and when she threw back her shoulders a regular "ravine" was created between the rolls of muscle on each side of the spine.'[49]

The Jordans left New York for Australia shortly after the troupe was embroiled in controversy when the North American Society for the Prevention of Cruelty to Children claimed that physical training would retard mental growth, and tried to stop 8-year-old Nellie from performing. In defending the humane training of young gymnasts in 1896, a journalist compares the Jordans' training to a game, and the speed of the 16-year-old female as she climbs a rope to a trapeze, swings and turns a somersault, to that of a sailor, and of a monkey on a rope. An accompanying drawing of a 16-year-old, probably Lena, shows her flexing her well-developed muscles, like a bodybuilder (see Figure 2.7). Answering a query about how 'the muscles [are] hardened, the nerves steadied, the

New Big Thrilling Aerial Sensations
A Special Separate Circus Given High in the Air by Sixty Incomparable Artists

EVERY NOVEL, UNIQUE, DANGEROUS, SENSATIONAL, HAZARDOUS FEATURE KNOWN TO THE GYMNIC WORLD MADE TO CONTRIBUTE TO THIS BIG, NOVEL, THRILLING SHOW.

A PERFECT CARNIVAL OF AERIAL SPECIALTIES PRODUCED BY THE FOREMOST SPECIALISTS IN THEIR LINE.

More money paid for New Aerial Features than the entire Salary List of any other show in the world. Many new Startling Innovations produced now for the first time in America. Marvelous Trapeze Performances. Hazardous Aerial Bar Feats, Wonderful Return and Catching Acts. Daring Teeth Ascensions at Dizzy Heights. Thrilling High-air Equilibrium. Exciting High-wire Exploits. Laughable Aerial Comedy scenes. Sensational Bicycle Riding on high-tight ropes, and Dangerous Dare-Devil Episodes, Feats, Contortions, and every Conceivable form and manner of High Air Achievements by an army of Human Beings Flying, Darting, Climbing, Leaping, Diving, and Somersaulting through the air like birds.

The World-Renowned Jordan Aerialists

As a special feature of a big aerial display in which 60 world-famous artists appear, Ringling Brothers have secured the celebrated Jordan Family, beyond all doubt the largest and most sensational number of the kind ever seen. Their thrilling performances in mid-air have never been equaled, and it is probable that they will never be duplicated, for it seems out of the question that ten such remarkable aerialists as compose the Jordan family will ever again be found acting together as one company.

THE CELEBRATED CLARKONIANS

With exquisite grace and the utmost celerity they accomplish feats that seem impossible, and so sure and certain are they in every movement that their marvelous flights and evolutions appear to be executed with absolute disregard of danger. Among the many astounding feats accomplished by these incomparable artists is their famous "Twisting Double Somersault." This marvelous exploit is performed high in the air, midway in a thrilling vault of over 40 feet from one swinging trapeze bar to another. Their wonderful display is impossible to describe. It is different from all others and easily the most astounding, most amazing aerial act ever seen.

A COMPLETE COMPANY OF AERIAL SPECIALISTS CULLED FROM THE GREAT AMPHITHEATRES OF EUROPE AND SUPPLEMENTED BY AMERICA'S LEADING GYMNASTS

Figure 2.6 Jordans and Clarkonians, *Courier*, 3 June 1907, Circus World Museum.

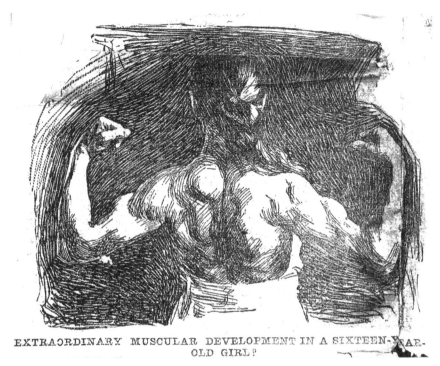

EXTRAORDINARY MUSCULAR DEVELOPMENT IN A SIXTEEN-YEAR-
OLD GIRL?

Figure 2.7 (Probably) Lena Jordan, *The NewYork World*, 6 September 1896: 16, Circus
World Museum.

eyesight made keen, the courage developed to a pitch of daring', Lew says that
young performers emulate adults seen in rehearsal from an early age, and gymnasts develop better mental faculties because a firm hand needs a well-nourished
brain.[50] This article's lack of comment about the gender of the aerialists is
revealing.

Carolyn Steedman cautions against assuming that a nineteenth-century spectator distinguished 'the child' by gender as dependents were feminized (1995:
8–9). She also argues that the amorphous child acrobat became a dispropor-
tionate focus of social anxiety (ibid.: 16). Given the emphasis in England and
North America on the age of acrobats and aerialists, was greater liberty still
possible for female aerialists than subsequently eventuated? If so, this might in
part account for the successes of female performers in the nineteenth century.

Enjoying kinetic freedom

The muscular action of female aerialists provided ongoing resistance to the feminine spectacle even as the latter gained momentum. Regardless, all action by

female aerialists defied beliefs in female weakness and inactivity even if this was accompanied by justifications that they were naturally good at balancing. Two young flyers, the Flying Fitzroys, talk knowledgeably about their physicality and seem oblivious to social expectations and legislative age limits; they contradict Le Roux's perception of naturalness with their detailed explanations of technique and training. A description of the Fitzroys' act at London's Aquarium describes how, 60 feet up, 13-year-old Maude flies 32 feet towards her 14-year-old sister Adeline, the catcher, breaking through a suspended paper cylinder drum in a trick similar to Alar's. Maude performs the same trick blindfold, encased in a sack, claiming it was her idea. She explains,

> 'The great thing is to judge your distance beforehand and to calculate the exact time when to leave the platform and the bar. I don't know anything until I'm in my sister's hands.' 'And I can't see her coming,' interposed Adeline. 'You see, the drum hides her completely.'[51]

Adeline hears Maude crash through the drum a moment before she sees Maude's legs. Adeline explains that the hardest trick to catch is when 'my sister turns *forward* off the bar on to my hands'. Despite what her trainer father calls her 'wonderful strength', even if she lifts her shoulders, this catch is dependent on the quickness of her eye. Adeline explains that 'when I'm hanging from the bar, head downwards, I can hold *three* 56 lbs . . . without pain'.[52]

The pride and enjoyment of the sisters in their feats and their attitude of fearlessness should not be discounted as naïveté or promotional hyperbole. Instead, it might be considered a personal quality that typifies the performers described here, and which allowed them to undertake these acts and to theatrically enhance them to appear easeful and exciting.

Female aerialists were increasingly advertised with poster imagery of floating bodies, and circuses up to the 1910s often utilized posters with a generic female doing nondescript aerial action at some distance above an audience. Romanticized imagery made the action appear to happen without exertion. In a 1907 poster, birds fly and the Flying Grigolatis Girls float with fairy wings in the air without any visible aerial apparatus, described as 'the wonderful winged women of the sky' (see Figure 2.8).[53] Yet it was a well-paid leading male soloist, Aeriel, who wore large mechanical wings as 'do the birds' (Durant and Durant 1957: 155). There was an increasing gap between a visual association of ethereal flight that implied involuntary action, and a performer's strenuous exertion that could still be seen in the execution of many aerial acts.

To what extent did femininity linked to cultural notions of danger detract from the recognition of actual athletic achievement? As Day writes, performers were doing acts of 'skill and bravery' in 'a period of intensive repression that questions most female activity outside the home' (1992: 138). She asks how performers in circus could possibly be role models of female achievement, given that female daredevilry was socially unacceptable (ibid.: 138). In addition, aerial

Figure 2.8 The Flying Grigolatis Girls, *Courier*, 3 June 1907. Image courtesy of Ringling Bros and Barnum and Bailey® The Greatest Show on Earth®, Circus World Museum.

performers punctuate the act with smiles and salutes, so the performance of enjoyment may have diverted attention from its serious social implications. Certainly the performance of enjoyment and feminine display made female aerial action more socially sustainable, but the significance of body development was nonetheless recognized within the wider culture.

The 'New Woman' was the nineteenth-century term for women who supported and campaigned as suffragettes for the controversial rights to vote, work and own property. Her presence was unmistakable within the movement to improve women's health through exercise (Todd 1998). Mary Beaumont's short story 'Two New Women' (1899), a conventional English romance set in Venice, presents Betty as a doctor and Daphne as a gardener, also trying to build up her muscles through 'Sandowing' exercise, and whose romantic inclination is undecided at the end (1899: 3). Only theatre and, in particular, circus acts routinely modelled an expanded female physicality for nineteenth-century spectators in contradiction of social practices. Increasing numbers of women in London's theatre audiences from the 1880s coincided with what Viv Gardner (2000) explains were changing patterns of movement in social spaces for women. Exciting aerial performances in which women bodily demonstrated spatial freedom slightly preceded the advent of wider changes in women's social mobility.

An expansion of opportunities to view female physical exertion in performance coincided with an increasing interest in undertaking exercise. Jennifer Hargreaves explains that middle-class women's participation in sports was a gradual process brought about by increased leisure (1985: 46). She writes that 'the female body was redefined to symbolize a more active, yet nonetheless still subordinate role' (ibid.: 40). Systematic exercise regimes had certainly increased in England by the 1880s with enlightened medical advice (McCrone 1988), and spread to North America along with Swedish and German calisthenics (Park 1987: 59). In order to reach working-class children, educators campaigned to have female teacher training include gymnastics on horizontal bar and rope – the ropes look like an aerial descent rope (Fletcher 1987: 148–9). In addition, middle-class American women, like Charlotte Perkins Gilman, with suffragette sympathies sought solutions for physical and mental ill-health through exercise manuals, and they attended gymnasiums (Lancaster 1994: 36–7). Ideas expanded from a belief that women's moral virtue was enhanced by physical education to a justification for exercise based on scientific measurement of the ideal body (ibid.: 39). Gymnastics drew on circus skills in the social encouragement of exercise; Doctor Dudley Allen Sargent was a circus performer who eventually became the influential director of Harvard University's gymnasium (ibid.: 40). Sargent collated his measurements for an ideal female body achieved through gymnastics with those of the 'Venus de Milo' statue, and a female statue with these combined dimensions was displayed at the 1893 Chicago World's Fair (Atkinson 1987: 38–9).

The female physical prowess demonstrated in all aerial performances and with other circus skills contributed to a milieu in which women sought increased physical freedom. In turn, there are direct references to the New Woman in circus publicity. In marketing all-female acts, BBC opportunistically exploited an idea of the New Woman as being physically freer. A poster that was probably used for its European tour reads, 'The New Woman in the Arena. A Complete Ladies' Circus . . . 20th Century girls in 20th Century Costumes'.[54] Janet Davis also finds comparable examples of the New Woman in circuses (2002: 82). Circus was reflecting but also contributing to the New Woman's profile in unambiguously demonstrating female physical capacity as the promise of the new century. Even then, signalling physical ease and enjoyment may have been anomalous in relation to what was still a social struggle for physical freedoms.

If the cliché of a nineteenth-century New Woman was a serious, bookish, middle-class bluestocking without a sense of humour, smiling female performers who were extremely physical and sexually alluring might have seemed antithetical. Early feminists subscribed to respectability. As working women who attended venues like the Crystal Palace or New York's halls preferred dancing in their leisure time, however, the social stigma of enjoying physical activity in public lessened (Peiss 1986: 90–7). For women who could afford bicycles, as suffrage drama reveals, bicycle-riding was a version of the idea that a demand for social rights also involved the right to mobility and freedom of movement (Pfisterer and Pickett 1999: 66). Bicycle trick acts with women became common in circus alongside aerial acts. Physical activity as spectacle impinges on its adoption in social practice, as attested by the young women who followed Sandow's and alternative exercise regimes.

By the 1920s the identity of the New Woman had expanded to include a hedonist, exhibitionist flapper as frenetic dancer. Aerial action provided one precedent fostering a social idea that females might find the physical freedom of fast action inherently enjoyable. By the 1920s a performance of enjoyment unquestionably enhanced interest in adopting that physical activity.

In an example from the 1920s, Lori Landay describes the potent pleasure effect for female spectators of 'a new kinaesthetic' of early cinema's dancing flapper (2002: 224 (Schwartz)). Aerialists also created performances that delivered 'kinetic power' (ibid.). While early cinema's female stars were compared to circus performers, freed from the 'laws of physics' in their stunts, and aerialists were not, yet as Jennifer Bean explains, spectators were aware of distinctions between stunts (2002: 405, 413). Cinema's female characters endured more stunts than males, but they had to be terrified (ibid.: 414); the emotional context overpowered depiction of adventurous physicality. By comparison, a female aerialist executed her action unencumbered by an imposed narrative – spectators might create their own narratives for action – and she performed enjoyment with her risk-taking. Consideration of the social impact of female aerial performances should encompass the accompanying kinetic spatiality, which was integral to the overall effect. They presented a comparatively free physicality as a kinaesthetic pleasure.

Contradictory, convoluted social attitudes permitted female aerial displays. On the one hand, female aerialists appealed because they were shown to be strong-bodied like men; on the other hand, perfected womanhood was deemed as subordinate to manhood. Female aerialists approached their training in a disciplined way, and willingly displayed their muscles, although double standards meant that female muscularity was often attributed to male training rather than self-determination. Nonetheless, in performance they demonstrated muscular strength and power as they fuelled cultural fantasies of erotic allure. Anonymous female choruses also contravened the limits of social mobility even as they undermined the esteem for aerial athleticism – although not within the profession at this time. From a distance, aerial bodies might be rhetorically recast as phantasmatic ideals and sublime entities in cultural reception, but they were unavoidably produced within athletic and artistic practices that coincided with changes in the wider social experience.

The residual effect of performing physical freedom should not be discounted. The increasing prevalence of a New Woman who might also be a gymnast may have compounded cultural fears about a seemingly unstoppable, increasingly stronger physicality. From the 1870s the New Woman was accused of wanting to turn women into men (McCrone 1988: 22–3 (Maudsley)). A masculinized female was considered abnormal and unnatural and aroused anxiety as a femme fatale who had male characteristics of dominance, cruelty and toughness (Mosse 1985: 103–4). This impression was compounded by fast aerial action. Female aerialists led until, coincidentally or not, the New Woman was gaining legal recognition through suffrage in New Zealand in 1893, Wyoming in 1894 and Australia in 1902 (Pfisterer and Pickett 1999: 35). The female gymnast doing strongman aerial acts may have become too socially dangerous. The more curtailed muscular freedoms of pleasurable feminine display would at least continue.

Nineteenth-century theatre performers, with the exception of celebrities, did not work much past their mid-30s, limited by role opportunities, and female aerialists were further curtailed by the strenuous demands of performance. Of the female performers discussed here, I could only find (superstar) Zuila still touring at the turn of the century, at 45. Although wire-walking might seem less spectacular than flying acts, it held comparable risks, and Zuila did have a serious accident falling from her velocipede in 1904 in Dublin (Tait 2003a: 81). If her fame kept her in work for 30 years, like all the acts discussed here, her performance was one of great skill and technical mastery including walking a 90-foot high-wire with a full body blindfold.[55] A blindfold might have provided a final flourish of physical mastery, but as a gesture in which the performer could not see where she was heading, it became metaphoric of the female aerialist after three decades of exceptional achievement.

Chapter 3

Cross-dressing and female muscular drag

Bird Millman was celebrated for performing popular dance steps on the wire and when she left RBBBC in 1923 the world's biggest circus hired 'dainty dancer' Berta Besson.[1] Like Millman, Berta wore a softly feminine, calf-length dress with flounce and fluff, except that Berta was Herbert, a female-impersonator wire-walker who had worked in circus since at least 1916. It was as if the physical action, the dancing on the wire, had acquired a feminine look but did not require a female performer. While cross-dressing was common in nineteenth-century theatre, what made aerial acts distinctive is that muscularity blurred gender identity, and therefore it was, and is, staged as part of an act's heightened physical action. Cross-dressed male aerialists and highly muscular female aerialists challenged prevailing social assumptions about the body's gender identity, but their practices were also artistic strategies.

The representative solo acts discussed in this chapter made gender identity ambiguous; these were performances of queerness with aerial action. Male aerialists cross-dressed from 1870 because female performers were more popular, but cross-dressing could only be perpetuated as a credible disguise because females were muscular. Two acts with queer aesthetics are described in detail: female impersonator Barbette, who remains well known, and his contemporary, Luisita Leers, well known during the 1920s and 1930s. Interestingly, Leers's milieu in circus reveals broader identity ambiguities especially to do with nationality and historical events.

Gender tricksters

In 1881 aerialist Lulu was 'the Beautiful Goddess of the Air, who at each performance, actually flies with the ease and grace of a dove, entirely across the vast Hippodrome Tent. Audiences amazed, Astounded, Astonished.'[2] And not surprisingly. A sketched image and photograph reveal Lulu dressed in her frilled costume with a moustache. Lulu was the protégée of Farini, who would later manage Zazel. In 1870 Lulu had become a feminine celebrity in London, and by 1874 Lulu was known to be Sam Hunt, cross-dressed. The continuing popularity of this cross-dressed performer is fascinating given that the adult male body hardly looked like a delicate white bird; 'the goddess' Lulu was certainly a queer bird.

Between 1870 and 1874 Lulu's cross-dressed identity was kept secret. Only Farini's rope-walking rival, Blondin, said publicly that Lulu was Farini's young male partner, El Niño (Peacock 1996: 197). As an adolescent performer in London, Hunt's Lulu was acclaimed for her refined pale beauty, her flowing curls and frills (ibid.: 189), and she instigated a look and act that female aerialists copied and Farini opportunistically exploited. To become a star of Lulu's magnitude in 1870 needed more than feminine beauty and required a particularly inventive aerial act, and this was what the crowds also came to view a decade later.

The act was performed between three trapezes and two covered mid-air wooden platforms, 18 and 16 inches wide. Tricks 1 to 12 were striking, with body revolutions, somersaults between trapezes, a half-somersault to a platform, a forward somersault and a drop to a leg catch.[3] For trick 13 Lulu was propelled, by Farini's newly patented invention, 25 feet straight up in the air to land, feet first, on to a platform. The eight-foot-high spring propulsion mechanism was hidden under the stage so it appeared as if Lulu's stiff body jumped up, unaided – Lulu stood on a pedestal above a piston that was released by stretched rubber straps. For trick 14 Lulu uniquely executed three somersaults from the platform down to a net – Farini invented a net, as did the Hanlon-Lees and others.

With Lulu, Farini and Hunt created a performance phenomenon that helped forge an impression of feminine weightlessness. A drawn image of Lulu shows her mid-air, her arms up at an angle, with an almost supernatural look.[4] Lulu was one of several apprentices trained by Farini, and worked as El Niño in the mid-1860s in an act imitative of Little Bob with the Hanlon-Lees. When Lulu appeared, El Niño was presumed to be a cross-dressed girl, and as Lulu, repeatedly sang the line, 'Wait till I'm a man' (Frost 1881: 186).

With Lulu's gender masquerade exposed in 1874, public suspicion about the gender identity of circus performers unsurprisingly seems to increase, supported by the evidence of gender duplicity elsewhere. In North America the trapezists Lila and Zoe De Lave, mentioned in Chapter 1, were touring with Dan Rice's Paris Pavilion in 1871, as was Monsieur De Lave, who was probably a wire-walking rival of Farini and Blondin. Zoe, blindfolded in a sack, was swung out from a trapeze, did a somersault and caught a rope in what was described as the most 'desperate and startling feat' ever attempted (quoted in Slout 1998b: 17). William Slout's research reveals that the daring Zoe in Rice's circus was male, and Lila disappeared before her gender was verified (ibid.: 18). The cross-dressing of young males with upper-body strength for competitive advantage made the aerial act appear impressive 'for a woman', and ensured its hire over other male acts. The financial rewards were significant and Lila and Zoe advertised in 1870 that they would meet the Leopold family's challenge of doing their leaps for $500.[5] Geraldine Leopold copied Lulu's leap (Slout 1998a: 174). In

1869 Zoe was mentioned alongside Azella and Sanyeah.[6] Exposure of gender trickery mattered because it was part of the aerial act's theatricality to confound ideas about female physicality.

The widely cited precedent for male-to-female cross-dressing in circus was an equestrienne, Ella Zoyara, also Ella Stokes (Senelick 1993, photograph 11; Moore 1994: 127–8; Senelick 2000: 296–7). Peacock implies that Farini copied Ella's cross-dressing (1996: 197). Ella was Sam Omar Kingsley, cross-dressed by Spencer Stokes and working in 1850s Europe and in 1860s North America. Kingsley also performed in the same programme alongside his feminine persona, Ella (Slout 1998a: 158), and she was rumoured to be male (Munby 1972: 35). After the cross-dressing exposure in 1861, Kingsley married, had a family, and continued managing and working in circuses touring extensively to Australia and East Asia.[7] Frost writes of Ella in 1849 in London that the 'charms of face and form were a never-ending theme of conversation and meditation for the thousands of admirers who nightly followed them around the ring with enraptured eyes' (1881: 126). In noting male attentiveness to Ella's movement around the ring, Frost implicates her action in her desirable appeal.

Most male performers who cross-dressed were young and frequently reluctant to do so. It was relatively easy to effect but not always to keep secret, and led to identity confusion. In a less common reversal, Frost recounts that Little Corelli is 'supposed to be a boy; but I have since heard that it was a girl' (ibid.: 186). Laurence Senelick reiterates a nineteenth-century view that troupes preferred cross-dressed males because their muscular strength was more consistent and reliable (1993: 84 (Le Roux)). The explanation most commonly given in circus biographies, however, is either that the act needed a substitute female performer at short notice or that to be competitive it needed to compensate for a lack of women. This practice was instigated by older showmen pandering to the (male) audience's demand for young female performers. There are examples of male cross-dressing across a range of circus skills; for example, Janet Davis describes equestrian Albert Hodgini as Miss Daisy (2002: 115–16). Photographs of the esteemed English equestrian and aerialist family, the Clarkes, show Alfred (Augustus) in a pale, calf-length ballet dress, and the acrobatic John Frederick in a sombre, 1890s long dress holding a whip, and there is a clear record of Alfred John performing with Lord Sanger's in 1889 as Madame Isabelle, fraudulently billed as the only equestrienne doing somersaults, and receiving letters from enthralled male admirers seeking clandestine meetings (Coxe undated: 5, 8). Studio photographs of named performers held in archive collections without further information suggest similar male cross-dressing practices in aerial work.[8]

There was very little advantage for females to secretly cross-dress, and acts of female-to-male cross-dressing in circus were far rarer than in theatre. But in a 1906 BBC show '[t]hree of the girls impersonated male characters' in the Vorlops' spinning act.[9] Tight-wire-walker Mary Miller, working with BBC, cross-dressed as George because males got better opportunities (Moore 1994: 123). The paucity of female cross-dressed aerialists should be contextualized in relation to the widespread practice of male impersonation of varying degrees in nineteenth-century theatre, in particular female performers cross-dressed as boys and for clowning (Bratton 1992: 83, 89). Female identity in circus gained from less rather than more clothing and it was displays of female physicality that dazzled audiences. The female's costume was an adaptation of the original male tights, trunk-hose and sleeveless vest, which dressed down to reveal the anatomical body rather than camouflaging it.

As indicated, female circus performers were engaged in a more profound challenge to body identity through their developed muscular shapes and athleticism – aerialists and other circus performers preceded physical culture enthusiasts and bodybuilders. In 1895 the journalist interviewing Adelina Antonio, at that time the star at London's Aquarium, describes a finale with a 90-foot dive and a double somersault to a net, and quotes Antonio proudly saying that she is muscular. It was lifting the weight of the body up by the arms to the trapeze bar that had developed her muscles:

> As Madame spoke, she drew up her forearm, causing her splendidly developed bicep to rise and display itself to full advantage. 'Between elbow and shoulder the circumference of my arm is thirteen inches.' . . . 'My eyes must be open and my head clear during the fall. As you have seen, I bend backwards as far as possible before I let go, and my toes are the last to leave the platform. Then I watch for the net as I descend, and must calculate the exact moment when to turn, that I may land on my back. If I landed on my feet I would break the net. My weight is just doubled by the fall: I weigh ten stone, but strike the net with the force of twenty. I effect the turn with my back, which is the hardest-tried part of my body in this performance.'[10]

Antonio is describing the precision of each move and her concentration during the performance. She was from a family of Hungarian aerialists and because she had had accidents, her husband now did a safety check each time. Antonio's 20-year-career took her all over the world, including to Australia and New Zealand.

Female muscularity continued to attract attention. Alison Kibler recounts that in response to an American journalist's question about women's suffrage in 1916, Ruth Budd of the Aerial Budds duo showed her biceps with a claim that she could lift up men in the street (1999: 143). Kibler's thoughtful analysis of the Budds' act explains how it contravenes gender norms; firstly because Ruth supported her male partner Giles's weight and secondly because, in Ruth's solo, she manipulated an idea of femininity by using song and dance before her aerial and acrobatic action to make the latter seem more remarkable. The position of weight-bearing on trapeze, however, was still widely done by female aerialists up to the 1930s and it only became a largely masculinized role and body position by the mid-twentieth century; acts with females lifting males were more evident in the decades following their 1870s antecedents. In the film *A Scream in the Night*

(1919) Ruth appeared as a female Tarzan, Darwa, swinging through the trees and outwitting an ape in a confused social Darwinism that produced headlines calling her a 'monkey' (Kibler 1999: 160). Kibler's analysis finds Ruth's film performance at the nexus of a regressive generalized Woman who is elided into an idea of animal, and synonymous with a category of nature. The fictional narrative and setting of the film for the aerial action generate ideas of feminine primitivism and of a chimeric circus body (see Chapter 5). The female aerialist would seem to have lost her god-like mystique by the 1910s, but unlike a costume, her muscularity could not be removed at the end of the act.

Man-woman and spaces in between

Barbette (Vander Clyde) is known for an act of female impersonation, and nominally also as an angel; she ended with a trick called 'angel's dive' (Senelick 2000: 507–8; Leslie 1973: 203). Described in publicity as a 'man-woman', and billed as an enigma, Barbette was acclaimed for the act's effect on the audience. Descriptions of the act in theatres and circuses vary as commentators interested in its drag downplay the aerial skills, while the circus commentators are less concerned with the costuming. Barbette walked on low tight-wire, swung on trapeze and turned on Roman rings to music by Wagner and Rimsky-Korsakov's *Scheherezade*. Francis Steegmuller comments 'Barbette's act played with masculine and feminine attributes using the aerial apparatus as "vehicles"' (1986b: 525, emphasis in original). Jean Cocteau writes that Barbette's parodic pantomime captured all women by 'becoming himself *the* woman – so much so as to eclipse the prettiest girls' (quoted in Steegmuller 1986a: 366, italics in original). Barbette was technically skilled though not outstanding; she executed a hock-catch, grabbing the bar with the knee from either a standing or a sitting position (Coxe 1980: 159). Was the Barbette phenomenon simply immaculate female impersonation and striptease that stood out when combined with skilled aerial work?

Barbette claims Shakespeare's heroines as her influence: 'I wanted an act that would be a thing of beauty – of course it would have to be a strange beauty' (Steegmuller 1986b: 525). She sought an artistic ideal as a fashionable woman, and for Cocteau and Paul Valéry the act was art. Cocteau describes her as 'no mere acrobat in women's clothes, nor just a graceful daredevil, but one of the most beautiful things in the theatre. Stravinsky, Auric, poets, painters and I myself have seen no comparable display of artistry on the stage since Nijinksy' (Steegmuller 1986a: 365). The quality of Barbette's movement was being praised.

In a well-cited, somewhat florid review by Velona Pilcher (1930), she is a bird, supernatural like the mythic Orion, and a muse for Sapphic verse. Usefully, though, this description is specific about muscular action:

> the most masculine of muscles are moving like levers, folding and unfolding as if their very friction would burn away the flesh. And observe that long

bone of the back, when arched at its acutest angle . . . the cord of this spine is taut.

(Pilcher 1930: 1034)

She points, spins, pirouettes and dances. Undressing as if in a bedroom, she is 'two lovers in one body', who are lifted by light; then 'Barbette is a boy' (ibid.: 1036). The act's appeal also seems to be the visible tension between muscular effort and its feminine costuming.

Barbette's costume transformations delivered a sensuous experience that inspired viewers to compare her with mythic figures. She was perceived as mysterious, and no doubt in part because of what Jacques Damase terms 'sexual mystification' (1962: 30). Even Damase, who gives a more literal description of Barbette's act in Parisian music hall, confirms the staging of a femme fatale suggesting exotic otherness. He writes,

> The woman then rose, naked except for the gems on her breast and belly, and began walking a steel tight-rope. Her eyes shaded green like some mysterious Asiatic jewel, she walked backwards and forwards along the tight-rope, dispensed with her balancing pole, and contorted her thin, nervous body as the entire audience held its breath . . . Then Barbette leapt down on the stage, gave a bow, tore off her wig and revealed a bony Anglo-Saxon acrobat's head: gasps from the astonished audience shattered by the sudden brutality of the action.
>
> (Damase 1962: 30)

Barbette did 'a wrestler's salute', one arm raised with a clenched hand to reveal maleness at the finale (Leslie 1973: 203). Like most aerial performance, Barbette's act cannot be disengaged from the wider offstage context and, importantly, publicity and programme notes. Initially she was billed as a 'deceiver' and a 'mystery'. By 1926 Barbette is 'The Supreme Sensation of Circusdom', and the programme tells the audience that the costumes cost £3,000.[11] In programme photographs Barbette is standing in a long dress, her head turned at an angle, her arms in the air so that her muscles are less apparent – Barbette's specially made hose masked her skin's roughness and protected it from the apparatus.

As an adolescent, Vander had been inspired by aerialists to practise wire-walking, and subsequently stepped in at short notice to the Alfaretta Sisters' act as a sister.[12] Later Vander developed a cross-dressing solo act as Barbette for vaudeville. Barbette was working in England by 1921 with BMC but would become acclaimed in Paris in 1923. As Damase explains, she was 'a jazz-age Botticelli' with a 'disturbing, dreamlike perfection' (1962: 30). For this transformation, Barbette earned ten times the average acrobat's wage (ibid.). The act created a feminine spectacle with a visual aesthetic that catered to 1920s tastes. One of the most famous American female impersonators, Julian Eltinge, was at the height of his career just before the First World War when Vander was developing aerial skills. Cross-dressing had become a sophisticated act as one of Eltinge's contemporaries, female impersonator Ray Monde, shows. Monde as a woman removed his wig to become a man, then removed a second wig to become a woman again (Laurie 1953: 90). Eltinge was reported in the media to dress offstage as male, to be a 'manly' man, which gave him the license to stage what was called an 'ambisextrous' gymnastic female identity (quoted in Senelick 2000: 310). Audiences were meant to perceive Eltinge as decidedly male offstage. This both protected the performer from accusations of sexual impropriety and heightened the act's artistic achievement. There was even publicity about Eltinge's fights to verify his masculinity. Barbette adopted similar strategies, even fighting, and appeared dressed as a male offstage.

In Man Ray's (1980) famous photographs, Barbette is bare-chested in front of the mirror, wearing make-up and a short blonde wig. She looks provocatively sideways or upwards, innocently angelic. Only large veins in her muscular arms reveal a body capable of strong, forceful action. Barbette also stands, her legs spread apart, putting on suspenders and stockings, then descends a staircase in a long dress. She is balanced on a wire wearing point shoes and a ballet skirt, right arm up, left arm out, and then with her arms upwards; she is stripped to satin shorts and jewelled bikini top, a beaded star radiating from her crotch. There are also photographs of Barbette in a man's suit.

Barbette changed gender identity from feminine to masculine during the act. The feminine effect was the first part and it was accentuated by aerial action. Barbette explains, 'In the circus there's a long tradition of boys dressing as girls, and especially in a wire act women's clothes make everything more impressive – the plunging and gyrating are more dramatic in a woman' (Steegmuller 1986b: 525). While it is clear that the costumes and associated staging underwent artistic development, the extent to which the aerial skills changed is unclear.

In an era of variety shows with the 'girlie' and Ziegfeld revues, Barbette's trim muscularity had to outdo these undulating female bodies. Her entrance was a Ziegfeld-like illusion of excessive decorativeness. She explains, 'I went in for lamés and paillettes with trimmings of feathers and lace' (ibid.). A successful Berlin designer first offered expensive gowns, but when this happened is unclear (Foster 1948: 119).

The carefully observed drawings of Barbette's act at the Paris Empire by the two circus artists Marthe and Juliette Vesque confirm that she descended a high staircase in a gown and then removed it in order to do the aerial action (1977, 1 December 1927 – see Figure 3.1). On the wire she is drawn in a sequined bodice coming down to her hip-line, and on the trapeze and on the rings she seems to wear a jewelled body-stocking and shorts. A photograph in Man Ray's (1980) archive collection showing Barbette on a swing without the shorts (see Figure 3.2), however, also corresponds with Damase's description, so there may have been occasions on which she was on trapeze costumed as naked. Barbette's

Figure 3.1 Barbette à l'Empire, 1 December 1927, by Juliette et Marthe Vesque, Paris, courtesy of the Musée des traditions populaires, © Photograph RMN – P. Pitou.

Figure 3.2 Barbette 1926, ©Man Ray, licensed by VISCOPY, Australia, 2004.

second identity was created when she stripped to a body-stocking and shorts in sexually evocative action.

Barbette's swing photograph is reminiscent of the dream-like aesthetic of boy-girl figures in idealized classical landscapes created by American painter and commercial illustrator Maxfield Parrish. As one of the first mass-produced prints, Parrish's *Daybreak* (1922), with its naked figure of undetermined gender bending over a sleeping girl, was estimated to be hanging on the walls of a quarter of American households by 1925 (Yount 1999: 15). It is Parrish's *The Dinkey-Bird* (1904), however, with a naked body of undetermined gender mid-air on a swing and a fairytale castle behind, that seems closest to the aesthetic of Barbette's photographic performance on the swing. Parrish's androgynous fantasy figures in twilight settings conjure up a playful dalliance and curiosity as if existing outside the polarized gender identity of social worlds. A genderless sensuality implies sexual innocence, and yet in its depiction the body becomes eroticized.

Barbette's undressing and unfolding action implied a space of identity that was in between feminine dress and masculine physical action. The performing body's physical suspension on trapeze echoed identity suspension. Barbette exploited the inherent potential of a muscular aerial body to seem androgynous, and her costumed double skin, her fake nudity, was explicitly suggestive of an androgynous body in between gender. This expands on the spectacle of gender exploited by covert male cross-dressers, who relied on the potential of adolescent muscular gymnasts to appear as either gender depending on the costuming. An idea of a body that is neither gender, or both together, became emblematic of 1990s queer identity, and Barbette's 1920s girlish maleness might be comparable to boyish femaleness of 1990s aerial body identity (Chapter 5).

Barbette made transitions from feminine to androgynous to masculine as she concurrently performed aerial action, and this elided physical and social identity spaces. Her act built up from displays of precision in balancing and pointed footwork usually deemed feminine, to swinging on trapeze in body suspension, followed by tricks on rings which displayed upper-body muscular strength and, on descent, she delivered masculine gestures. The sequence of the aerial action could be effectively arranged to support the transitions in costumed cultural identity. Its progression added to the performance of mysteriousness.

Open secrets and silences

The 1926–7 BMC programme in London had a starred footnote: 'The Management would appreciate it if the Guests would preserve the Barbette secret.' If BMC meant the revelation of maleness at the end of the act, the larger open secret would seem to arise from how gender identity transformations were produced by a body in continuous physical action.

The irony of the request to preserve Barbette's secret is not lost in hindsight. The assumption accompanying a show like Barbette's was that a manly man could be a skilled cross-dressing performer without being homosexual. Nonetheless the performance of cross-dressing was perceived as coda for homosexual identity. In what seems like a reliable but somewhat boastful first-hand account, circus performer Frank Foster, who greatly admired Barbette's act, says, 'At every performance I was asked by fops and dandies smitten with Barbette's charms if I could arrange an introduction to the fascinating creature. I could have retired on the bribes I was offered' (1948: 119). He recounts that Barbette punched a circus worker on the jaw and sent him reeling for adopting a 'pansyish attitude' (ibid.). Foster explains that this made the worker respectful, and there was no repetition of 'the mimicry'. The aerialist was not 'effeminate' but 'attracted sexual perverts whom he helped' and gave generous tips to the venue staff because his 'heart dictated his life' (ibid.).

Foster's account of why Vander (Barbette) stopped performing in Europe explains that Vander returned to America and the Cines-Variety Circuit, on a very large salary, and was expected to work five performances daily, which was too strenuous. The dancer, Anton Dolin, claimed that the rumours about why his friend stopped performing included that he had broken his legs, paralysed his back, contracted pneumonia or infantile paralysis and had to learn to walk again or that he had even died (1938: 305–6). It was osteomyelitis that hospitalized Vander in 1938 for 18 months.[13] But Dolin is also quoted saying that Vander was unable to get another English work visa following an indiscretion.[14] Regardless of the circumstances, Vander was in New York in 1935 to perform in *Jumbo*. Billy Rose produced this popular musical at the Old Hippodrome theatre with 40 showgirls, a score by Rogers and Hart and staging by John Murray Anderson, who would later team up with Vander in circus (Albrecht 1989: 97). Francis Steegmuller describes meeting Vander in 1966 in Austin, Texas, and finding a fastidious, well-groomed, thin older man with jerky, stiff movement, the result of illness.

Vander continued working in circus and other large-scale entertainment for over 20 years, specializing in directing feminine spectacles. After 1943, as artistic director, he reinvented the aerial ballet and human butterfly choruses of RBBBC and other American circuses for mainstream audiences (see Figure 2.5). He directed numerous female aerialists from beginners through to solo celebrities, although Sverre Braathen complains about this emphasis on the chorus spectacle in what is 'more of a girl show with production numbers rather than strictly circus'.[15] As well, Vander advised on a number of successful films in the 1950s, including *The Big Circus* (1959), and the cross-dressing of Jack Lemmon and Tony Curtis as disguised musicians hiding from thugs in *Some Like it Hot* (1959). Vander devised the aerial ballet for the hit *Disney on Parade* in America, and rehearsed it in Australia in 1972, although with difficulty since he was allocated non-professionals to train.[16] Most accounts of Barbette omit the ensuing decades of Vander's significant artistic contribution to the development of American circus and feminine choruses.

If Barbette's cross-dressing was an open secret, Cocteau finds Barbette's 'secret' to be the machine-like precision to his work (Crowson 1976: 85). Lydia Crowson explains that Cocteau is interested in theatre as illusion, where sensory 'perception changes completely' and is deceived, in an 'intimacy' between audience and performer (ibid.: 81–2, 85). She writes that Barbette suppressed masculine body movement until the end of the act in order to be feminine (ibid.: 81), although suppression presumes that masculine body action was naturally present. The artistic secret to identity in Barbette's act is that it was created with the body in action as well as with costumed dress. She developed a choreography of gender identity in conjunction with her aerial action.

Barbette's body movement in between aerial actions received few comments until the final surprise gesture of the raised fist. This suggests that either the body's action was not registering with spectators or could not be put into words, or, more likely, that it was close to how identity is perceived in lived experience, and therefore did not warrant comment. A journalist might only be expected to comment on the specialized movement of bodies within dance, sport and circus.

Did Barbette's feminine and androgynous costuming make the body's non-aerial movement less visible? If the performing body's action seems like a social experience of perceiving masculine and feminine identity, then it may not be received as also part of the artistic creation. The function of physical action in the performance of gender identity becomes like an open secret.

As with most live aerial performance, only traces of Barbette's routine remain. Nevertheless accounts and drawings of the performance confirm that feminine and masculine identity was physically performed as part of the action, and that the space in between was one of androgynous identity. An aerial body with multiple gender identities was especially mysterious.

Unavoidable identity risks

Luisita Leers became internationally successful at 17 years of age after John Ringling saw her performing in Havana, and had her debut in the 1928 RBBBC circus. Her solo act on trapeze was programmed in the ninth event as the girl who 'astounded all Europe'. It exemplifies the strenuous physical exertion of solo acts by leading females throughout the twentieth century, although this quality is only rarely acknowledged outside circus in later decades. A publicity agent labelled Leers as 'The Physical Culture girl' in a circus show 'fairly glowing in its Achilles sturdiness, its healthy complexion and its vigorous strength'.[17] An emphasis on healthiness in circus promotion suggests wider social acceptance of the benefits of physical exercise by the 1920s, even for women.

For the RBBBC programmes, Leers wears a simple white, sleeveless leotard of the kind also worn by male aerialists, and Leers is photographed from the waist up flexing her biceps and trapezius muscles to maximum visual effect. Leers's muscularity was part of her attraction. While the physical risks that she took in performance were admired, she was looked at when she walked in the street because her muscular shape and movement made her stand out in the 1920s and 1930s. In everyday public spaces, her muscular appearance was even socially risky. Accordingly it is not surprising to find a sympathetic commentary describing Leers's cultured outlook, her moral propriety and, above all, her innate femininity, which could not be seen. Nor is it surprising to find an expression of unease about her muscles.

Solo female aerialists may have been becoming more muscular as strenuous endurance standards increased. The use of feminine costuming to camouflage muscularity was pioneered expertly at that time by celebrity aerialist Lillian Leitzel (see below). It was not yet prescribed as it became in 1950s circus. To some extent, female circus performers up to the 1930s were freer in their display of muscular development because of its continuing novelty, but it also marked them as socially different.

An aerialist copies males and females in aerial action, and a muscular female obviates gender separation with her action as well as her shape. Although this is not the intention, the muscular body seems imitative of masculinity. Annette

Kuhn writing on 1980s female bodybuilding in film suggests that '[m]uscles are rather like drag' (1988: 17). Steven Cohan utilizes Kuhn's work to explain that muscularity 'is as much a performance art as any drag show; both activities theatricalize the body itself so that it becomes marked with gender signs' (1997: 186). The term 'drag' was formerly used to mean males in dresses (Baker 1994: 17), but broadened to encompass females impersonating males with costuming. Masculinity, however, is also widely depicted by a bare muscular chest. Kuhn explains how female 'bodybuilding is an active production of the body' that calls into question 'the naturalness of the body' and 'the natural order of gender' (1988: 17). Accordingly, a female aerial body with visible upper-body muscles in minimal costuming manifests muscular drag.

Leers performed an endurance act (see Figure 3.3). In a number of sports, women have proved very effective endurance athletes (MacClancy 1996: 14–15). Luisita, the name is a Spanish version of Louise, was born into a family of German acrobats, and became known as the 'Wonder-Girl. A youthful aerialist of prodigious strength and amazing skill in a trapeze offering that has astounded two continents'.[18] Her father, who worked on the Roman rings, was also a contortionist, and her mother, an acrobat. Her physical training, for two to three hours a day from six years of age, was supervised by her father, and she began trapeze in early adolescence.[19] As an adult, Leers lived in close quarters with her parents and only had one week off a year. She had to be careful with food although, ironically, circus food sometimes made her sick.[20] She was careful with exercise too and rarely swam as it took strength needed for the act.

Leers's solo trapeze act without a net included record-breaking tricks with a long high giant swing, a neck hang from the high trapeze without a safety line, and a muscle grind in which she rotated around the bar with her elbows against it. These repeated actions were painful and damaging for the body as well as dangerous should she slip when the apparatus became wet with perspiration.[21] She writes,

> The most times I turned over in my muscle grind were 139, I think I maybe could do about 180 but naturally not every day, my arms would get too sore and it would make me to[o] tired . . . My arms got sore very often, naturally it also is painful but the people do not need to see that. The most difficult part of my act is the neck [word unclear; hang] with the split you know on trapeze is street [word spelling; straight] and the neck is round so there is just or very little place to hang by and it makes it still so much harder, when I take one leg to make that split, the one arm[e] planihes [planges] are hard too almost on hot days.[22]

Leers's letter conveys how her act was physically arduous, causing muscle strain and pain, especially from repetitive movements that bruised her skin. Although Natalie of the Foucart Sisters is accorded an early version of the muscle grind in

Figure 3.3 Luisita Leers on trapeze, Milner Library.

1862 (Speaight 1980: 72 (Munby)), and Verrecke was at least photographed in a neck hang (Gossard 1994: 11), nineteenth-century aerialists were not working at comparable height or against endurance records.

While Leers executed these aerial tricks using her muscular strength and without theatrical effects, a letter states that there was at least one contemporary who copied her act but theatrically faked the muscle grind.[23] Performers who used a short cut for the muscle grind with a revolving bar on a second trapeze detracted from Leers's acts because at a distance the audience could not necessarily tell the difference. In this faked version the female body would be passively turned by the apparatus, rather than turning with its own strength. The implication here is that muscularity provides proof of authentic action in aerial performance.

Although admiring of Leers's athleticism, some 1930s journalism reflects anxiety about a female aerialist's muscularity. An experienced reviewer of circus acts, Stern, is perturbed and seeks outward feminine signs from a smile, an attitude, and in the body's gestures. When Leers debuts in Paris in 1935, Stern is greatly impressed:

> Luisita Leers stops the show at Medrano this fortnight. Girl trapezist, in best aerial single act seen in Paris this year, is in secondary spot – right after intermission – but she walks away with the works, eclipsing everything else on the bill . . . Girl is not only a remarkable performer, from a purely acrobatic viewpoint, but has one of those smiles that knocks 'em over, and a body which remains beautiful in spite of its extraordinary muscles. She works high, without a net. Muscular control is so perfect that her stuff looks easy, but when she hangs by the back of her neck, apparently just as easily as she did her simpler introductory turns, audience realizes there was something to it all along.[24]

Stern recognizes the aerial body's beauty by exempting its muscles.

Stern gives a second account of Leers at the Alhambra, Paris, for an International Vaudeville Festival, praising her achievement but criticizing how the raising and the lowering of the curtain during the muscle grind trick undercut appreciation of the quality of endurance. Stern writes, 'Powerful young lady, with eerie smile and graceful, madonna-like attitudes'.[25] While the Madonna might be the supreme exemplar of feminine gentleness, why does Stern find Leers 'eerie'? This unease might derive from a perception of gender disturbance; either the body's action was unsettling because it displayed signs of both genders simultaneously or its impression of masculine power cancels out one of smiling feminine tenderness. A perception of unease might also arise if visible muscularity short-circuits conventional female objectification.

A female athletic physique was still uncommon outside the circus despite the physical-culture movement. A journalist writes of Leers in her early twenties,

> When Luisita Leers walks down the street in a short-sleeved Summer dress, women stare at her arms, hardly believing their eyes when they see the bulging muscles and the dark burns inside her elbows. But Luisita only

smiles, and there is a soft look in her brown eyes. For her there are none of the outward aspects of femininity. Eighteen years on the high trapeze in circuses all over the world have robbed Luisita of those feminine traits that women jealously guard and men look for in the ladies.[26]

Lawyer Sverre Braathen, a knowledgeable circus fan and friend of Leers, may have been the writer of this newspaper article headlined '18 Years on the High Trapeze but Circus Star is Afraid to Sleep in an Upper Pullman Berth, Gambles Her Life Each Day in Dangerous "Neck Hang"'. Is it credible that Leers's strength work, performed at height with fearlessness, coexists with neurosis about top bunks on trains? Anecdotally, aerialists do not generally have a fear of heights. While this might be interpreted as a manifestation of a performer's unconscious fear of the body's falling, and/or the performer's fear of a loss of control over the body while sleeping, and even her dislike of the circus train's cramped quarters, it also narrates psychic weakness. This information is given in a discussion of professional work that demonstrates female physical strength. Far from being voyeuristic in alluding to bed, the revelation of a fear of the top bunk provides Leers with feminine behaviour to make her seem approachable to (male) readers or audience members who would presumably have no fear of top bunks. The journalist also writes that the pain reduced her to tears after the act. The reference to tears reinforces an idea of femininity, and it is hard to find a comparable comment about male aerialists.

To further dispel an inference that Leers's requisite muscular exterior indicated unorthodox social behaviour, the journalist testifies as to her sensitivity, education and good character. She is well read, with the socialist Maxim Gorky's novel *The Mother* among her books; she has a record collection that includes Beethoven, Bach, Wagner and Brahms, and she speaks four languages. This journalist, who testifies to her inner femininity from his offstage contact, seems reassured. Irrespective of all these concessions to social attitudes about physicality and gender, the 1933 newspaper article praises Leers's professional achievement: 'She is one of the great athletes of the world and one of the supreme artists.'[27]

The article also states that she 'is not really like that' as if 'like what' is obvious to readers without further explanation. It is not for contemporary readers. The writer may be defending her against any potential accusation that she has masculine character traits because she has a muscular body shape, and instead proclaims her feminine traits. Inadvertently, the article is refuting the belief that an interior self's gender is automatically indicated by the body's appearance with its inference that muscularity is not Leers's true identity. The statement implies a separation of the body and the self. It is probable that behind this protestation is a rebuttal of an insidious social fear that an overly developed muscularity equates with masculine urges. This becomes especially socially dangerous where sexual desire is assumed to mean only desire for the female body.

This speculative extrapolation on female muscularity should not be mistaken as in any way making an inference about Leers's personal life or her sexual orientation. This is an argument about how the appearance of female muscularity, despite its central function in aerial performance, was socially provocative in relation to conventional expectations of gender identity. Leers may even have been aware of the implications of her muscularity. In a 1936 letter she comments on the photograph of a woman mistaken for her. She writes, 'I think it is Herma Canastrelly, she looks a little bi [*sic*] like me and the[y] must have made that misstake therefore.'[28] Is this a misspelling or is Leers noting that her muscular shape and those of other aerialists implied a body with a dual gender identity? Where a body is interpreted as presenting meaningful social codes (as a text) for communicating (reading) cultural identity, female muscularity remains ambiguous and resists prescriptive ideas of male and female physical difference.

Posters of Leers show her in a neck hang, her legs apart, in a pose from her act (see Figure 3.4). In Havana in 1927 her posters had to have an additional pasting across the leg area to protect her reputation from graffitied insinuations (Morris 1976: 87). By the 1920s photographic images of a performer's full-length body were commonly used in Europe and the USA, but such an overt display in public space was not necessarily acceptable internationally. In Cuba a poster of the performer in a leotard during her performance provoked shame. The image captures a momentary suspension of the athletic action so that a promise of unfolding physical action also becomes implicated in sexualized reactions to it. Significantly muscular drag can contain a promise of physical action.

The writer of the article '18 Years on the trapeze . . .' avoids any impression that might imply a sexualized body, even sexiness, in Leers's act. She 'is a Beethoven symphony on a trapeze'.[29] The act is compared to an uplifting experience of classical music – it was accompanied by live circus band music. The journalist would seem to be explaining a sensory receptiveness to aerial performance in that its action is experienced with and as sensory phenomena, albeit with sight transposed into sound. The journalist romanticizes the act with the music analogy, which evokes an impression of hearing pure cadence and over-rides the voyeuristic implications of what might be taken as a lower order of cultural behaviour.

Conversely, the performer's body in the Havana poster was unromantically eroticized. Perhaps an image of female muscularity was threatening, and a sexualized response was one way that the gender hierarchy could be restored. Judith Halberstam claims that masculinity only becomes intelligible as an identity text when it appears removed from the (white) male body (1998: 2). Honi Fern Haber explains that the 'muscled woman makes visible the artificiality of the norms of masculinity and femininity' because seeing female muscles brings into question male domination and leads to political change through the aesthetics of bodily appearance (1996: 142). In Haber's elaboration of Foucault's

Figure 3.4 Luisita Leers poster, Milner Library.

ideas about the body as the site of power, the contemporary female bodybuilder provides an example of social empowerment. Kuhn suggests that these body-based practices might bridge a category of Woman as spectacle and as object, and women's participation in identity-making (1988: 22). The Cuban poster example of sexual objectification, however, would not support the argument that female muscularity might at least confront social prejudices. The female bodybuilder's lack of femininity puts her outside regimes of social power and makes her susceptible to what Chris Holmlund describes as the paradox of 'a fear of visible difference and a fear of the abolition of visible difference' (1997: 149–50). The persistence of male objectification of female bodies leads Haber to propose a re-eroticized look in relation to muscular females, one which expands on notions of male desire and the male gaze. Certainly female muscularity might represent bodily sameness to a male viewer and thus be imitative of self-same desiring. It also implicates two-way desire by representing a female body that is potentially an active seducer and not passively feminine. Physical identity slippage might fulfil sexual fantasies as it spans social categories. Thus female muscularity may disturb objectification, belie identity classification and confront orthodox configurations of sexual desire.

Muscular drag in aerial performance, however, presents identity that is a consequence of the body's physical action. Whether female muscularity invites or repels, it is perceived – in body-to-body encounters – either in the delivery of physical action or in its promise. This has implications for how bodies are sexualized even with gender identity slippage. Where a muscular body with a capacity for energetic physical action is sexualized, its action becomes part of its appeal. Physical action might be nominally considered integral to a muscular body's desirability.

Slippery work and nationality slippage

Leers's performance career was ended abruptly by the Second World War (1939–45), which also caused the loss of her muscularity when she became malnourished. Leers's muscularity and physical strength could not be recouped. The wider social and historical context impacted on Leers's work, and that of her contemporaries, in ways that reveal further contrasts and complications between an act's technical skills and its theatrical techniques of identity formation, between personal and professional nationalities and between social and physical risk-taking.

Leers starred in the centre ring at the pinnacle of American romance with circus, typified by RBBBC's 1930 show that brought together some of the most famous aerial performers: the German–English Siegrist-Silbons, German-born Lillian Leitzel, the Mexican Codonas and Aboriginal Australians Con Colleano and his older sister Winifred Colleano. Although Leitzel was unquestionably the big female star, Winifred was Leers's main rival with a spectacular heel catch first done by Edwardo then Alfredo Codona. Fred Bradna explains that after

20 years on trapeze, Winnie was the greatest heel-and-toe aerialist as she 'swung down from it, hanging on by her hands, and then let go while executing an upward somersault and a simultaneous half twist of the body, catching the bar by her heels' (1952: 312–13). She also rotated from a sitting position and caught herself by her heels, and finished with a somersault from the net to the floor.[30] Winnie's extreme physical action in performance brought accompanying social liberties and mobility denied to many other indigenous people in Australian society at that time, since they were excluded from voting, economic rights and travelling around freely. Circus provided a comparatively safer social enclave in relation to racial difference (Holland 1999).

An association with Germany prior to 1940 was an advantage for the highly skilled Leers and Leitzel, because of that country's centrality to the development of gymnastics. A female leisure pastime of dance gymnastics, popular during the 1920s, subsequently became absorbed into the Nazis' institutionalized spectacles of nation building during the 1930s (Manning 1993: 8–9). While Leers's aerial career was ended by changed political circumstances, the abrupt end to Leitzel's life reveals the full extent of the risk in both their acts. Sadly, Leitzel fell in Copenhagen, on 13 February 1931, when a metal ring broke, stressed by a temperature change, and she died two days later. Anecdotal stories suggest that apparatus and rigging failure is the major cause of aerial accidents and most are extremely injurious although not fatal. Ella Harris survived apparatus accidents with iron jaw, trapeze and wire in the 1930s (Beal 1938: 77), and Australian Angela Ravelle, well known for a one-heel hold, survived a fall due to equipment failure in 1982.[31]

In contrast to Leers, Leitzel used theatrical gestures and costuming for feminine effect to offset her muscularity as she executed an exceptional display of endurance and strength. As a child performer, Leitzel had similar physical training to Leers, working with her mother and aunts in the Leamy Sisters (Culhane 1990: 187–8).[32] Leitzel's solo act on Roman rings was graceful and skilful. She climbed the ascent rope using one arm to turn her body three feet at a time in order to reach the suspended rings. Her hands and arms supported her weight on the rings in moves that included a legs split as the band played Gioacchino Rossini's 'William Tell Overture'. Leitzel dismounted, and for the act's second half she was winched up to a web with a hand loop at the higher end. She began plange turns in which she swung her whole body up to shoulder level and over itself with increasing speed, from 60 to 100 times, accompanied by a snare drum and Rimsky-Korsakov's 'The Flight of the Bumblebee', and letting her hair out. The crowd chanted her turns; Leitzel's record was 249 (Culhane 1990: 187). Even from a distance in the tent, spectators routinely describe the ugly jerkiness of this turning action (May 1963: 271).

Leitzel's third husband, flyer Alfredo Codona, explains how this act

> requires muscle – a great deal of it. Of course it requires endurance, and a certain sense of fatalism, in as much as no bandage ever has been devised

that can protect her arm from the constant danger of blood poisoning from rope burns. But more than this, it requires a knowledge of breathing as expert as that of any opera star.

(1930: 13)

Leitzel's tricks were as dependent on muscular strength as Leers's, but Leitzel deliberately gestured to a feminine identity with her costume, her movement and her routine. A perception of awkwardness may also have come from her performance of femininity set against strenuous muscular action. Billed as 'dainty' on her RBBBC posters, to do her act she had the shoulders of a 'middle-weight boxer' (Verney 1978: 205, 202). But she was small-bodied, 4 feet 10 inches in height, and this was highlighted to enhance her act when she entered the ring in a white cape with a 6-foot-4-inch man at her side, some- times even carrying her. In a gesture of frailty, and to the annoyance of the ring director, Fred Bradna, Leitzel used to fake a faint after her act on occasions. As a forerunner of the popular young Olympic gymnasts of today, who are per- versely celebrated because they are small but extremely athletic (Chisholm 2002), the adult Leitzel achieved this impression through cuteness. She is described as 'looking like a little girl in her pink tights and short jacket bordered by silver beads', 'a fairy princess' (Bradna 1952: 180, 182), a 'little rag doll' (Culhane 1990: 185 (Taylor)).

Leitzel clearly controlled the composition of identity in her performance, and was independently minded about her personal life. While she cultivated a public impression of youthful frailty, this also made her muscular action seem more difficult, more exceptional, and less masculine. Leitzel was greatly mourned when she died.

Leers's act had little theatrical embellishment in its presentation of bodily identity. Nonetheless her performance delivery was improved by working in RBBBC, and possibly from the competition around her. Wire-walker Helen Wallenda, herself one of the great twentieth-century aerialists (Morris 1976), explains that Europe, where ability is crucial, admired Leers's unequalled tricks. Helen explains, 'It isn't that she has greater ability but she has developed her showmanship and personality and the ability to sell her act to the public . . . Leitzel's super showmanship made her a star.'[33] Braathen confirms to Leers, 'Your act was truly wonderful . . . so much more colour and showmanship . . . You seem to enjoy your work more.'[34]

From 1927 to 1937 Leers worked most summer seasons in North America and returned to Europe to work during the winter months. In 1932 Leers sought advice from Braathen about problems with a summer season contract, possibly with RBBBC. The contract may have been agreed to by an agent, but it only permitted its performers to do winter season work in indoor vaudeville theatres. Leers last worked at RBBBC for the 1933 season.[35]

In 1932 Miss Tamara, executing a toe hold on trapeze, debuted in the centre ring with Leers. After opening night Leers was quickly moved to a later place in the programme that reinstated her pre-eminent status.[36] Did management initiate this shift or did Leers or her parents express dissatisfaction with the programming? Perhaps her act had become too expensive to rehire in 1934 because she needed to earn more American dollars, which had devalued in Europe, in order to support her parents.[37] Certainly she had other work offers, and in 1934 Leers worked in England and in German theatres, and in picture houses, and performed in Paris in 1935.

Leers continued working some summers in the USA after 1934 in fairground circuses and recalled later that these were harder work with more performances and extra work with rigging. In 1947 she expresses regret that she did not stay with RBBBC when she had the opportunity or even in America, given marriage proposals, but her family home was in Germany and she did not feel it was 'egoism' that made her leave. She implies that she could not make her own decision when she writes, 'I did not do what I really wanted. I often made the misstake [*sic*] in my life having been too good to people who did not deserve it.'[38]

It is possible that Leers was also discouraged from staying in North America by salacious publicity once she was performing away from RBBBC. Circus publicity announcements in 1934 and 1937 read,

> Young lady would like to meet handsome and persistent masher – object, not matrimony, but assault and battery . . . Louise Leers . . . a quiet and demure young person . . . Let the curbstone Charlies who are interested in Miss Leers first gaze on her as she appears in her first professional role of trapeze performance above. Note the biceps and shoulder muscles – and ponder the playful wallop they pack.[39]

The marketing ploy of promoting powerful female muscular action as sexually alluring but an object of derision, and unsuitable for marriage despite Leers's demureness, is informative about ambivalent cultural attitudes. It confirms the attractions of female muscular physicality in performance, but also its social rejection because of the capacity to punch a male. 'Charlie' was taking a social risk in viewing a spectacle of female muscularity.

During the war, Leers lived with her parents in Germany. Some circus acts in the USA, however, managed to avoid the issue of the originating nationalities of their performers. There were repercussions for offstage nationality in war-time; during the First World War the USA's Secret Service watched circus performers, and fingerprinted the Bradnas because Fred was from Alsace and Ella from Czechoslovakia (Bradna 1952: 93), and there were at least 18 different nationalities at RBBBC (May 1963: 286). The Second World War Allies' policy of internment of civilians from hostile countries may have been ineffectual for circus. Acts could adjust their professional nationality through costuming and nomenclature. Anecdotally, Connie Clausen claims that a 'Japanese act suddenly changed its costumes, music, and name, and became the Chinese Wizards' (1961: 180). Nationality and/or ethnicity can be difficult for spectators to determine without external signs. Further, performers slipped in and out of acts that maintained distinctive national identities. Identity slipperiness in circus performance lent itself to opportunistic exploitation at times, and yet became necessary in other circumstances.

The nationality and ethnicity of performers had become a source of their appeal in twentieth-century circus business, which presented acts of costumed difference; that is, exotic bodies. In the 1920s A. H. Kober specifies German circus had teams of Arab acrobats; horse spectacles with American Indians on US government-imposed bonds for their return; Chinese contortionists, knife-throwers and aerialists suspended and spinning by the hair; Japanese perch-performers and wire-walkers; and Australian wood-cutters (1928: 72–96). In an extended discussion of how America's big tenting circuses exoticized other nationalities in increasingly grander spectacles from the 1890s until the 1930s, Janet Davis explains that proprietors utilized political events, especially wars, promoting socially conservative agendas of patriotism and articulating commu-nity 'dystopian racial anxieties' (2002: 224). These attitudes reflect vested management interests rather than the politics of the performers since circus has a long-standing parallel tradition of political satire by individuals.

The circus continued to tour in the USA during the Second World War when most circuses closed in Europe and elsewhere, including Australia. The war also impacted on family acts, such as the Italian Cristianis with RBBBC, because indi-vidual performers were conscripted (Hubler 1967: 176). RBBBC contributed materially to the war effort and to patriotism, providing free tickets to people who bought war bonds and to the armed forces. Roland Butler writes,

> And, while the circus contributed to the public morale by diverting the minds of its patrons from the tragedy of war, it stimulated war bond sales tremendously . . . and helped defray the cost of victory to the extent of one hundred million dollars.
>
> (1943: no pagination)

As this indicates, abstract acts of physical skill can be effectively deployed within a wider nationalistic purpose. Yet even in 1943 – Barbette directed the aerial ballet – there was a concerted effort by RBBBC to promote the circus as a mix of nationalities, albeit with the proclamation 'Let Freedom Ring' for all peoples of the Earth in circus; in which 'the United Nations March and Engage in Fes-tival Ceremonials, Garbed in Native Holiday Finery, Rich, Exotic' (ibid.). Lest audience members were uncertain about how they should respond to the spec-tacle, the 1943 programme photograph shows the Statue of Liberty in centre place with a comment encouraging a 'high note of Emotional Fervor' (ibid.).

Leers probably could have continued performing in the USA as she claimed. Participating in the RBBBC 1943 United Nations March were the German Wallenda Troupe (Leers's friends Karl and Helen and their children) and others. They had taken out citizenship in the USA shortly before the war. Their high-wire act was famous for three tiers of acrobatic shoulder balances using poles and chairs with seven performers and no safety equipment, which led to two fatalities in a famous tragic collapse in 1962 (Morris 1976). This is dramatized in the film *The Great Wallendas* (1978), with Lloyd Bridges as Karl. In the grand wire-walking tradition of Blondin, Karl worked and died setting himself successively greater outdoor challenges, and one of his performance heirs would surely have to be the anarchic Frenchman Philippe Petit (1991) and his walks between skyscrapers.

In 1946 Leers resumed contact by letter with the Braathens and conveyed some of the difficulties encountered by circus performers during and after the war in Germany.[40] The Leers's family house was bombed, which destroyed Leers's apparatus and costumes. She had been sending circus programmes to the Braathens since 1931, and after 1946 asked her American and English circus friends and acquaintances for food, clothing and footwear parcels. She had few misgivings, explaining that she needed to help her parents. She writes to thank the Braathens at the beginning of 1948, because rationing was decreasing the amount of available food and a malnourished Leers could not undergo necessary arm surgery.[41] Eventually Leers found work in an office, then as a translator, married, and in 1954 opened her own translation bureau.[42]

In 1934 Braathen writes with regret about Leers's RBBBC replacement, 'What a change from your act as a center ring attraction to an ordinary cloud swing which is nothing more than a double.'[43] He writes that Dexter Fellows 'made the remark that you were a much greater aerialist than Leitzel. Now how is that for a patron . . . one who has seen all the greats come and go during the past forty-three years'.[44] Perhaps Fellows was complimenting Leers for an extremely skilful slower endurance act that avoided identity trickiness. Leers's muscularity was a vital part of performing aerial identity, but its requisite display would subsequently become less socially acceptable even in circus.

Chapter 4

Gender competition, camp spectacles and impossible machismo

Throughout the twentieth century male flyers were considered the leading aerialists, even though most aerialists were female and continued to demonstrate comparable athletic capacity. Male performers became an athletic elite and females, with a few rare exceptions, were perceived as an extension of the aerial ballet even within the profession in the post-Second World War era. Gender differences were magnified in films about circus imbued with emotional conflicts, in turn influencing social perceptions of aerialists. There is some fascinating intertextuality between film narratives and aerialists' stories, and yet circus is routinely overlooked in critiques of film in relation to other art forms.

Flying troupes were the most esteemed aerial acts, and an individual flyer's prized goal was the execution of a triple backward somersault to a catcher's hold and, after the 1970s, a quadruple somersault.[1] Circus venues provided the height and expanse needed by troupes. During the 1930s these included the Clarkonians, the Codonas, the Concellos, and three Ward troupes, all based in the USA. Despite their accomplishments, troupes working in western Europe and out of eastern Europe and Russia did not effectively challenge this dominance until the 1960s, but Mexican family troupes in the USA continued to produce the top flyers well into the 1980s.

Aerial performance was popularly feminized and bodies became coded within a hierarchy of gendered flesh. Flying and catching were done by both males and females up to the 1930s, but by the 1950s and 1960s the 'shapely' female aerialist standing on the platform was integral to the spectacle but not to the important flying action between the male flyer and male catcher. From the 1930s male flyers with admirable physiques performed bare-chested with Tarzan-like machismo. It was the catcher, however, who came to typify 1950s muscular masculinity in fashions attuned to body shapes, and this dictated that female aerialists wear sequined bikinis, fishnet stockings, feathers and false eyelashes. Beliefs about gender identity distorted aerial history and the visible evidence of acts. When circus championships began in the mid-1970s it became evident that female flyers had remained formidable competitors. In outperforming them, and up against cinema's heroes in impossible stunt action, male flyers in the 1980s and 1990s performed to painful extremes.

Pretty tough competition

In Cecil B. DeMille's Oscar-winning film *The Greatest Show on Earth* (1952), new-comer the Great Sebastian (Cornel Wilde) is openly challenged by female aerialist Holly (Betty Hutton) to compete for star position in the centre ring, which has been allocated to him instead of her. Sebastian is also trying to seduce Holly away from her dour boyfriend, the safety-conscious circus manager Brad (Charlton Heston). The two aerialists compete as soloists on trapeze and web, and as the competition escalates, they take increasing risks with their swinging and flying tricks during performances. The setting for the film is its namesake, John Ringling North's three-ring RBBBC The Greatest Show on Earth. The plot involves a four-way romance between Sebastian, Holly, Brad and elephant performer Angel (Gloria Grahame), and a subplot in which the gentleman clown, Buttons (James Stewart), is wanted for medical manslaughter by the police. The aerial competition escalates and Sebastian attempts a double somersault over a bar through a paper hoop without a net, and falls to the ground badly injured. A remorseful Holly vows loyalty to the maimed Sebastian until a major circus train disaster reconciles her with an injured Brad. Subsequently Sebastian proposes to Angel.

The fiction of an ego-driven competition between a bare-chested male and a shapely sequined female aerialist mimics what happened in aerial history during the twentieth century. The female aerialist knows her performance to be as good as his; he does not doubt that he is the greater aerialist and star, except that he can only establish this with certainty by pushing himself dangerously further. The promotion of competition between the sexes is a fascinating subsidiary thread to the athletic competition driving aerial history. In an early example from 1870, the three French Foucart Sisters on trapeze, horizontal ropes and rings were promoted as outperforming males from the British navy (Speaight 1980: 72 (Strehly)).[2]

Circus films are invariably about masculinity in ways that are comparable to sports films (Baker 2003: 3). Holly is particularly dangerous competition for Sebastian in *Greatest Show*'s surprisingly athletic depiction of a temptress. Both characters share the larger purpose of seducing the audience. Sebastian, as a womanizing playboy with a European accent, is too much like a Latin lover to be a 1950s American hero. When Sebastian's injury stops him performing and prevents him from marrying Holly, the physical pain becomes interchangeable with the emotional pain of losing his real passion, his act (his sport). While Holly is sidelined from centre ring by 1950s values, comparable ideas of masculinity and in particular fears of effeminacy also impacted on the artistic treatment and status of the male aerialist.

Aerial performance and circus sought to amuse, delight and excite, and circus films additionally provided scenarios of romantic love, jealousy, revenge, sadness and violent anger.[3] In literature and films, female aerialists on trapeze and rope are repeatedly depicted as a romantic interest, and commonly between rival circus performers. A male character's love personifies cultural fascination with the female aerialist, and ideas of physical danger are transposed onto her role as seductress. She embodies danger; love is like the aerialist (for males). Circus becomes a space for sexually transgressive women; the scandalous love affairs of nineteenth-century dancer Lola Montes, in Max Ophuls's *Lola Montes* (1955), are framed by action in a circus ring (Russo 1994: 46–7). Circus love stories invariably show emotional pain manifesting with physical pain.

If a plot about extremes of aerial risk-taking in front of audiences in *Greatest Show* lacks credibility, the portrayal of circus is considered accurate – live circus still attracted large audiences at that time. The film's tricks are executed by accomplished aerialists: Wilde's flying tricks are by North America's pre-eminent male flyer of the day, Fay Alexander, and Hutton's by Danish La Norma (Fox), a star soloist with RBBBC from 1949 to 1951.[4] At one point in *Greatest Show* the world's leading woman flyer, Antoinette Concello, appears on the aerial platform handing the trapeze bar to Alexander. Behind the scenes Antoinette had taught Hutton some basic flying movement (Higham 1973: 295–6). Both the Flying Comets and Artonies make brief appearances, as do the wire-walking Alzanas.

American circus adapted easily to Hollywood cinema. Richard Dyer writes that even though entertainment is 'hedonistic, democratic, vulgar, easy' and considered a secondary leisure pursuit, it is a major economic activity (1992: 2, 12). Cinema as entertainment offers 'the image of "something better" to escape into' in its arousal of emotional utopian sensibilities (ibid.: 18). Circus spectacle might be said to have long served such economic and emotional social functions and, like cinema, must continually reinvent itself to avoid becoming dated. The production of cinematic entertainment about circus peaked in the late 1950s, and overshadows the athletic action with melodramatic emotional conflict.

Live aerial entertainment throughout the twentieth century, however, remained an athletic contest to master increasingly difficult tricks typified by the flyer's mastery of the triple somersault. As outlined, although Lena Jordan was first to do the triple, Ernie Clarke deserves his acclaim as the seminal twentieth-century flyer because he performed a triple using a fly bar and other complex moves over a 35-year flying career.[5] The triple was enhanced by the uncertainty as to whether it would be missed or caught. Convention dates Ernie's first triple somersault to his younger brother Charles at Publiones Circus, Cuba, in 1909. Ernie's own performance history disputes the Cuban debut date as he was probably doing a triple as early as 1902 at Nouveau Cirque in Paris. Edith Kenward writes that Ernie 'has a triple somersault and return which is entirely his own' (1902: 339). The reviewer seems knowledgeable and is preoccupied with the difficulty of his return pirouette, which moves out of the line of the flying and thus strains the catcher.

Ernie came from English circus family the Clarkes, famous for equestrian acts (Sturtevant 1938). Ernie, Charles and Percy Clarke emerged as the Clarkonians (see Figure 2.6), working in a BBC programme alongside the Siegrist-Silbons. By

1909 Ringlings were boasting the world's highest paid aerial troupes, including the Clarkonian duo without Percy, and by 1910 Ernie was attempting the triple to Charles at most performances. The duo reportedly practised 9,000 somersaults over two years before they could exhibit the trick to a high standard of artistry (Fargo 1926: 48). A trick may only last 30 seconds, and the Clarkes had 20 tricks (ibid.: 48–9). Extreme repetition is required to develop fine aerial artistry.

The invention and then repeated reproduction of difficult flying actions requires relentless practice and a long-standing partnership. Extra dedication is needed for a trick to look easy. A catcher hangs upside down with his or her legs curled around the cables of a catch bar or cradle to sustain the impact of the flyer's body weight travelling at speed. To catch a somersault, the catcher makes each swing even and reaches the extended position of an upward swing, a second in time after the flyer reaches the top point of his or her swing out-wards. The flyer lets go of the fly bar and moves downwards, and the flyer and catcher's wrists lock together. The catcher cannot necessarily see the body part being caught. A flyer's body becomes compact for multiple somersaults back-wards; forward somersaults are harder to control and considered dangerous. Alexander did the forward double somersault over the bar until injury stopped him (Culhane 1990: 304). If flyers miss the catch, they must land with their backs hitting the net to prevent injury, the neck braced by holding the head up, and arms at the side. The important point here is that the flyer is moving across the arena and, after a missed catch, unless he or she immediately corrects the trajectory to move downwards, runs the risk of hitting the net wrongly or missing it altogether. The threat of injury is constant, but fatalities due to per-former miscalculation are less likely than audiences might expect, with risks comparable to extreme sports.

At the beginning of the twenty-first century, the triple by males and females is considered part of the standard repertoire for leading flying troupes. But Antony Hippisley Coxe estimates that there were under 30 flyers worldwide able to catch a triple by 1980 (1980: 150). Because flyers move so fast, audience members may be unaware of the degree of difficulty in a trick without an announcement beforehand. A leading flyer should present artistic qualities of graceful smoothness in his or her movement, avoiding irregular jerkiness, and these qualities are perceptible to audiences.

An assumption that male aerialists would attempt the most difficult tricks, including somersaults, was apparent in the 1930s. Within the flying profession, however, divisions in the action according to gender were still not evident and it would appear that social perceptions of gender differences were achieved through oversights in the historical record, distorted accounts of aerial perfor-mances, and the public reiteration of prescriptive ideas about bodily difference.

A caption accompanying an extensive article in a culturally influential 1930s magazine observes that a 'woman catcher' (unnamed) has just released one flyer to catch a second, the first man returning to the fly bar as the other leaves in a passing trick or double passage (Kelley 1931: 499). Women's catch bars were rectangular while males commonly used the catch trap with padded cables.[6] Regardless of the effectiveness of the catch, the caption repeats the viewpoint that this female catcher's body position is inferior and states that '[m]asculine performers' only have to intertwine their legs in the cable (ibid.). In accompanying photographs of unnamed aerialists, including one of Alfredo Codona, a female performer executes the splits mid-air, her legs horizontal, her feet in two rings in a nominal female soloist's trick, and a man swings on a rope from her waist (ibid.: 498). The strength, stamina and technique of females in weight-bearing and catching positions evident in the photographs contradicts the dismissive commentary.

A claim in the 1930s that female aerialists needed to be smaller than males suggests artificially imposed criteria. While admitting that many aerialists did not conform to this pattern, Arnold Jackson recounts the view that flyers should be small – ideally males should be 5 feet and 6 inches to 6 feet, and females should be between 5 feet 2 inches and 5 feet 6 inches – and male catchers need more weight than male flyers (1937: 5 (Silver)). Both males and females should have well-built upper bodies and thin legs. Sometimes there was an additional requirement that women should have narrow hips and slim buttocks because 'a heavy posterior does not permit a graceful somersault' (Bradna 1952: 174). For technical reasons, a wider, heavier bottom might inhibit the body's tuck in somersaults, and fractionally slow down its pendulum swing-effect. Even given such qualifications, and accepting that some male and female body shapes are more suited to aerial work, this commentary reflects the social beliefs valuing a proportionally smaller female. While acts needed to satisfy social preferences for 'pretty girl' flyers, bodies in competitive performance-making do not fit neatly into such cultural selection. Regardless, both male and female flyers in action must look 'pretty' (ibid.: 175).

Expressions of surprise by observers of female acts reveal resistant public sentiments. In English newspapers in the early 1930s, the foremost circus proprietors, Bertram Mills of BMC, and his son Bernard, vehemently defend female circus performers. After a female flyer executes a double somersault, Bernard recounts, '"Fancy a girl being able to do that", comments somebody, falling into the common error of thinking that women are more for show than work' (1933: 6). Bernard writes that he could mount the most extraordinary circus using only innovative female performers. In response to questions in private, Bertram writes that he is thought to be joking when he says, 'it is my firm belief that women are equal and occasionally even superior' (Bertram Mills 1933: 7). These clearly articulated defences also needed to verify the domestication of circus women and their fear of losing their femininity from 'ungainly masculine muscles' (ibid.). As Lillian Leitzel outlines, women have a double burden of physical and reproductive labour, and she points out that they must be physically fit to do their 'hazardous work', look their best and work without domestic privacy, 'under conditions which would drive the average woman frantic' (Leitzel 1932: 32). These commentaries would seem to be responses to ongoing criticism and confirm that female circus performers provoked unease. Strenuous movement in dance could be veiled with costuming to make it more socially acceptable, and while aerial performance had become similarly feminized in the cultural imaginary, contradictory evidence of the unfeminine athleticism of female aerialists was probably unavoidable, and female muscular action challenged a fundamental tenet of the social order.

The discrepancy between a female's capacity to do all aspects of aerial work and prescriptive ideas of female physicality could not be sustained. There were few female catchers by the 1950s and seemingly no female flyers doing the most difficult tricks.[7] As a business, aerial performance appeared to comply with wider society's expectations of male dominance and female decorativeness. Similarly, catching and weight-bearing became male roles so aerial body positioning was effectively gendered. The renowned catcher Juan Vazquez reiterated in 2003 that each of the three woman catchers that he has seen in performance 'look more like a man'.[8]

One further consequence was that female flyers were not ranked in relation to male counterparts. While it had been advantageous to the earning capacity of female performers in the nineteenth century to be identified as the first female, such labelling worked against women by the mid-twentieth century, unfairly allocating them a secondary status. Lena's triple is labelled 'first woman' rather than 'first performer' in *Guinness Book of Records* (Ross McWhirter 1972: 177). The prevailing assumption came to be that the serious athletic competition happened between an elite of male performers.

Action hero scandals

By the late 1920s Alfredo Codona, from a Mexican family troupe, had established a reputation as the world's foremost flyer, and successor to Ernie Clarke. For the first time, Alfredo's triple somersault was consistently caught by his catcher and brother, Lalo. In addition, Alfredo worked with revered lithe lightness, and a special 'lift' on letting go of the fly bar, and became a major artistic influence on aerial arts in the twentieth century. He was very good-looking with an upright posture and a 'naturally classic' well-proportioned muscular body: 'Flying develops a muscled, lean, graceful torso' (Bradna 1952: 192). He had the body shape esteemed during the 1930s. His public persona, however, became caught up with contradictory attitudes to masculinity and aerialists, and the feminization of aerial performance in popular perception. These were prefigured by Alfredo's stunt work for two major films – *Variety* (1925)[9] and *Tarzan and His Mate* (1934). The two films depict extremes in male action hero identity: Artinelli, the suave sensual flyer as seductive lover in *Variety*, and Tarzan, the seminal muscular action hero swinging through the jungle.

Representations of male flyers in twentieth-century films reiterate a polarized tension between perceptions of aerial performance as a highly athletic male domain and as one of feminine spectacle. Graceful flying transforms a muscular body's solid density and weight, which are usually apparent in sports with their aggressive competitiveness. The male flyer was certainly ripe for 1920s film narratives about a romantic seducer who could be both physically active and emotionally sensitive. Accordingly, this was received as atypical male behaviour.

The male flyer initially appears in cinema as a flawed hero. The prototypes are characters found in the silent film *Variety* (1925) (*Variété*), directed by Ewald Dupont and based on Felix Hollaender's novel, *The Oath of Stephen Huller*.[10] This is a semi-expressionist film about a heavy-bodied catcher–husband, Boss Huller (Emil Jannings), whose wife, Berthe-Marie (Lya de Putti), is seduced from domestic bliss by the trio's lighter-bodied star flyer, Artinelli (Warwick Ward). The catcher–husband imagines dropping his rival, the flyer, but murders him instead in a fight, and goes to prison. The seducing male flyer is the provocateur of extreme passion, a position subsumed by female aerialist characters in later films. But the male aerialist as a criminal, even murderer, intermittently reappears in representation because he epitomizes a capacity for extreme risk-taking, which is translated into socially risky immoral behaviour.[11] But it is the male flyer who becomes especially vulnerable to depiction as a fallen hero, literally and for losing emotional control.

In analysing the contrasts between 1920s male film stars and their roles, Gaylyn Studlar discerns '*transformative masculinity*' that can also be a performance, in a process of reaction against the threat of feminization (1996: 4, 7, italics in original). Studlar finds cultural unease with the atypical masculinity of the numerous film characters created by John Barrymore and Rudolph Valentino; she specifies criticism of the depictions of a sensitive lover as a sportsman or gymnast who is not belligerent in his fighting, and especially towards the identity of the immigrant Latin lover or dancer (ibid.: 16, 151, 185). Moreover, the sexualizing of the male body, with his bared chest, was counterbalanced by a narrative of suffering, and emotional '*actions*' to avenge or protect (ibid.: 138, italics in original). Contradictorily, a male gymnast (flyer) overwhelmed by emotional pain is not heroic; excessive emotion counteracts masculinity.

Alfredo's participation in *Variety* outlines some significant convergences and confusions: between early film stunt action and live aerial action, between a melodrama and a tragic personal life, and between a fictional character and a performer's public identity. Alfredo's reputation as a celebrity aerialist is comparable to that of a 1920s silent film star who acquired a textual identity from the merging of film roles with a media-created private life; this was a 'star persona as a marketable commodity' (Studlar 1996: 2). Alfredo, from a Mexican circus family, aspired to the flyer's dream and had mastered the triple by 1920 (Culhane 1990: 186). In 1913 the Flying Codonas, with Steve Outch and Ruth Farris, and with Victoria Codona on slack wire, started out at Wirth's Circus in Australia, with Alfredo practising for the triple. They were working with the Siegrist-Silbon Troupe by 1916–17. The Codonas achieved star status in Europe in 1922, and in the USA during the mid-1920s, and the troupe, including Alfredo's first wife, Clara Gron (Curtin), were well established in RBBBC's

centre ring by 1927. By 1937 both Alfredo and Lalo had given up aerial performance; Alfredo snapped two shoulder muscles in a shoulder dislocation in 1933
doing the triple and could not return to flying, and Lalo developed muscle
strain in 1936.[12]

Alfredo's tricks included a single somersault with a one-and-a-half pirouette
on his return, and his triple somersault was followed by the double pirouette on
the return. The Codonas worked 100 feet up with a net 25 feet from the
ground and Alfredo describes split-second timing and how 'psychology and
muscle are mingled in the triple' (Codona 1930: 76). He makes his well-known
claim that his body had been measured travelling 62 miles an hour turning
three somersaults within 7 square feet (ibid.: 12). Claims for the flyer's speed in
a triple range from 40 to 60 miles an hour and depend on the height, weight
and fly bar's length. Alfredo emphasizes the loss of mental control as the body
in a second somersault turns faster – faster than the speed of thought, he suggests, in a 'momentary dream' space where vision and memory distort (ibid.:
79). While acknowledging the trick's difficulty, other flyers dispute that the mind
goes blank, and emphasize that achieving height and having muscles and a
skilled catcher are crucial.

Alfredo did all his actions smoothly and seemingly effortlessly. Bradna describes his pirouette,

> The trick here is to propel the body, once it leaves the catcher, with a
> double motion: forward and upward towards the trapeze, and simultane-
> ously around in a circle. To make the turn beautiful, the arms must be
> close to the body, the legs artistically posed, lest the whole effect be
> ungainly rather than romantic. All these muscular co-ordinations, exerted
> in precisely the proper order, within a space of one and a half seconds
> demand much more finesse than most flyers develop.
>
> (1952: 169)

The artistry is achieved by keeping the limbs and arms close to the body in a
streamlined compactness and maintaining fluid, even movement.

In circus annals, Alfredo's personal story effectively upstages his work. He
divorced his first wife, and married Leitzel in 1928. Both Alfredo and Leitzel
had been child performers and became aerialist celebrities but did not work in
the same act. Leitzel's tragic death in 1931, and Alfredo's 1937 murder–suicide,
in which he shot his third wife and Australian ex-Codonas flyer Vera Bruce in a
lawyer's office while she was negotiating their divorce settlement, ensured that
their personal lives are retold.

Alfredo's and Leitzel's feats represented the outer limits of aerial physicality,
and adoring audiences celebrated their offstage union. While husband and wife
partnerships are unremarkable in a field of constant touring and training,
Leitzel and Alfredo's short marriage was played out as a public affair that exemplified celebrity romance. The popular, diminutive, feminine Leitzel became an

ideal love match for flyer-hero Alfredo. An explanation for Alfredo's subsequent violence was more readily found in the emotional pain of losing an idealized lover like Leitzel rather than in losing an aerial act through injury. The depiction of Alfredo as a victim of grief that leads to his subsequent scandalous behaviour confirms that, like Artinelli in *Variety*, the male flyer emotionally flouts the moral code, by which stoic masculine heroism becomes imbued with honour. In all likelihood Alfredo's extreme violence four years after the loss of his aerial act was due to depression from compounded disappointment, and possibly also physical pain, a legacy of injury.

All three of Alfredo's wives were aerialists and two worked in the Codonas act, although descriptions of Clara's work are difficult to locate. Ruth Manning-Sanders describes Vera's competent flying in a double passing trick (see Figure 4.1):

> Lalo hangs from his trapeze, swinging Vera by the ankles. Alfredo swings from his trapeze by the hands. The two trapezes swing towards each other; Lalo releases Vera's ankles and flings her forward; at the same moment Alfredo shoots over the top of his trapeze, and passes above Vera in mid-air. The next moment, Vera has caught the trapeze that Alfredo has just left, and Alfredo's wrists are gripped by Lalo's strong hands.
>
> (1952: 241)[13]

The Alfredo described in circus annals is like a mythic Greek hero reaching physical perfection but denied his 'true' love by fate; the flyer is the solitary Icarus who might fall. This story has assumed mythic dimensions because it suggests ideal love thwarted by death. Emotional pain dominates the Alfredo narrative when the aerialist and the aerial act converge into loss that merges melancholy about an unattainable love and mourning for a dead lover.

Aerial artistry generally masks any discomforting physical pain, especially in performances like those by Alfredo that appear effortless. A spectator, however, might perceive, for example, Leitzel's work as having a painful effect, with her staged femininity that heightens an impression of difficulty. Even though a spectator might fear the consequences if a male performer should fall, physical pain is not easily reconciled with the impression of lightness and ease in flying action.

Interestingly, Alfredo was also the stunt double for the first Johnny Weissmuller Tarzan films. Alfredo executed some of the aerial swinging of the prototypical masculine action hero, joining the elite ex-swimming and football champions who were cast as Tarzan (Essoe 1972). Aaron Baker (2003) explains that American cinema's representation of sports asserted both masculinity and values of individual heroism. The numerous and popular Tarzan films made from 1918, based on Edgar Rice Burroughs's novel *Lord of the Jungle* (1912), presented their hero living in wild jungle, that is, he was in untouched nature and fighting its corruption from an encroaching civilization. Tarzan is the 'gentleman' in a schismatic masculinity that maintains species and race hierarchies. On

Figure 4.1 Flying Codonas, Alfredo and Lalo Codona and Vera Bruce, courtesy of Special Collections, Milner Library, Illinois State University.

film his eroticized, albeit white, body delivers unsmiling monosyllabic responses (Morton 1993: 112–13). But Tarzan becomes heroic only by rescuing Jane, who is emblematic of white womanhood faced with physical and social dangers from non-white villains in narratives with racist implications (Newsinger 1987: 44).

Maurizia Boscagli's astute psychoanalytical interpretation of the Tarzan character as a successor to Sandow finds that while Tarzan does circus stunts, as a muscular Nietzschean superman his wounds are indicative of masochistic masculinity (1996: 121–2).

Cinema carries on the nineteenth-century circus tradition of defining Africa (Pollock 1995: 128). When Tarzan and his chimpanzee (friend) do eventually venture to the centre of civilization, New York, to save Tarzan's adopted son in *Tarzan's New York Adventure* (1942), he ends up at the circus fighting the villainous kidnappers. Circus functions as culture's symbolic place of nature since it presents tamed wild animals who become intelligible through performances of human-like behaviour (Carmeli 1997; Kwint 2002). But a social space where the actions of animal and human bodies overlap also becomes one of depravity.

Tarzan personified culture's ongoing efforts after the 1880s to recoup a 'primitive masculinity' (Bederman 1995: 157). Gail Bederman discerns how the early twentieth century's white manhood in the USA was constructed in racist responses to boxing action, and through the reconciliation of identities that were 'civilized, manly and undervitalized' and 'primitive, masculine and passionate' (ibid.: 102). Kristen Whissel argues convincingly that physically building up the male body in early American cinema also equated to building the national character through 'kinetic movement and circulation of the male body-in-motion' (2002: 147). Later, the Tarzan character also featured in American nationalist, anti-Nazi films during the Second World War (Essoe 1972: 115).

Boscagli writes that by the 1930s the shape of the male body was changing in response to ongoing perceptions of a masculine identity crisis, and became visible as a tanned, muscular, even unclothed 'spectacle of untamed natural strength' in places of leisure like the gym and the seaside (1996: 1, 4). Even in the late 1920s Tarzan still had to partially cover his chest with a leopard skin, as his undressed body merited comment (Essoe 1972: 61, 70). His inarticulate aerial action of the rescue became prototypical of masculine action in cinema, and his bared chest set the precedent for the systematized look that became particularly accentuated in 1950s films.

If Tarzan's action initially mimics the flying action of an aerialist, the increasingly exposed chest of the male aerialist began to mimic Tarzan's body. The male 'body genre' came to involve 'sweat, muscles, shows of strength, tunics and loin cloths' (Hunt 1993: 66). But this foreshadowing of cinematic action hero identity highlighted ongoing contradictions in male aerial identity caught between the masculinized solidity of muscularity and feminized lightness of flying action. Nonetheless cinema's doubling of body genres placed male aerialists in competition with action heroes without female equivalents.

Double fashions in triples

The male aerialist's female counterpart, however, was still performing live in the circus. In a ground-breaking double act, husband and wife flyers Arthur (Art)

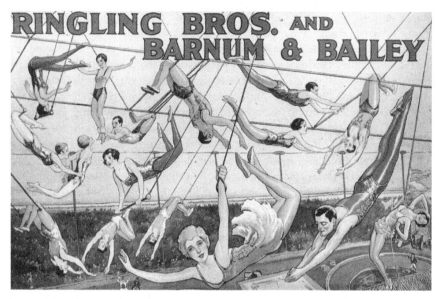

Figure 4.2 1937 poster of 16 aerialists including Concellos, Comets and Randolls, image courtesy of Ringling Bros and Barnum and Bailey® The Greatest Show on Earth®, Milner Library.

and Antoinette Concello were performing triple somersaults with RBBBC in 1937 (see Figure 4.2). They were the core partnership of the Flying Concellos, one of the most highly regarded aerial troupes during the 1930s and 1940s with four flyers doing triples. These included Alexander, who later formed the Flying Alexanders, and Wayne Larey, who trained the Flying Waynes during the 1960s (Couderc 1964b; Gossard 1994). Antoinette was the only woman doing the most difficult tricks in the first half of the twentieth century. At a time when gendered expectations in aerial flying made Antoinette stand out, her achievements were measured against three of the world's leading male flyers.

As early as 1932, the Concellos' male flyers were photographed bare-chested, a male performance fashion that continued into the 1970s.[14] (Female aerialists might appear to have exposed legs and skin although they usually wear protective flesh-coloured tights, and sometimes a second flesh-coloured leotard.) By the 1940s the unisex leotard and tights, worn by Antoinette, Leers and others in the early 1930s, was outmoded costuming for a star female flyer surrounded by a sparkling chorus. Changing costume fashions also corresponded with an increasingly gendered demarcation of action within flying troupes.

Arthur and Antoinette were trained by the Wards, whose flyers, the Wards and the Ward-Bells, dominated North American aerial performance until the 1960s (Gossard 1986). Brother and sister Eddie and Jennie Ward started as a trapeze duo pioneering a breakaway trick in which Jennie dropped suddenly down only to be caught just in time by cords from her ankles attached to Eddie's wrists (ibid.: 5–6). After 1912 the duo became the Flying Wards when Eddie married Mayme Kimball, and Jennie married Alec Todd from the Flying (ex-Silbon) Herberts, and Alec taught them the flying return act. Jennie did a two-and-a-half backward somersault with an ankle catch, and Mayme did a double somersault blindfolded (Bradna 1952: 169). Tragically, Jennie died in the Hagenbeck-Wallace circus train accident in 1918. Subsequently Eddie and Mayme Ward's training barn in Bloomington, Illinois took performers from outside circus, and offset the training advantage held by European troupes who had access to municipal hippodromes over long seasons. One reason for the USA's developing dominance of flying was that the rigging was 4 feet higher than in Europe. The Wards trained most of the hundred aerialists to come out of Bloomington, and importantly they trained male and female flyers to do the same work. The era of rapid invention had long passed and professional performers needed time, specialist teachers and a dedicated space for training. A high level of aerial skill remains dependent on the most accomplished aerialists teaching others; an aerialist also passes on his or her artistic style of movement in the choreography of a routine.

Arthur became an outstanding flyer (even reportedly executing a triple-and-a-half somersault), a skilled trainer and a notable success as a circus manager. He was training in the Wards' barn when Antoinette was starting on iron jaw and swinging ladder. She was a younger sister of web performer Mickey King, working with the Flying Wards (Gossard 2003).[15] Arthur and Antoinette married in 1928, left the Wards' flying troupe in 1930 and worked with Sells Floto in 1931 and RBBBC from 1932. Arthur was doing consistent triple somersaults by 1928, and to catchers Eddie Ward Jr and George Valentine in 1930. In 1935 Arthur was achieving four out of five triples and Antoinette was described as the 'only femme' doing a two-and-a-half somersault.[16] From 1937 she performed triples, although not as regularly as the males.

Before she was trained as a flyer, Antoinette was taught to work as a catcher. Like Eddie, Mayme Ward was an aerial catcher as well as a flyer, and she could catch a triple somersault. Antoinette explains, 'It helps a lot to have had experience of both ends of the rigging . . . so much depends upon the catcher and a good one will make all the difference to an act' (quoted in Toole-Stott 1935: 10). In the 1930s Raymond Toole-Stott watched Antoinette in a practice session at the Cirque d'Hiver working with a safety line and being caught by the feet in a hocks-double somersault. He prophetically predicts 'possibly the greatest woman aerialist' for her grace (ibid.: 8). Arthur explains, 'she is unusually quick, mentally and physically. Flying and somersaulting come naturally to her, and she has plenty of confidence' (quoted in ibid.: 9). Antoinette may not have achieved Arthur's technical mastery and athletic consistency, but she was more highly praised for her style and ease of movement; that is, her aerial artistry.

Toole-Stott asked Antoinette if she was afraid of falling:

I never think of it . . . a delay of even a tenth of a second can make a difference between a successful catch and a faulty one . . . 'Keep your head up
. . . half turn . . . now GRAB . . . It helps you to concentrate' . . . People
who've got nerves should leave trapeze work severely alone. But I guess
every artiste gets a 'kick' out of the danger, it gives him a feeling of accomplishment. I love my work.

(quoted in Toole-Stott 1935: 10)

Significantly, Antoinette is a direct link between many of the world's top male
flyers in that she had also practised with Alfredo, and in 1973 flew with Tito
Gaona's act (Culhane 1978: 25). She was still supervising aerialists with RBBBC
in the 1980s when Miguel Vazquez joined.

Female flyers and catchers did continue to be recognized as leading aerialists
in the 1930s. The Edythe Siegrist Troupe was even named after its catcher (see
Figure 1.3). Valentine formed the Flying Valentinos, with his wife Lorraine
Mather and Sue Pelto as the female flyers (Gossard and Valentine 1987). In
1939 they won *The Billboard* magazine's readers' poll for the best flying return
act. Lorraine did a double somersault and a twister, and a two-and-a-half
somersault blindfolded.[17] The Flying Melzoras had Jane (Ma) Melzer working
as catcher on a man's catch bar to her son Buster, a heavy 220-pound flyer.
From the 1930s Australian Nellie Perry worked as the weight-bearing performer
for the Sylvester Four's acrobatic act, and as the catcher in aerial acts for both
male and female performers.[18] Contemporaneous fiction based on circus
depicted a female catcher of a male flyer's double somersault (Liebovitz 1946:
145). In circuses everywhere there was ongoing visible evidence of the all-round
skills and mastery of complex tricks by female aerialists until the 1950s.

This significant female contribution was largely ignored by the popular press.
By the 1940s a standard flying act might have two or three males and a female
only expected to do simple flying and the 'necessary femininity' (Devenney
1947: 13). Peter Waring writes about how gender identity itself creates a drama
as females twist and somersault:

There's an air of tragedy in the great trapeze act – that is, if the girl is
fragile and looks at the mercy of the masculine wrists. The act is considered
the top because the girl is slim, pretty and apparently helpless.

(1948: 16)

Despite expressions of distaste for female muscles, some female flyers persevered
with difficult tricks in the 1950s and 1960s. An interview in 1962 with RBBBC
aerialists Mary Gill of Australia from the Flying Waynes, married to flyer Stanley
Gill (Fogarty 2000: 86, 88), and soloist La Toria (Victoria Unus), emulating her
predecessor, Lalage, suggests how females straddled the restrictions imposed by
wider society while striving for physical mastery.[19] The article contains comments
typical of the 1950s and 1960s, specifying whether the performers are brunette or

blonde and reassuring readers that their muscular appearance does not destroy their feminine figure. They are described as the prettiest two of the 125 girls; 'both are "for-real" blondes, blue-eyed, and shapely as well as muscular' (Fields 1963: 42). La Toria works 45 feet up without a net and does 60–75 Leitzel-like one-arm planges. Mary explains that to do La Toria's act 'you need the strength of a man' (ibid.). La Toria explains that Mary does a passing leap and is learning a double somersault while '[a] lot of girls just drop the trapeze bar to the men and decorate the act' (ibid.).

Connie Clausen (1961) joined the American aerial chorus as an adult per- former in the mid-twentieth century. Increasing social awareness of double standards led Clausen to write about a significant gap between what female performers achieved in their performances and the traditional patterns of rela- tionships behind the scenes in their personal lives – this could include domestic violence (Frega 2001: 30). In a commentary that echoes the conservatism of the nineteenth century in which women could excel physically as long as they were considered socially subservient, Clausen writes,

> No matter that SHE (weighing ninety pounds) caught and held HIM (weighing two hundred and twenty pounds), while hanging from her knees on a swinging trapeze . . . no matter that she was the low man in a human pyramid or just completed a forward somersault on a slack wire (that would cut her in two if she missed) . . . with every breath [she] assured him how much smarter, stronger, hard-working, and better looking he was than she . . . Circus women might be as strong as Amazons and smart as whips, but they camouflaged their muscles in lace and ribbons and put their brains to sleep lest their ideas conflict with HIS.
>
> (1961: 160–1)

Clausen observes critically that male performers promised to make the female performer a star by re-teaching her the routine that 'she'd been perfecting since age three, changed her hairdo, told her that her costumes would *have* to go, rewrote her music, negotiated her contracts' (1961: 192, italics in original). Clausen's account accords with an accentuated femininity in 1950s society and renewed post-war cultural belief in male dominance and compliant female domesticity.

As male aerialists had to contend with cultural preferences for bare-chested action heroes, females confronted changing fashions in clothing and body shape. While nineteenth-century women had worn versions of everyday dress to do sports, by the 1920s and 1930s sports, swimming and evening clothing that exposed the skin had become everyday wear. To stand out, the female chorus performer in a one-piece or two-piece costume needed to shimmer. Similarly, water ballets and musicals with showgirl choruses in sumptuous costuming raised the competitive standards in entertainment fashions. By the 1930s aerial ballets were up against the impact of filmed chorus spectacles, such as Busby

Berkeley's films in which the camera panned across formations of female dancers in swimming costumes or flowing gowns (Thomas and Terry 1973).

While there is clear evidence of two-way exchanges between fashions in clothing and theatre costumes (Troy 2003), and film designs, and to a lesser extent dance costumes, any exchange with circus remains hard to verify.[20] Aerial costumes were far ahead of the broader fashion for one-piece and two-piece sports costumes up to the early 1930s when the female star's costume ranged from frills to unadorned simplicity. But aerial costumes subsequently followed beachwear trends and film costumes after 1946 with sequined bikinis, and then hi-cut bikinis after the 1970s. In summarizing complex theoretical interpretations of the exchanges between fashion, cinema, consumerism and pleasure in relation to gender identity, Jane Gaines points out that films produce styles of dress (1990: 11 (Debord)).

French fashion designer Coco Chanel's aesthetic of boyish hipless bodies with broad shoulders was popular after 1922, and this body shape suited female aerialists in the 1930s (Rubinstein 1995: 154; Seeling 2000: 110). In the late 1940s, however, fashion was once again emphasizing a curvaceous body. By the 1950s female sex symbols played aerialist characters in films. Betty Hutton, Gloria Grahame and Dorothy Lamour (as a web performer) were in *Greatest Show*, Gina Lollobrigida in *Trapeze* (1956), Rita Hayworth and Claudia Cardinale in *Circus World* (1964) and Doris Day in *Billy Rose's Jumbo* (1962). Cinema's preference for a curvaceous body in the 1950s distorted female aerial physicality, while it also brought enhanced ideas of glamour to action entertainment previously considered low culture. As an institution, American circus replicated capitalist ideals of mass consumption, so perhaps it is not surprising to find that circus became integrated into post-Second World War Hollywood cinema's glamour, and its casting of Italian performers like Lollobrigida and Cardinale, who exemplified its reinterpretation of European glamour (Gundle 2002: 346). Hollywood 'glamour', as 'a structure of enchantment deployed by cultural industries', created 'the language of allure and desirability of capitalist society' (ibid.: 338–9). Cinematic entertainment now set aerial precedents. Notwithstanding an aura of glitter and sparkle, female muscularity could not be easily reconciled with 1950s glamour.

Between the 1950s and 1970s fashionable glamour seemed to obscure the skilled muscular action. Costume was part of the increasingly complex apparatus in live aerial performance as prominent female aerialists outside the chorus had to be fashionably glamorous, like film stars, while maintaining distinctive physical accomplishments. Since aerial performance was already deemed feminine, the female aerialist performed a double identity act with fashionable femininity (see Figure 4.3). While circus relied on illusions of adventure and risk, decorative femininity counteracted these impressions. This set up a contradiction that could only be reconciled by female athleticism becoming subservient.

Cinema's glamorous female aerialist also reflected fashions in cultural behaviour. She could be physically active as long as she was not demonstrably better

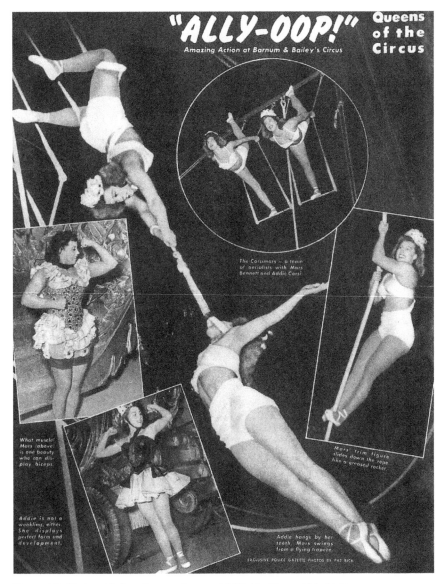

Figure 4.3 National Police Gazette, August 1947: 12. Circus World Museum.

than the male. In *Billy Rose's Jumbo*, based on the 1935 musical *Jumbo* about a star elephant in a nineteenth-century circus, the equestrienne, Kitty Wonder (Doris Day), is trying to save the circus from her gambler father (Jimmy Durante), as well as romantically interest rigger Sam Rawlins (Stephen Boyd), who is secretly a spy from a rival family circus. At short notice, Sam, in black with an eye mask, replaces a male solo aerialist. Later, Kitty finds Sam in the empty tent working on the aerial platform, and he is surprised when she flies across to him on trapeze and asks, oddly, how she learnt flying – Kitty is circus-raised. The film's circus action subsequently becomes incoherent because Kitty performs with the expertise to transfer from a moving horse up into the air on trapeze and back again in a very difficult trick. Nonetheless, an aerial rig provides the symbolic social space for romance, and for heroic action. When a storm destroys the tent, Kitty and three female aerialists in a human butterfly act are stranded mid-air, and must be heroically rescued by Sam.

Cinema's presentation of offstage life reinforces an impression of gender difference. As Clausen explains, however, audiences at live performance do not see backstage life or management. They see the performance. If they look beyond the fashionably feminine double act, they could not avoid seeing accomplished muscular women in action.

Catching pains in cinema

A flyer's struggle to achieve the triple somersault in Carol Reed's cinematically innovative box-office hit *Trapeze* (1956) became an inspiration to young flyers. In this melodrama, artistic integrity and the quest for the triple are the ambitions of the two muscular male aerialists, while the female aerialist seeks and attracts the male flyers and the audience's attention with some basic 'tricks'. Flyer Tino Orsini (Tony Curtis) achieves the triple, and catcher Mike Ribble (ex-acrobat Burt Lancaster) wins Lola (Gina Lollobrigida). Orsini's pursuit of the triple is not in Max Catto's novel *The Killing Frost* (1950), from which the film's three characters and love triangle are loosely drawn. In the novel, a priest, Father Francis, investigates the murder of a seductive, female aerialist, Sarah Linden. Orsini is wrongly executed for her murder and is assumed to be carried away with his passion, while Ribble, the murderer, eventually commits suicide. But both the novel and the film make the female aerialist guilty of competing for the affections of the two males, thereby destroying their true partnership as flyer and catcher, one that has homoerotic undercurrents. The point of the action is the completion of mid-air male-to-male body contact. Love for the aerial action and the female aerialist merge as enmity develops between the two men.

Importantly, *Trapeze*'s plot is derived from aerial history with its depiction of a flyer striving for the triple. Despite his physically flawed body, his limp from an accident doing the triple, Ribble is ironically the more masculine figure. Eventually Ribble protectively chastises and goads the younger, boyish Orsini to help him achieve the triple at the film's climax. *Trapeze* reveals the physical strain of the action alongside heightened emotional interactions; it adds (close-up) muscular pain to a performance of flying routines and reveals aerial bodies with interiority.

Although gendering the aerial action, *Trapeze* contributes to social knowledge about it. Filmed on location at the Cirque d'Hiver, once again Alexander did the flyer's (Curtis's) tricks, working to Eddie Ward Jr as the catcher (Lancaster, see Figure 4.4). But as evidence of the extreme difficulty of routinely executing a triple, Alexander's triple had to be an editing trick because he was not caught by Eddie during the filming – Eddie and Alexander were not a regular partnership, which increased the trick's difficulty.

Lollobrigida's flying work was done by the cross-dressed Alexander in wig and bra.[21] Feminine identity is faked through decorative display in contrast to the exposed chest muscles that authenticate masculinity. A cross-dressed Alexander did comic trapeze action for fortune-teller Lulu (Martha Rae) in *Billy Rose's Jumbo*. Aerial femininity becomes camp embellishment that can be done by either gender. Camp, as a decorative style to attract attention, but of dubious artistic merit, suggests excess, and circus in particular suggests 'camp-as-zircon' with its costuming that uses fake jewels (Cleto 1999: 4–5, 8). Accordingly, even the styling of gestural flourishes and limb positioning become camp since they seem surplus to the aerial action. The femininity and masculinity of the aerial body is visibly marked and exaggerated in 1950s narratives of competitive aerial action.

Between the 1950s and the 1970s males in flying groups, like the Steeles, Artons and Merilees, routinely performed bare-chested (Couderc 1964b). The male aerialist was not competing with the physique of the bodybuilder but working in a body genre that became caught up in the broader esteem increasingly accorded to a bodybuilder's shape. In one revealing synthesis of 1950s hyper-masculine display of muscle, catcher Kenneth (Dick) Anderson combined bodybuilding, gymnastic training, stunt work and aerial catching (see Figure 4.5).[22] Male bodybuilders in bikini briefs had become the 1950s male equivalent of the showgirl (Cohan 1997: 185). Annette Kuhn (1988) argues that bodybuilding is an impersonation of gender, although as Steven Cohan expanding on this idea points out, 'gender is an effect of social *reception*' (1997: 175, italics in original). As indicated in the example of Sandow, performers who perform bodily both influence and respond to culture's transformations of the body. It was the catcher who displayed a more solidly muscular male body in line with 1950s masculinity, and catching had physical stresses that made it heroic.

Catcher Bob Behee of the Flying Behees, with Ward-trained flyer Clayton Behee and Clayton's wife Rose, describes a catcher's efforts hanging upside down for 20 minutes for six catches: 'He grasps this steadily increasing weight and his shoulders snap and stretch from the strain, while his legs suffer silently from the unaccustomed load' (1947: 11).[23] Such physical management might have more in common with a 'chronic pain subculture' and its concealment by athletes and manual workers (Williams and Bendelow 1998: 166 (Kotarba)). The convention for live performance is that an aerialist must endure rather than show physical discomfort. A mystique arises with artistry of seamless fluid action when it falsely looks easy and painless, and the muscular male body is particularly susceptible to an expectation of invincibility. The aerial body's dis-

Figure 4.4 Fay Alexander flying to Eddie Ward Jr, courtesy of Steve Gossard's
private collection.

comfort remains hidden behind expansive gestures and smiling delivery; he (or
she) performs enjoyment.

The mid-twentieth-century bulkier male body shapes actually did not suit
aerialists and especially flyers and their work. Male aerialists should be 'broad-
shouldered, bee-waisted' (Johnson 1974: 103), but short, because they look
bigger in the air (Culhane 1978: 26). The typical male aerialist, however,
remained slim and lithe with visible ribs below upper-body muscle definition. At
this time, the five men and one woman in the Flying Otaris performed a four-
way cross-over, and Amy Porter writes admiringly that Frank Otari might be 68
with dyed hair but his 'well-proportioned body was sleek and slender, well
muscled, flat of stomach' (1946: 16). Unquestionably there were degrees of
prowess. The Mexican Palacios divided male flyers into principals and ordinary
leapers according to the degree of physical difficulty in the aerial tricks, like a
test of macho identity within the profession.[24]

A proliferation of American circus films during the 1950s and 1960s including *Greatest Show, Trapeze, The Big Circus* (1959) and *Circus World*, present tenting
circuses as sites for heroic action for male performer-characters at a time when
its live equivalent was going through a period of stagnation. These circus
films promoted the male circus performer, but not the aerialist, as a he-man in
what Cohan reiterates is 'the age of the chest' denoting virility (1997: 164–200

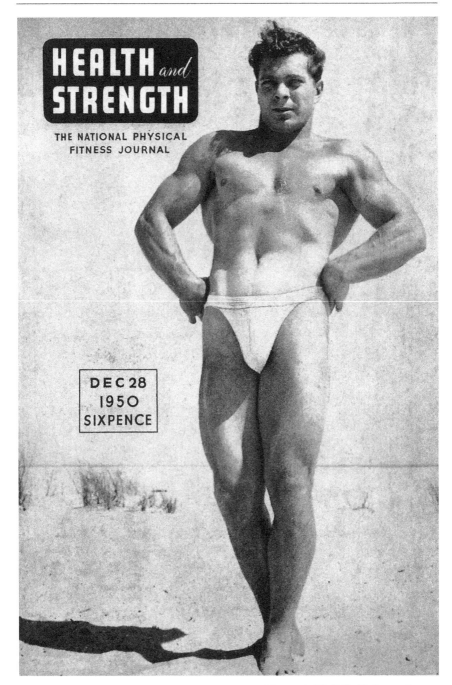

Figure 4.5 Catcher Kenneth Anderson, *Health and Strength*, 79 (26), 28 December
            1950: front page, Circus World Museum.

(Armour)). Masculinity was represented by accentuated muscularity. For example, Lex Barker, the 1950s Tarzan, exercised to achieve muscle definition and pectoral muscles in contrast to the midriff largesse of his popular predecessor, Johnny Weissmuller (ibid.: 185). In the post-Second World War context of American manhood, with widespread male access to physical training during the war, a male film star was valued for the impact of his upper body, and the effeminate male became a negation of the heterosexual norm (ibid.: xii–xiii).

As *Trapeze* reveals, male aerial athleticism in the 1950s was only partially amenable to the deep-chested masculinity of American cinema that presented 'multiple masquerades' (ibid.: x). Culturally ambivalent attitudes typified cinema's depiction of flyers. In the flawed and convoluted plot of *Circus World*, John Wayne stars as circus owner Matt Masters, staging Wild West shows in an 1890s-style circus. Wayne's iconic, authoritative, manly economy of body movement may have been miscast in circus (Wills 1997: 21–3). The plot concerns the tragedy of an aerial accident 14 years before in which aerialist 'Alfredo' died, and his wife Lily (Rita Hayworth), in love with Masters, returns to Europe leaving her daughter by Alfredo, Toni (Claudia Cardinale), to be raised by Masters. (It is worth noting the somewhat blatant naming of the dead aerialist as Alfredo, and of the live Lily for Leitzel.) The film's characters are reunited on tour in Europe after boat and fire disasters and there is a finale with a refreshing contest between mother and daughter doing one-arm planges (like Leitzel) which the mother wins. The film's deceased flyer, Alfredo, is remembered as a brute, making him reminiscent of *Variety*'s Artinelli, while the ultra-masculine horseman, Wayne as Masters, is a devoted father figure.

An expression of the full implication of 1950s American cultural fears of effeminacy associated with male-to-male flying action would not be evident until Marion Zimmer Bradley's novel *The Catch Trap* (1979), which portrays a homosexual relationship in an aerial troupe. It describes a lifelong passion between a male flyer and a male catcher, with all the complications of forbidden love and lack of self-acceptance, girlfriends and ensuing domestic violence between the two male characters. A literary precedent for aerial performance and lesbianism, however, is found 80 years earlier in Frank Wedekind's *fin-de-siècle* plays about femme fatale Lulu (Boa 1987; Ritter 1989b; Goodall 2002: 199–204). Lulu becomes an increasingly grotesque figure as her femaleness is metaphorically crossed with animal identity to suggest a chimeric circus identity. A more intriguing depiction of a lesbian as an aerialist is Djuna Barnes's Frau Mann in *Nightwood* (1937), who is described as having a 'slight and compact' body that could 'seem much heavier than that of women who stay upon the ground' (Barnes 1961: 13).

Although the male flyer no longer fitted idealized masculinity, circus, with its action and decorative femininity, was an ideal spectacle for American cinema of the 1950s and 1960s. This glittering fantasy circus developed its own momentum as a genre, contrasting with the bleaker European depictions of circus life, and even live circus.

Girls with muscles of steel

In 1977 the Flying Cavarettas, then called the Terrells, competed against two other troupes in London for the title of world champions. The flyers were sisters Terry (then Lemus), Kandy and Maureen Cavaretta, and Terry consistently did a triple somersault to catcher Jim (her brother).[25] The programme describes the troupe as having 'three of the world's prettiest – and athletically most accomplished – girls'.[26] Competing against them were the Romanian Flying Ganeas, reportedly with a quadruple somersault, and the reigning 1976 world champions, the North American Rock-Smith Flyers.

The Cavarettas won the 1977 World Circus Championship and Terry became the reigning world champion flyer. This triumph should mean that women flyers were once again fully reinstated. Greg, with the Rock-Smiths, however, did a triple-and-a-half; a trick done consistently after 1962 by Tony Steele to catcher Billy Woods with the addition of a leg catch, and in the 1970s by Don Martinez at RBBBC (Couderc 1964b: 17; Culhane 1990: 303). Did the Flying Cavarettas win because there were three female flyers, and Terry was the leading female? In other words, were male flyers expected to execute more difficult tricks than females to become winners?

The Cavarettas' history, however, completely supports their reputation as a leading troupe, with entries in the *Guinness Book of Records* for Terry's triple with one-and-a-half twist on return.[27] She performed about 1,600 triple somersaults to Jim, mostly at the Circus Circus Casino Hotel in Las Vegas where they worked for 23 years. Successive flying troupes are expected also to do difficult tricks like triples in what can only be described as a gruelling performance space with the deafening sound of the gaming machines below. Perhaps it is not surprising that performers who continually defeat the odds should be one of the founding entertainments in a centre synonymous with gambling. (This alliance of circus and gambling greatly expanded in the 1990s with Cirque du Soleil's permanent Las Vegas shows.)

The Cavarettas were given basic training by Faye Moses and Fay Alexander, and then were largely self-taught. Terry was the youngest professional trapeze artist when she started at five years of age in 1958, and did her first triple at 13 years of age – 15 is considered an appropriate age for flying. As teenagers, in 1965, the Cavarettas did a double cross-over aerial trick and a trampoline act.[28] In 1984 the Cavarettas were awarded a Silver Clown at the Monte Carlo International Circus Festival (started ten years earlier), which had, by then, become the only ongoing championship. An invitation to perform at Monte Carlo continues to be an indication of top world-class achievement.

Terry discusses her triple:

> Before I do it, I go through the whole trick in my mind – exactly how it should be done . . . I must make sure I get far enough over for my brother to reach me and to stay in the third somersault until I feel his hands touch

my arms. It takes a lot of concentration and when I lose it, that's usually when I miss . . . My emotions run quite high throughout the whole thing. Before the trick I am very nervous. I'm not afraid of getting hurt, only of failing. When I catch it, I am thrilled, relieved and very, very happy. The feeling is just as when I caught the very first one.

(Jamieson and Davidson 1980: 74)

In a televised close-up of Terry before her triple, she wears false eyelashes and she tucks her long hair into the strap of her bikini top before leaving the aerial platform to do the triple – long hair is potentially dangerous (Gaona 1984: 31–2). Terry is working with the added complication of identity fashions.

The Cavarettas' achievement is remarkable and Terry is clearly one of the twentieth-century's leading flyers. This still leaves the question about the judging criteria for the 1977 championship. The more members of a flying troupe able to do each trick, the more accomplished the group, and the troupe demonstrated more than one performer crossing mid-air. The programme states 'The judges will be looking for style and precision in the work, for passes and somersaults executed with ease, for smoothly held catches and for well timed returns to the trapeze bar.'[29] Artistic qualities influenced the judging. Terry's triple was caught smoothly by Jim in a wrist-lock, and she did a twist-and-a-half on her return. The act was noted for the impact of its up-to-date music, with the performers entering to Andrew Lloyd Webber's music from *Jesus Christ Superstar* (1973), rising to film music from *Rocky* (1976) in an inter-textual salute, and performing three tricks to Beethoven's Fifth Symphony.[30]

The 1977 championship was won by the high standard set by all the flyers, Terry's work with Jim's catching, and the act's overall theatricality.[31] Importantly, what happened is that both the Ganeas' flyer and Terry attempted quadruple somersaults, and both were unsuccessful, landing in the net. Terry attempted hers after the Cavarettas' routine ended. The potential for Terry and Jim's quadruple was there but not practised, which raises a question as to why they did not attempt to achieve it earlier. Even given scarce opportunities to practise, the physical risks of training for such tricks were incompatible with maintaining a livelihood from ongoing performance commitments.[32]

For televised circus extravaganzas in the 1960s and 1970s, including some for the Disney studios, live aerial bodies and their action could be seen clearly. The standard ritual of identity coding whereby female performers discard their high heels with their capes before climbing up to the aerial rig was now followed throughout the act with camera close-ups.[33] On the aerial platform female aerialists continued to display identity with their hand gestures, stance, make-up and false eyelashes in ways that were surplus to the aerial action but not the act. This camp display was a response to the tension between close-ups of required female upper-body muscularity and the social expectations of an aerial spectacle.

Such identity display could not disguise how the muscular female circus performer was ahead of her time in not conforming to the image of the fashionable thin waif of the 1960s, and long pre-empted the social movement towards healthy athleticism in the late 1970s and gym exercising in the 1980s. She was also well in advance of the 1990s fashion in western societies for sexually alluring and frivolous clothing and make-up for their pleasurable and fun effects in combination with physical dynamism.

Identity display aside, by the 1980s top female flyers were again expected to train to perform difficult tricks. Diane Valentine was performing a triple in the early 1980s in the Flying Valentines, with three girl flyers and a male catcher related to the Valentinos (Hofsess 1987–8: 43). As triple somersaults became a standard feature in routines during the 1980s, groups like the Flying Caballeros had three men and a woman doing triples. Among the half dozen female flyers who mastered the triple in the 1990s are Australian Bekki Ashton, daughter of flyers Nikki and Mervyn Ashton, granddaughter of aerialists Phyllis and Doug Ashton, with a circus family lineage back to the 1850s (Cannon 1997). Bekki was doing the triple to her brother, catcher and circus owner Joseph Ashton in a troupe that includes his flyer wife Michelle.

At the beginning of the twenty-first century, South American male and female flyers, duos and soloists in the USA, as well as eastern European and Russian aerialists also working in Europe and Australia, make a major contribution – more recently there have been aerial troupes from north Asia. The opportunities for the sustained training needed to do difficult tricks may be diminishing for both males and females in the shift away from traditional circuses, family-based aerial troupes and state-funded circus schools in eastern Europe. Most importantly, the mentorship of accomplished flyers is required for the narrative of record-breaking flying to continue beyond twentieth-century circus.

Quadruple macho acts

If Tarzan haunts cinema's images of masculinity, and becomes an impossible ideal in the body action genre (Kirkham and Thumim 1993b: 11), cinema's action heroes ghost live aerial performance. In neat symmetry, Tito Gaona explains that he was taken as a child by his father, Victor, a circus clown, to see the film *Trapeze*, and Orsini's cinematic triple inspired Tito to become a world leading aerialist (1984: 17). His efforts, in turn, inspired Miguel Vazquez to attempt the quadruple, which he achieved in 1982, to his catcher and brother Juan. Male dominance of flying and the centrality of Mexican family troupes were once again not in doubt as it was another decade before Jill Pages executed a quadruple in rehearsal. By the late 1980s the Russian Flying Cranes had two male performers, Pyotr Serdukov and Vladimir Shumilin, consistently doing the quadruple to catcher Vilen Golovko, and Pyotr doing a four-and-a-half, coming close to a quintuple (Collins 1990: 12). But the Cranes are significant for another reason in that their emotionally heightened act exemplifies how live aerial performance now sought to deliver emotional moods more commonly associated with theatre and cinema – the Cranes claim both gymnastics and acting (ibid.).

As flying troupes progressively set new records, Mexican family troupes continued to produce the top flyers. South America has a rich circus tradition and the oldest Mexican circus, Atayde, often presents two flying acts. Nationality labelling became advantageous given aerial achievement since the Codonas. In the 1960s the Mexican Ibarra Brothers, Vicente and Ignacio, were leading flyers (Couderc 1964c: 16), and the Gaonas developed a flying act from a trampoline act to become internationally recognized; Tito (Victor) Gaona did the triple in 1966 in Sweden. Their act, with several catchers, had Tito doing a triple somersault blindfolded, as well as triple pirouettes on his return to the platform. Tito's brothers and sisters were highly skilled flyers, Lalo, Armando and sister Chela doing a double somersault and a triple in practice, and younger brother Ritchie doing a triple (Gaona 1984). By the time Tito was trying for the quadruple, he was already a celebrity, and his 25-year flying career included working with RBBBC, Circus Knie, and New York's Big Apple Circus. Tito now trains aerialists, and is renowned as one of the most inventive aerialists for having created over 15 new tricks. He trained carefully, conscious that he did not want a 'hard' inflexible muscle that might break, or '*too much* muscle' (Culhane 1978: 28, italics in original). William Johnson calls Tito a 'genius' and leader among aerialists, who 'are the finest athletes in the world' (1974: 104).

Tito Gaona was hired by John Ringling North for RBBBC in imitation of the way Orsini was hired in *Trapeze*. Alexander, who performed the aerial stunts in *Trapeze*, was very briefly a catcher for young Tito (Gaona 1984: 11–12). Alexander's live triple that had only been caught six times is upstaged by his stunt triple for Curtis in *Trapeze*, which has a ghostly echo through Tito's mimicry of the cinematic struggle – his ultimate prize, the quadruple. Alexander is reported to have perceived Tito's ability to be the first performer to do the double-double, considered the most difficult trick, which he mastered in 1968; this involves a full twist inward and one outward while turning around in a double somersault. Tito describes how he imagines his own body's movement in a trick as if he is watching a film or at times he dreams his action (Johnson 1974: 104).

The bare chest was outmoded for male flyers by the 1970s. In cinema, the shaved chests of Lancaster and Curtis in *Trapeze* had become superseded by the 'hard bodies' of the 1980s (Jeffords 1994), in what Yvonne Tasker terms 'muscular cinema', which had also developed a few heroines of 'muscularity' (1993: 1, 3). Circus could not compete with the robotic adventure action of celluloid heroes created by Arnold Schwarzenegger, Sylvester Stallone and others, who displayed an oversized muscularity of characters in plots which merge a social conscience with combat duties. These heroic hulks appear indestructible within dramatic circumstances that minimize physical and emotional pain.

In contrast, aerialists actually execute their increasingly risky stunts for live television. For example, Ryan Kelly did a balance from his calves on a trapeze suspended below a helicopter. Although a male aerialist did not present a

Figure 4.6 The Flying Vazquez, image courtesy of Ringling Bros and Barnum and
        Bailey® The Greatest Show on Earth®.

message beyond striving for athletic and artistic triumph, he did remain culturally competitive within the USA's international agenda because he could still
outperform Russian aerialists during the last stages of the Cold War in the
1980s. Tito Gaona (1984) describes some of the personal problems caused by
the restrictions on eastern European performers hired by American circuses
during the 1960s and 1970s. Top male aerialists would still make national headlines working in the Feld family-managed 1980s RBBBC spectacles that
continue to fill sports stadiums. Perhaps it is not surprising that aerial athleticism
peaked again in the 1980s when the quadruple somersault was mastered.

The working context for Miguel Vazquez's striving for the quadruple was not
reassuring (see Figure 4.6). Flyers, including women, suffered major injuries
such as broken backs in attempting the triple (Gallagher 1982: 20; Culhane
1990: 318), which continued to have a reputation as being especially dangerous
after Ernie Lane died working with the Wards in 1921.[34] Aerial acts remained
the aspiration of performers, although the increased prevalence of child flyers
raises questions about choice in family businesses. As an adolescent flyer,
Miguel did not stand out. He technically mastered difficult tricks like the triple
and then executed it blindfolded, but still had to make his style smooth and
streamlined (Gallagher 1982: 36). John Culhane's detailed account captures the
struggle and thrill of how Miguel and catcher Juan achieved the quadruple,
which was thought impossible (1990: 315–20). The Vazquez Troupe came from
five generations of Mexican circus acrobats and in 1981 they were hired by

RBBBC for ring three; the Flying Farfans were in ring one, and the promising 12-year-old Tata Faria mastered a triple at eight years of age. Miguel learnt to get the height to throw four somersaults and then he practised being caught (ibid.: 319, action photographs). He trained with boxing for reflexes, rope-jumping, push-ups and weights, although the muscles must not get stiff or they lose their speed in the air (ibid.: 317). Miguel tried 200 times before doing the quadruple finally in front of an RBBBC audience on 10 July 1982 (Collins 1982: C11). On a subsequent night the force of impact as Juan caught Miguel dislocated Juan's shoulder. This world-leading flyer and catcher still epitomized superb lightness of action and precision in 2003, in an act at Circus Circus that included Juan and ex-Vazquez flyer Patricia Segrera's twin daughters, 18-year-olds Veronica and Victoria.

The aerial body moves in a clover-leaf shape for the quadruple, and should it be fully mastered, the quintuple requires three somersaults as the aerialist flies up and out into an arc and a further two as he or she descends towards the catcher (Collins 1990: 15). Once the precedent for the quadruple was established, others followed. Ruben Caballero did so in 1985, as did Douglas Ferroni with the Flying Martinez between 1988 and 1992 in the USA, Asia and Australia, venue height permitting. Bruno Vargas performed it to catcher Peter Gold, of the Flying Vargas, who has large hands with which to grab the flyer but skinny wrists, which are easier for the flier to grasp (Collins 1994: C15). It is the catcher 'who must calculate angles and speeds and aggressively snare the flier', catching four somersaults (ibid.).

The story of the first woman to challenge a decade of flying machismo is even more remarkable because Jill Pages (née Flinders), of the Flying Pages, did not have any of the advantages of a circus family upbringing. She joined a YWCA youth training programme with circus skills to compensate for the learning difficulty of dyslexia, and had the opportunity to work with Circus Fantasy at Disneyland, where she was discovered by Armando Farfan. Jill joined the Flying Farfans, and on her 18th birthday, 11 October 1986, became the first woman to perform three-and-a-half somersaults.[35] Her catcher, husband Willie, caught Jill's quadruple in rehearsal in 1992. She was invited to perform at Monte Carlo in 2002, and also performs a solo act on rings.

During the mid-1990s the Pages flying act had four catchers and six flyers for an act in RBBBC, and also worked at the Big Apple Circus (see Figure 4.7).[36] Despite Jill's renown, traces of a patronizing attitude towards women flyers remained evident in a journalist's comment that after her triple 'the audience's sigh of relief is almost louder than its applause'.[37] Jill was seriously injured in 2002 after landing badly on the net and, despite doctors' pronouncements to the contrary, she overcame considerable pain to return to flying in 2003 with a troupe including her 12-year-old son, Antony, in training for a triple. As a testimony to her exceptional achievements, Jill says the most difficult thing that she has done is to come back to flying after giving birth twice, and resume doing triple somersaults.[38]

Figure 4.7 Jill and The Flying Pages, Big Apple Circus 2000–1, ©Bertrand Guay/Big
    Apple Circus.

As the outer limits of flying tricks became physically more difficult, there was
a compensatory artistic shift towards expanded theatricality, emotions and
choreography. Russia's Flying Cranes developed their international reputation
in the 1990s for their poetic mood of sadness, emotional pain, mourning and
pathos, in combination with their highly proficient athletic technique. The 1995
Monte Carlo Golden Clown winners, the Cranes' seven members included one
female and, although three work as catchers, all trained as flyers at the Soviet

sports academy, six receiving the Russian title of Master of Sport (Collins 1990: 27). (Adolescent gymnasts will often retrain for circus.) Injuries were numerous, and Shumilin had even worked with a broken hand. Organized by Golovko and his father, and with the artistic direction of trapeze Washington performer and ex-soldier Pyotr Maistrenko, their act had been the Victory Day act at the Kremlin's 40th anniversary in 1985 to mark the end of the Second World War. The act was inspired by Rasul Gamzatov's poem about dead soldiers whose souls become white cranes, a well-known symbol in Russian cinema. The choreographer, Valentin Gneushev, also claimed inspiration from the film about the Vietnam war *Apocalypse Now* (1979), especially its soundtrack (Albrecht 1995: 115). The act was highly technical, with electrical winches, strobe lighting and smoke. It used classical music by Tchaikovsky, Bach, Liszt, Ravel, Stravinsky and Wagner, and the performers wore plain white leotards and tights. Live aerial performance has traditionally used comedy but complex emotional tones of sadness combined with this level of flying athleticism was a major innovation. The Cranes did the quadruple consistently in performance from 1985, with Serdukov and Shumilin doing over 100 each. Catcher Golovko was knocked unconscious by Serdukov attempting to do four-and-a-half turns on 10 December 1989 at Fort Worth (Collins 1990: 10).

An aerial performer's compulsion to excel comes in part from his or her passion for doing the action despite the physical consequences. Muscular tenderness might be logically predicted from stretching and pushing a body but instead, aerial performance invites spectators' projections of emotional tenderness that obscure the muscular body. Physical pain presents a problem for body-to-body(ies) communication and needs externalization (Scarry 1985); pain is conveyed by cultural languages of emotions in performance. The gender of the aerialist further complicates a perception of pain. The social idea of pain is contradictorily implicated in 'male power and female fragility and weakness', and a male conceptual division of pain between mind and body (Williams and Bendelow 1998, 166–7 (Morris)). As the aerial body flies, bends and turns, it arouses emotional affinities that displace muscular strain. A performer's aches and pains, the physical effort of difficult tricks, remain unseen and accentuated by a cultural perception of lightness, of insubstantiality. If narratives of emotionality also render the aerial action feminine, the aerialist embodies (feminized) love and a (masculinized) masking of pain.

At the beginning of the twenty-first century, the production of emotionally varied moods, either within classical aerial acts or in new circus, expands performance possibilities and deflects the emphasis from (im)possible tricks. In new circus in particular, aerial feats are often secondary to the theatricality and its emotional impact. There is an expectation that aerial acts can also be emotionally evocative like those in films; that is, male and female aerial bodies will be athletically, artistically and emotionally moving.

Chapter 5

Androgyny to queer violence: Cirque du Soleil, Archaos and Circus Oz

New circus relies on aerial artistry to deliver impressive skills and thrills. As part of new circus after the mid-1980s, some aerial identity became overtly sexualized and intended to shock. As well, there were significant developments in aerial technique and apparatus. If a potential for presenting transgressive identities with aerial skills can be traced to the Hanlon-Lees Brothers' macabre pantomimes, new circus diverges when it sets out to be deliberately socially provocative. Radical new circus also finds artistic inspiration in twentieth-century cultural ideas of circus and sideshow, the imaginary circus of books and films removed from actual circus performances.

By 1990 the artistic and economic importance of new circus as an art form in its own right was undeniable. Its internationally acclaimed organizations include Archaos from France, Cirque du Soleil from Canada and the USA, and Circus Oz from Australia, with some exchanges of artists between them. This chapter discusses aerial performance in the work of these three companies in order to illustrate trends and contrasting aesthetic forms; some smaller physical theatre groups provide further examples of a much larger field. Distinctive circus aesthetics are created by the irreverent and frightening bad behaviour of early Archaos performing to heavy rock music, the androgynous charming fantasies of Cirque du Soleil dancing to lyrical popular music, and aggro femme clowning in the brassy cabaret circus of Circus Oz. Unlike traditional circus, each of these new circuses develops an overarching emotional tone: Archaos shows around 1990 delivered anarchic intimidation, Cirque du Soleil continues to offer romantic exuberance and Circus Oz presents witty silliness. In some new circus, an aerial body's identity seems queer because of the physical action and, in particular, violent interactions. Some new circus explores a politics of underlying violence in circus.

The first new circuses challenged establishment values, and 'banned' decorative femininity. It was as though aerial work picked up from the 1930s traditional circus when female and male aerialists worked interchangeably. New circus remains closer to theatre in its aesthetic and thematic purpose and unity, and because performers work in relationship with others displaying qualities that range from quaintly charming to outrageous and obnoxious. In theatrical terms they are more types than characters, and are perhaps more accurately described as body-types. Physical theatre developed out of the new circus movement, most noticeably in England and Australia, when smaller ensembles integrated acrobatic and aerial skills into more seamless performances of movement and dance. Both new circus and physical theatre self-consciously refer to the form of circus in artistically and politically inventive ways.

Banned

In 1990 Bristol Council banned Archaos following tabloid descriptions of nude trapeze artists and 'men dancing together' (de Jongh 1990: 2). London's Islington Council tried to ban Archaos's *Bouinax*, and in 1991 officials in Toronto, Canada sought to relocate and contain Archaos to a football stadium on the margins of the city, out of sight (Little 1995–6: 19). These efforts are indicative of a new era whereby animal-free circus was transgressive of social identity, values and, importantly, circus norms. Efforts to ban whole circuses rather than selective acts had previously come from animal rights groups. Archaos, with its nightmarish aura, had completely replaced the family-friendly, showgirl aesthetic of sequins and smiles. In this punk, post-apocalyptic circus created by Pierrot Pillot-Bidon, motorbikes, makeshift tanks, cars and robot toys roared instead of animals, in an urban wasteland accompanied by loud, live rock music. This was circus that sought to pierce the veneer of civilized cordiality in everyday life rather than offering an entertaining escape. It established a trend of performing abjection in new circus.

Although Archaos shifted in aesthetic direction over the next decade, and the company's 2000s shows are no longer highly controversial, in 1990 it spearheaded neo-gothic grunge aesthetics and queer behaviour in circus across North America, Australia and Europe. Archaos productions around 1990 were *Le Cirque de Caractère* (1986), on the poetry of travelling; *Le Chapiteau de Cordes One*, on loneliness and violence (1987–8); *The Last Show on Earth* (1989), on love and tenderness; *Bouinax* (1990–1), on loners; *Metal Clown* (1991–2), on slavery and colonization; and *Méchanique et Transpiration* (1992), on cruelty.

By 1990 two shows were touring widely; one in Australia, and another in Edinburgh and London. The thematically unified shows depicted urban street life and its inhabitants, often in violent interaction, and convey some of the company's outlandish extremes. The sizeable 90-strong *Bouinax* had performers appear in cages; chainsaws also rushed at the audience, guns were brandished and a car was firebombed. The programme notes explain that *Bouinax* means 'beautiful absurdity, a comic cock-up' and state:

> When the aerial act catcher is working from the end of a swaying crane-boom, his job is just as difficult as it looks . . . it represents the sort of difficulty that has to be faced and surmounted in our mechanistic age.[1]

With male performers spinning on webs deemed female apparatus, female duos, and females in the weight-bearing positions with male partners, new circus reversed the gendering of aerial body positions. Archaos's aerialists included Ramon Fernandez on rope wearing black lace, flyer Sophie Kantorowice in a dress that flew up to reveal her underwear, and a blind singing aerialist who was assaulted. In the violent mayhem, a fiendish female terrorist mimed acts of abjection, wielding a chainsaw to behead or castrate males (*Archaos Two* video, 25 April 1990). A thug female aerialist was lowered on trapeze to manhandle performers up from the ground and then dump them again, one into a rubbish bin. Scenarios included a woman and a man fighting violently on the ground, and the strikingly original tin clowns wearing roof-metal on their backs for sliding and colliding. Archaos's style did have less confrontational but nonetheless bizarre moments that included an adult little person being carried like a child, a housewife dusting discarded metal rubbish, a lost explorer on a bicycle and an old lady knocked to the ground.

From 1986 to 1992 Archaos's shows presented a burlesque aesthetic of sexualized interactions tinged with violence. Peter Wilkinson writes of a performance at Dunkirk in 1990: 'In one scene, two swarthy men recline in a basket, smooching; in another male courtiers woo a bald-headed Roman senator garbed in a diaphanous skirt and green lipstick' (1990: 51). In this example, a queer identity was presented via the sexualized interactions of (presumably) same-sex performers. Other unconventional sexual behaviour was suggested when Pascualito (Lionel Hassin) in a leather G-string and a neck chain is pulled along in a sado-masochistic ritual by a leather-dressed female.

The efforts to ban Archaos confirm Pillot-Bidon's view that a meaningful show can offend some spectators (Wilkinson 1990: 48). By replacing clown noses and glitter spangles with macho leather, tattoos and chains, he intended to expose an underlying violence in circus, and reflect a larger edgy social reality. Slapstick circus action is not benign when some young spectators find traditional clowns frightening. Circus developed in England around the time of team sports, and Norbert Elias and Eric Dunning's (1993) sociological history argues that the twentieth century's aggressive violence by sports players and spectators is the legacy of its own history. While acknowledging Jennifer Hargreaves's (1986) criticism of Eurocentric modernist linear narratives that avoid consideration of class tensions, the argument that the development of team sport allowed for an institutionalization of social violence (Elias and Dunning 1993: 151) suggests a broader context in which circus was also a cultural diversion for such tendencies. Moreover, the depiction of violence in Archaos was hardly gratuitous or formulaic. *Metal Clown* included a Bahia dance troupe, Aze Bahia, and content about oppressive governments after early European colonization. It alluded to death squads murdering children. The efforts to ban Archaos, however, may have been indicative of the difficulty of delivering an unambiguous message with physical skills, music and minimal speech, which became open to misinterpretation as inciting violence and sexualized behaviour.

Archaos's productions suggested complex layered resonances in their representation of violence through a sophisticated adaptation of circus. Also, the fluidity of the physical form suggests how the representation of ethnic identity becomes that of fusion rather than interculturalism.

While it is possible to proclaim a politics of violence with some new circus, it is difficult to claim a radical political effect. Yet more than ever, with the unfolding wars and terrorism of the early twenty-first century, there is an urgency about artistic efforts to grapple with violent action and its consequences.

Circus is a business venture and new circus is no exception. By 1991, despite controversy or perhaps because of it, Archaos had become very successful internationally. A fierce storm in Dublin destroyed the Archaos tent, disrupted its performances and ultimately forced the company into voluntary liquidation. Interestingly, Cirque du Soleil also lost money touring to London in 1990 despite its popularity (Albrecht 1995: 145). Archaos revived but without the same scale of international touring. Under the direction of Guy Carrara, Archaos shows developed an aesthetic to appeal to young people's tastes for techno music and club culture. Shows include *DJ 93* (1993), and *Game Over 1* and *2* (1995–7), with multimedia images of game arcades. Carrara expects the performers, often graduates of the French circus schools, to be committed to the company and to be multi-skilled.[2] Archaos reflects an idea of circus as an age-old celebratory live experience created through human physicality in defiance of an increasingly technologically driven, alienating society, yet paradoxically, like circus traditionally, it utilizes new technologies.

New circus assumes its audience is familiar with the format of traditional live circus, and then takes its artistic inspiration from a cultural idea of circus as identity transgression and grotesque abjection, most apparent in literature and cinema. Early Archaos shows reflected a trend in new circus practice to include queer sexual identities and expand social ideas of freakish bodies. Artistic representation frequently exaggerates features of traditional circus, although a nineteenth-century clown was once termed a 'grotesque' or 'merriman' (Frost 1881: 68), possibly because of acrobatic contortion in acts which also included speech. Further, animals were often the partners of leading clowns (Towsen 1976: 214–15). Grotesqueness was conveyed by exuberantly messy bodies that overlapped with freaks in sideshows, and included bodies with an ambiguous gender identity (Russo 1994: 79 (Bakhtin)). Sideshow subsequently became sensationalized through its cinematic depictions (ibid.: 86–106). Mary Russo (1994) explores cinema that exemplifies an abject grotesque female identity polarized against a sleek, contained airborne body. Aerial action in new circus that is contorted, sexualized and/or involves black comedy delivers a grotesque aesthetic more reminiscent of cinematic depictions. Its gender reversals help compound an impression that some new circus is devoid of acts like glamorous feminine spectacles which have made traditional circus socially acceptable.

Kenneth Little questions the view that new circus belongs to large-scale cultural spectacles expressing the optimistic ideals of modernity claimed for traditional circus (1995–6: 15). Even when spectacles are paradoxical, they function as shared experience in a symbolic economy. Little draws on Guy Debord's idea that not only is spectacle metaphoric of modernity, but capitalist society is spectacle. Consequently, in 1991, Archaos's anti-spectacle was politically subversive because it threatened a city's unitary control of protocol in public spaces. Little explains that 'cosmopolitan popular' culture reveals the function of 'spectacle and the consolidation of the global economy, the world wide dissemination of cultural commodities and the emergence of new forms of economic and ideologically motivated migrations' (ibid.: 16). Circus performance has always operated in an international economy, and even radical circus like Archaos engages with cultural commodification. Challenging power relations through nonconformist gender behaviour and queer interactions, however, is particularly contentious internationally. A parodic evocation of circus form further contributes to an impression of a postmodern disintegration in formerly stable (national) societies.

Two Edinburgh city councillors campaigned to ban the all-female[3] Australian aerial group Club Swing from performing its show *Appetite* during the 1995 Edinburgh Festival, claiming it was degrading to women (Tait 1996b). The campaign against *Appetite*, which received UK-wide media coverage, was sparked by a poster photograph implying a naked female and therefore sexualized body in a trapeze act. Perhaps it was also the boyish femaleness of the muscular aerialists that might be taken for lesbian (body) identity, and sexualized food consumption that made it particularly controversial. The latent potential of trapeze acts to suggest sex acts reveals the extent to which such physical actions continue to be carefully negotiated in most aerial performance. As happens so often in aerial history, the origins of sexually explicit trapeze acts are unclear; Elinor Pelikan, Leitzel's mother, removed street clothes down to her aerial costume during a 1912 iron jaw act, and topless female trapezists performed in 1930s Paris (Damase 1962: 160).

Poster images aside, *Appetite* was performed by four fully dressed female aerialists in elegant costumes by Oscar-winning designer Angus Strathie, which consisted of white lace costumes and Gainsborough-style hats. Apparently, some of Club Swing's spectators complained because there was no nudity in the show. Instead it presented sensuous movement in solo and duo trapeze, cradle, web and cloud swing acts set to a soundtrack that included opera and British pop. The performers accentuated, and deliberately held, the transition positions between the recognizable aerial tricks and poses, which are usually minimized, and in this way the action became suggestively sexualized. They made the most of the sexual innuendo of bodies working in close proximity. On the ground there was a feast of fruit, chocolate and cakes that the performers consumed with erotically charged gestures. The four female aerialists who helped devise the performance were Circus Oz performers Anni Davey and Simone O'Brien, and ex-Legs on the Wall performers Celia White and Kathryn Niesche. It was directed by Gail Kelly, assisted by Circus Oz performer Robyn Laurie, and Lisa

Small. The Melbourne-based group toured the show from 1992 to 1997, and created other shows. In 1999 the group created *Razor Baby*, with guest artists Circus Oz performer Kareena Oates and English acrobat Jeremy Robins (Tait 2001). *Razor Baby* consisted of aerial performance set in a queer club with a techno mix provided by a live DJ; there was a trend during the 1990s of hiring aerial performers as entertainers for gay, lesbian, bisexual and transgender dance party events. The award-winning Club Swing typifies innovative experimentation in Australian physical theatre during the 1990s. Its visual texts of physical interactions parodied ideas of sexy circus body identity and the aerial form while delivering eroticism. Although Club Swing's fully dressed shows were visually beautiful and comically playful, their sensual aerial action belongs in adults-only circus.

Some physical theatre sought to reclaim queer circus history in the 1990s. For example, New York performance artist John Kelly created and performed the story of Barbette's early life and career and his friendship with Jean Cocteau in *Light Shall Lift Them* (1993).[4] This image-based multimedia performance had Kelly doing simple poses on low wire and on low trapeze. Adoration for the aerialist can also be considered part of queer history.

The artistic development of circus skills outside traditional circuses is particularly strong in France (Maleval 2002), and there are at least a dozen specialized aerial duos and groups.[5] The best known, Les Arts Sauts, presents a complete show of classical aerial work on a purpose-built rig accompanied by live lyrical singing. Bridging traditional and new circus in the USA are the one-ring circuses of the Big Apple Circus (Albrecht 1995: 50–1) and Circus Flora, bringing back more intimate circus with animal acts based on the long-standing European form. In England, a commercial adaptation blends traditional with new circus. After hiring ex-Archaos acts for their traditional circus during the 1990s, Cottles produced *Circus of Horrors* (1996) for young adults, featuring a live rock band, bungee cord aerials and adapted sideshow gimmicks, partially inspired by vampire films.[6] Gerry Cottle, who joined English circus proprietors in the 1970s when he started a traditional circus with animals, commissioned rock composer John Haze and Archaos's Pillot-Bidon to create *Circus of Horrors*, which toured to South America and continues seasonally in England. It features a gothic aesthetic of so-called 'undead' identities that include skeletons, and its revised productions make direct references to freak shows (McGill 1999: 35). The Cottle family contribute to the current vibrancy of England's circus entertainment with up to four circuses under their management annually, including Russian and Chinese tours.

Why did radical new circus become controversial? Efforts to ban it were not necessarily even specific to the content. It was as if the incompatibility of ideas of circus – that circus is for families and yet dangerous – was finally exposed and provoked an over-reaction. On the one hand, traditional circus is childhood entertainment and treasured nostalgically; on the other hand, it is surreptitiously instructive on what might be physically risky and sexually alluring. These ideas are part of the paradoxical allure of circus for performers and audiences alike, and traditional circuses remain socially acceptable as long as these ideas are covert.

The motivation behind the radical new circus movement of the 1960s and 1970s in Europe, North America and Australia was in part an attraction to the mythology of a self-contained world outside mainstream culture (Mullett forthcoming). It emulated circus skills but not traditional circus organization, where a performer's work regimes were extremely regimented and circuses were routinely televised for mass audiences. Performers and biographers repeatedly point out that circus life was often highly regulated by conservative values and familial relationships. New circus drew on circus skills long deemed working-class entertainments, which legitimized its western anti-establishment status, and this was underscored by the sanctioning of circus as state entertainment by communist governments. In addition, Ernest Albrecht argues that American new circus rethought circus by drawing extensively on the experimental theatre movement (1995: 10). Performers were inspired to acquire specialized circus skills in order to make popular (body) art.

The aesthetics and content of some new circus reflected an idea of badness – even bad circus skills. It encouraged sexually explicit acts and became socially outrageous. Instances of queerness evident in early Archaos and also English physical theatre DV8's early shows with Lloyd Newson (Burt 1995) would prove seminal to further exploration of gender and sexual identity in 1990s new circus and physical theatre. As this artistic movement matures, however, it becomes increasingly reliant on skill expertise and act specialization like traditional circus. Most importantly, however, new circus was bringing in new audiences.

Androgynous charm

At the beginning of the twenty-first century, Canada's Cirque du Soleil represents the apex of new circus achievement and economic power. Cirque did not reinvent circus, as is often claimed, but did reinvent its capacity to deliver a beautiful visual aesthetic with muscular action. Cirque productions still convey a radical motif through the androgynous body identity of acrobats and aerialists but within a distinctive non-confrontational performance style that includes original live music. Poetic interludes present a whimsical androgyny with echoes of Barbette's 1920s act. But Cirque's unique, artistically imaginative worlds are inhabited by bodies that stretch across human, animal, reptilian and even alien shapes with their appearance, athletic action and dance movement. Their struggles are against the elements – air, earth, fire and water – rather than with each other. The space is reconfigured with fog, fire and other visual effects so that it could be a cave or another planet; the bodies in mid-air are bird hybrids or superhuman. Fantastic identities are created with incandescent lycra bodysuits and sculptured headwear, masks and face make-up, which have an imaginative range spanning Renaissance mummers to futuristic worlds. The original music is crucial to the overall effect; at times the singing in a non-specific language suggests Celtic folk and medieval European choral influences. A large structure doubles as an imaginative set, with, for example, evocative metallic spikes or mesh, and provides the rigging structure for aerial apparatus as well as an overhead walkway for a singer, musicians and performers. An aura of other-worldliness suggests a place outside time with stylistic elements that are vaguely historical and yet also futuristic. This is serious circus – acrobatic, pole-balancing, contortion, clowning, juggling and aerials – that aims to be visually pleasing and technically accomplished, and to appeal to adult spectators.

Aerial and acrobatic artistry is central to each show's continuous action, and apparatus is imaginatively adapted or invented. For example, bungee cord – better known for recreational jumping from high places – was used by aerial acts in the early 1990s. Attached to the performers, it propels them outwards and downwards and back to the rigging with far greater mobility and spatial range than conventional flying equipment. Aerial bodies could bounce in a circular motion around a trapeze.

The youthful choruses performing identical choreographed action deliver an over-riding impression of androgynous sensuous physicality. With unisex costuming, the muscular gracefulness of male and female teams of acrobats and aerialists is indistinguishable. Costumes do sometimes specify identity, with frills on leotards distinguishing female clown-types. In solo or duo acts, however, male bodies seem more accentuated by bare-chested muscularity while females adhere to the general impression of androgyny delivered by the chorus. This is entertainment commensurate with an era in which young female Olympic gymnasts become celebrities. In addition, contortion acts heighten an impression of blurred species boundaries. Although casts are international, this non-verbal new circus, unlike traditional circus, does not present national and ethnic identity, and while the stereotypical sexy female circus body is absent, not so sensuality or eroticism.

Cirque is the world's foremost new circus in its popularity, multiple fixed venues and tented touring productions. It has annual budgets of hundreds of millions of dollars and employs almost 3,000 people. The shows originate in the company's headquarters in Montreal, where performers are trained. In 1984 the founding visionary, Guy Laliberté, with Daniel Gauthier, Guy Caron and acrobat Gilles Ste-Croix, collaborated to assemble 'le grand tour' of new circus performers that would develop into Cirque du Soleil (Albrecht 1995: 72–89). The company's successful formula brings together acts by highly skilled artists within the conceptually integrated artistic direction of Caron and, until recently, ex-Archaos member Franco Dragone, and the stage direction of Gilles Ste-Croix and more recently Dominic Champagne. Each creative team includes notable artists and the format of each show is carefully designed, and when the original performers leave, substitute performers learn the choreographed action. Interestingly, like new circus elsewhere, Cirque's founding members were associated with street performance and radical politics, and the organization continues to allocate funding for socially responsible youth programmes. The company produced *La Magie Continue*® (1986); *Le Cirque Réinventé*® (1987), *Nouvelle Expérience*® (1990), *Saltimbanco*® (1992–), and *Mystère*® (1993–) at Las Vegas's Treasure Island; *Alegría*® (1994–), and *La Nouba*® at Orlando's Disney World (1998–); and *Quidam*® (1996–), *Dralion*™ (1999–), and the water show *O*® (1998–) at Las Vegas's Bellagio Hotel.[7] In 2002 *Varekai*™ began touring North America and in 2003 the erotically charged *Zumanity*™ began in Las Vegas.

This discussion offers one interpretation (reading) of an androgynous aesthetic in the performance (text) of Cirque shows, and selectively about aerial acts. (Film versions are widely available.) Production concepts might be summarized as an innocent protagonist, often female, helped by an older identity, seemingly male, to face a challenging journey or search for identity; more generally, old versus young. Such conceptual through-lines provide an invaluable structure for making image-based work even if they sometimes elude a spectator. It is the imaginative and theatrical restaging of circus skills executed to a high standard combined with melodious music that makes these shows extremely impressive.

From early shows, the identity of the whimsical clowns was ambiguously fluid. *Saltimbanco* clowns in hooded lycra leotards performed like naughty pixies. They played acrobatically with the audience at the beginning of the show, pulling off T-shirts, rubbing bald heads, and even turning individual audience members in somersaults. The title evokes an ongoing tradition of artistically representing itinerant acrobats with, for example, the pathos of impoverished street performers found in Picasso's painting and Rainer Maria Rilke's poetry (Ritter 1989b). In contrast, *Saltimbanco* delivered a tone of joyful exuberance underscored with aerial acts: a pole act, a woman tight-rope performer leaping between wires, a four-person aerial troupe on bungee cords, and a favoured Cirque apparatus, the Russian swing, that propels teams of acrobats up into the air with twists and turns.

Mystère had a reptilian motif and performers descending bird-like over the audience, and it also presented a more conventional flying act including a flyer doing a triple somersault. Fantastic bird-types again make appearances in *Alegría*, although with fewer aerial acts. They predominate, however, in *Quidam*, haunted by a headless figure in an overcoat: Isabelle Chausse's wonderfully androgynous tissu act started slowly with leg splits, back arches, and graceful contorted poses with the tissu wrapped around the body and then unrolled; a chorus on large aerial rings; and a powerful cloud swing finale by Australian Christie Shelper.[8] *Dralion* was created with 34 acrobats and aerialists from the Flag Circus from south-west China, merging north Asian and western European circus practices, and also featured a performer who sang androgynously across low and high registers. The dynamic all-women teeterboard team bounced up into the air and into balances four bodies high. In response to an act adapting the North Korean cradles 'one's stomach is continually in a knot only to be unloosened with a gasp and a sigh'.[9]

O was an extraordinary, captivating and adventurous spectacle that brought together circus, sport and theatre. The purpose-built stage contains a one-and-half-million-gallon pool of water – acts in water tanks can be traced back to the nineteenth century.[10] A water setting, however, is a particularly dangerous environment for aerialists, who need dryness to grip properly. With complex lighting shifts, the Cirque setting evoked sky, earth and lake. The 75 performers worked between three spatial environments: in a deep diving pool or shallow water, on the solid floor and in the air. The show brought together champion high-divers, synchronized swimmers, acrobats and aerialists, who also moved seamlessly between ground, air and water. The movement delivered an androgynous physicality in a show in which circus and sport action became interchangeable as large choruses transformed into figures in a luminous fantasy of constantly shifting light and sound. A harmonious world was interrupted by rain storms, two clowns floated around on a flooded house, castaways appeared, Neptune danced by, and masked sirens swam in synchronized movement. The distances within the auditorium enhanced the impression of androgynous amphibian fluidity. Visually poetic, this live performance seemed wondrous in its imaginative physicality across athletic forms.

A trapeze duo, side by side, mirrored each other in movement before dropping from height into the pool, and the aerialist's lycra leotard became a wet suit. Performers appeared from under the water to rise into the air. They bounced down in bungee cords sometimes suspended by the feet. One performer, upside down in a head-stand, swung around rapidly in a motorized trapeze Washington act. An aerial rig, built like a ship, swung backwards and forwards and up and down as performers were cast across, underneath it – a flying boat with aerialists for passengers. A suspended metal grid had performers in zebra-striped costumes working across its flat surface. Acrobats leapt off a Russian swing from a height, somersaulting and pirouetting in dangerous free fall down white fabric slides ballooning like ship sails. In *O*, the remarkable aerial action includes diving into water.

In contrast, the touring tent show *Varekai* was full of edgy, fast action that used a circus format to engage directly with the audience and invite applause for tricks. Aerialists on a variety of apparatus moved up, down and around with speed on motorized pulleys, and the Russian swing act, again with white slides, was especially powerful because of its proximity to the audience. An angel with feather wings was cradled in an inventive netting apparatus, which was used initially like a cloud swing, and then as a vertical rope. Figures moved among the tops of poles in a metal forest. Two bare-chested males, in feather bird-like headdresses and ribbed black pants, initially worked on two straps and then as a duo, balanced together in holds from one strap (see Figure 5.1). A female undulated in very fast risky aerial action around a ring and finished with a neck hang.

Despite the company's phenomenal popularity and international artistic acclaim, there is some resistance to Cirque's highly choreographed danced style

Figure 5.1 Aerial straps from *Varekai*™ by Cirque du Soleil®, photograph
Véronique Vial, costumes Eiko Ishloka, ©2002 Cirque du Soleil Inc.

of circus. For example, while noting the performers' skill, Charles Spencer writes of 'soulless efficiency'; there is 'a continuous flow of loud, banal, jazz-tinged pop music, the costumes are gaudily gorgeous, and every movement has been carefully, if not particularly imaginatively, choreographed' (1990: 14). Appreciation of the Cirque aesthetic may be in accord with the way that 'taste' for ballet and modern dance is learned by different social groups (Desmond 1997c: 31 (Bourdieu)). Sarah Cottle – who together with sisters April and Polly ran the Cottle's Circus in the mid-1990s – explains, 'People come to see girls in fishnet stockings showing a bit too much bum and boys with big muscles' (Armitstead 1995: T10). Also, people want a sense of danger. There is probably a socio-economic distinction here because the Cottles' shows attract regular circus-going audiences, and Cirque reaches more affluent audiences who do not usually attend circus.

What are the implications of Gerry Cottle's claim that circus 'is all about sex and fantasy' (ibid.)? Entertainment everywhere is thoroughly sexualized; Toby Miller asks if sport has also become a sex industry (2001: 13). Certainly Cirque is redefining body identity and sensuous athletic action in popular entertainment. Is Cirque's wide audience appeal deemed bland by some because of its androgyny, and the absence of overt displays of conventional female sexiness long associated with notions of danger? Cirque confirms that highly skilled circus acts can reject traditional gender demarcations and be appreciated as beautiful; reviewers repeatedly praise the artistry and skill of Cirque performers. Because an occasional reviewer admits to finding some acts erotic, it may be that Cirque's appeal is less predictable than that of traditional circus. Two bodies balancing against each other in sensuous movement can be erotic; Cirque performers subtly suggest this possibility through their physical action.

From my observations, Cirque du Soleil presents a very exciting visual spectacle, but as a whole entity rather than selectively dispersed within particular acts. There are risks of injury for performers; acts are certainly arduous in North America, if not so obviously in the versions on the international tours once casts change. The shows that made the company well known accommodated formative innovations in risk-taking. For example, the clown, David Shiner, bodily engaged with spectators and established outrageous precedents for audience participation (Albrecht 1995: 81), while the wonderful Russian acrobatic teams flying off Russian swings up to the roof completely reconfigure and update aerial projectile action.

The presentation of body identity is potent when it tracks across the broadest cultural identity groupings. The potential for identity reconfiguration is most explicit when a performing body is physically bent in aerial or ground-based contortion acts. A contorted hybrid body may also create an impression of asexuality, and it has more complex resonances for race, especially with species fusion. Because there is a harmonious effect to the interactions in Cirque shows, these deliver a surreptitious subversion of identity.

Aggro femmes

At the beginning of the twenty-first century the physically adept aggro femme had become a recurring motif in new circus and physical theatre. She seemed to be everywhere. Flexing her muscles, she comes down from her aerial perch, runs across the ring, climbs up to chase and harass others. She is a bully, a bad-girl guerrilla, the dominatrix, and males falter and recoil in her presence. Her aggression is more often than not towards males, although she competes with other women. Thus the aggro femme is dependent on a demarcation between male and female bodies as she battles to dominate air and ground space. In the Argentinian De La Guarda shows, franchised in London and New York after the group's 1997 international tour, a group of aggro femmes in short skirts descended on motorized aerial apparatus to threaten the audience with their stare and stance. They hovered above menacingly, suspended from harnesses.

The female terrorist and thug in Archaos was a forerunner of the recent aggro femme activity, and aggressive physical action by female performers remains double trouble. It exposes the way that bodies are socially identified according to patterns of movement so that atypical action undermines gender demarcations. Accordingly, violent action can make a female body seem queer.

An aggro femme clown became a stalwart of Australia's Melbourne-based

Circus Oz productions after 1998 when Mike Finch became artistic director. Oz spends a third of the year performing overseas and in 2001 at New York's New Victory Theatre sold out its 10,000 capacity. The aggro femme made some earlier appearances in physical theatres (Tait 2001), and then appeared in Oz's productions as an aerialist and female clown. Her intent ranges across comically ridiculous, sly seduction and brutal harassment. But how funny is this aggro clowning?

There have been comic performers in aerial routines from the late nineteenth century, and these typically involve a male clown figure trying to imitate a flyer, and losing his trousers in a catch. The clown has to be a skilled aerialist before he (uncommonly she) can deliberately make tricks go awry. Clowning in the circus evolved out of comic action in rope and equestrian acts, and verbal exchanges with the ring master (Towsen 1976: 89). The physicality traditionally included comic aggression and perhaps for this reason, aside from 'glee-maidens' (ibid.: 47) and *commedia dell'arte* performers, the history of European clowning remained almost exclusively male. With a few notable exceptions such as Cecil MacKinnon with Circus Flora (Albrecht 1995: 103–9), black American Danise Payne, who also worked with the USA's Universalsoul circus, and Brazilian Angela de Castro in England, who have developed distinctive clown identities, most female circus performers did, and continue to, cross-dress, thereby adopting conventional male clown types. Yet comedy genres offer socially subversive possibilities, and physical clowning offers females ways to carnivalize authority with '*dialogic body language*' (Little 1991: 20, 22, italics in original (Bakhtin)).

Oz, formed in 1978, develops annual productions that combine circus skills with commentary about social justice concerns, and while their emphasis has changed over time with more skills and fewer rhetorical left-wing statements, this remains the company's identifiable formula appealing to its largely theatre-going audiences. Productions are called Circus Oz followed by the year date, and have a cast of twelve performers and musicians who have multiple functions within a sequence of acts that deliver circus cabaret in a ring. Oz's politically satirical clowning ranges from criticism of government decision-making to sympathy for the plight of unemployed people. Acclaimed for their irreverent humour directed at ideas of Australian-ness, the performers present naive and peculiar character-types doing circus skills, combined with live original music often with brass instruments echoing nineteenth-century circus band music (also see Tait 2004). The one-ring Oz show is not polished spectacle like Cirque du Soleil or confrontational like Archaos, but conveys thrill and risk in part because of its unpredictable theatricality. The physical style of comedy is often ironic direct address to the audience, who are placed in a position of knowing what might happen to unsuspecting performers. Oz performers excel at a burlesque idiocy, at brash self-ridicule and at outright foolishness. Quirky character-types doing accomplished skills typically threaten others in slapstick routines and/or fail spectacularly with their action. Doggedly persistent and imploring or knowingly bad but cute, most of the Oz character-types were endearing in their naughtiness rather than brutal; that is, until the aggro femme appeared.

Female performers with Oz have always resisted conventional portrayals of gender identity, especially in aerial acts that are susceptible to feminine stereotypes. They worked with awareness that circus is a domain in which women perform the same skills as men (Tait 1994: 111–19; Albrecht 1995: 10). Earlier Oz performers inspired successive casts. Their feminist agenda delivered through physicality, and in the demonstration of skills, avoids the polemicism of spoken theatre. The prevailing Oz style of female comic performers was accidental slapstick, hapless stumbling and bumbling without malice.

In a broad pattern of comic gender reversals, aggro femmes demand submission from startled males in their appearances between 1998 and 2002. Finch retains performers and their acts from year to year, such as the upside-down roof walking of Tim Coldwell, the only remaining founding company member, and group acts with Chinese acrobatic rings, acrobatic pole balances and unicycling.[11] Therefore the following performance identities reappear in subsequent years. In 1998 a serene John O'Hagan played his bass cello swinging mid-air on aerial apparatus; endearing Chris Lewis on the ground sounded honkers which are stuck in all the crevices of his near-naked body. Meanwhile tattooed female aerialist Oates, in a studded leather bikini, approached spectators with thug-like menacing and then transformed into an aerial femme fatale when she was hoisted into the air with fire-blazing hula hoops around her waist. The 1999 production satirized the national preoccupation at that time with preparations for the Sydney 2000 Olympics in an act where male and female performers hung upside down, to race in slow motion across the roof, as if doing competitive track and field races. Two aggro femme characters, Sera and Kera Tonin (Nicci Wilks and Sarah Ritchie), wearing black leather and cracking whips, chased Michael Ling, the wire-walker wearing a black tutu – two animal trainers after their human dog. A male trapeze soloist, Sebastian Dickins, had novelty value as 'the most gorgeous man in Australian circus' (Stewart 1999: O84). A breathtaking aerial dive merged into a water theme that included fisherwomen, fountain statues and mermaids.

Opening the 2001 Melbourne season were two Wurundjeri people representing the traditional landowners, and the show included juggling and contortion acts by Sosina Wogayehu, ex-Circus Ethiopia. In an acrobatic bearing act, strongwoman Mellissa Fyfe balanced four people on her shoulders while wearing high-heeled boots, and she was determined to win the juggling competition with heavy lawn bowls against two males.[12] Meanwhile, aggro femme Toni Smith played a comic destructive provocateur attempting to sabotage acts by other performers. Ling was under attack from Smith, as he repeatedly tried to reach the toilet at the other end of his slack wire. The show featured Anni Davey and Oates doing a trapeze act first performed in *Razor Baby* (see Figure 5.2). Davey's return to Oz was a personal triumph because she had broken her neck ten years

Figure 5.2 Circus Oz 2001, Anni Davey and Kareena Oates, ©Ponch Hawkes, 2004.

earlier in a serious fall owing to equipment failure while working with Oz at the Edinburgh Festival. Davey's larger-than-life drag persona, Adriana, in an over-sized costume and elevated shoes, also appeared on a television screen yelling arrogantly at her live body, while strongman Daryll John meekly appeared cross-dressed in a wedding frock. Images of powerful physicality and sexiness underscored a general impression of female dominance. In 2002 Ling wore a black tutu and leather jock strap, and Helen Thomson writes, 'Gender is a won-derfully fluid concept in Circus Oz, and the strength of its female bodies is positively inspiring' (2002: 18).

Violence may no longer be a straightforward topic for circus comedy in soci-eties confronted with the complicated mesh of international political alliances. The 2003 show marked a return of the company's milder sentiments, and the aggro femme was absent. Davey's Adriana became the ring mistress, and orga-nized audience participation with gentle persuasion in scenarios about the plight of asylum-seekers. The show included two extremely funny send-ups of aerial acts. A cannon act had all the inherent risks of projectile propulsion for the performer Matt Wilson, and aerial clowns in an inept flying act were dressed as white cockatoos – an Australian bird with yellow crest feathers. Making the bird's distinctive screeching sounds, they delivered a scenario in which a baby bird was desperately trying to stay on the perch in a series of slap-stick falls that ended with the rig collapsing. (Australian fauna has long been circus exotica, and in aerial work the cockatoo motif was used by Digger Pugh for his 10-to-20-strong female aerial ballets in Billy Smart's and European cir-cuses in the early 1950s; among the ballet's few Australian professionals was Aboriginal circus performer Dawn de Ramirez, who became its team leader in the early 1960s.)

Oz's comic aggro femme pursued dominance over awkward males with bravado. She was clearly dressed as female, and displayed distinctly anti-male sentiments in her comic antics. Acts with cross-dressed males and female bad behaviour parody gender roles, and yet why does the aggro femme's comic action in particular become unsettling?

Violence enacted in relation to sport has become delineated as ritualized and good or as destructive and bad (aggro), but both good and bad violence is over-whelmingly considered a masculine activity (Elias and Dunning 1993: 224). While sports need not even be competitive (MacClancy 1996: 8), the presence of aggression in most women's sports competition remains awkwardly integrated into sports science, which is a kinesiology of competition (Miller 2001: 21). Therefore the comic parody of competitive aggression by females is received uneasily when it is still largely considered masculine behaviour.

In Australia, the aggro femme identity arose within a wider group of works produced by new circuses and physical theatres that spread and evolved as per-formers moved between companies. For example, a version of an aggro femme identity was evident in Oates's earlier performances, and, together with her sexy hula hoop aerial act, originally toured with Rock 'n' Roll Circus's comic satire of freakery and horror films *The Dark* (1995) (Tait 2001). Similarly the infiltration of a queer identity into Oz came from precedents in early 1990s physical theatre. The aggro femme is generally more violent and comic in her actions than sexual. An absence of comedy in violent interactions can still create a cartoon-like effect (Tait 2003b); the sexualization of this violence becomes an additional feature in the queering of identity. A combination of violent and sexualized interaction points to a parody of sado-masochism instead of the gender dynamics of aggression.

The aggro femme is either imitative of artistic precedents, or a progressive development out of gender reversals, or both, but she is manifestly an international figure. In New York, Jennifer Miller founded Circus Amok in what she terms a circus theatre especially for public spaces, and attributes part of her inspiration to seeing Circus Oz.[13] Female leadership has been important to the development of new circus in the USA (Albrecht 1995). Amok presented an aggro femme clown with a split personality in the 1999 show. Two female performers wore one ingenious, reversible long dress as an apparatus to enact an acrobatic and spoken ground-based clowning routine. When one performer was standing, the other was hidden crouched under the dress. The performer on one side of the dress presenting a threatening identity and the performer on the other side, a loving one, made fun of stereotypes. Miller also appears in Amok as a bearded lady in a postmodern referencing that is parodic of sideshow queerness and freakery, and the 1998 show had male performers in women's underwear. Amok performances include juggling, fire-eating, unicycling and stilt-walking in pedagogical scenarios that comment on social issues ranging from the health system to junk food and mayoral politics. Audiences in public spaces respond very actively with calls and cheers to what Mark Sussman deems making a spectacle of difference (1998: 262).

A more abstract version of an aggro female aerialist is found in the all-female, award-winning group Lava under the direction of Sarah Johnson, who also worked with Circus Amok. Johnson acknowledges being influenced by Circus Oz when she visited Australia, and took up an offer of training. She is inspired by geology and plate tectonics and creates shows with themes about volcanoes and emotional relationships.[14] Lava presents females that wrestle and ram each other in live action set against video projections of volcanic eruptions. Performers work in acrobatic adagios and low trapeze duos, often wearing jeans and T-shirts. Lava's *Love* (1999) included film projections of beasts, reptiles, Hawaiian women and bodies rolling in a field behind the performers working live on trapeze. *Lava Love Cabaret* deployed feminine iconography that appeared camp (Valdez 2000: 51), and *High Tide* (2002) used Niagara Falls as a motif. Johnson considers her work more like creating dance, with a movement vocabulary in which performers hold the shape of a gesture rather than just execute an aerial trick. Lava presents acrobatic aerials, but there are at least four groups in the USA that classify themselves as performing aerial dancing. Additionally, New York-based choreographer Elizabeth Streb's acrobatic dance productions amplify the sound of bodies landing on the apparatus, and produce audio violence with their athletic action.

What makes this new circus and physical theatre stylistically innovative is that the violence of the interaction is manifest through the physical skills of female performers. The performance intention is central to its meaning since a physical action might be executed with either gentleness or aggression. Physical theatre and new circus are often developed from the performer's devised improvised movement and therefore are more dependent on artistic intention than is formulaic traditional circus.

What are the social implications of artistically presenting females imitating an idea of bad behaviour? They expose cultural beliefs that aggression only happens in masculine physical interactions and reveal the way gender identity is also constituted through the body's action. Regardless of the level of violence, females in body-to-body clashes seem overly more aggressive than male counterparts doing similar actions. Female physical badness heightens an impression of violence. When a female displays brute force towards others, this can imply a parody of masculine aggressiveness or feminine gentleness but both upset conventional ideas of identity. In addition, the actions of the aggro femme imply that violence underlies and maintains identity separation (Tait 2003b). Identity becomes destabilized by the interaction between bodies, and in particular females performing violent acts towards males and other females.

Women fighting with others suggest muscular development. Yet displays of female body strength and muscular power do not manifest as threatening in themselves. An aggressive female in comic action need not have a muscular shape, but for clash and conflict to become menacing, the female body must seem at least credibly muscular. Where a female takes on the dominant social position as a victor, her actions can seem serious even as a clown. Aggressive interactions combined with a display of muscular female strength and power seem particularly threatening.

Chimeric circus

Why did nineteenth-century ideas of the superior physicality of circus bodies become obscured by a twentieth-century idea of circus as symptomatic of abnormality, abjection and violence, to be subsequently parodied within new circus? As the nineteenth-century circus expanded, it separated from sideshow and carnival acts and their management to become identified with covered hippodromes and big tents.[15] The sideshow retained the open-air stages and closed booths of the fairground that pre-date eighteenth-century circus. The now largely defunct exhibiting of people in the sideshow accompanying circus provided before-and-after entertainments for audiences moving around the 'performers', in contrast to performers moving around the circus ring. Throughout the nineteenth and twentieth centuries individual aerial performers and group acts were employed at different times in circuses, theatres, fairs, world exhibitions, sideshows, carnivals and seaside venues. It was the performance space and the scale of the production that also established professional hierarchies for both the performers and audiences, and elevated circus above sideshow. The physical space, and its arrangements for viewing bodies, produced social separations.

The travelling circuses set up tents at the geographical periphery of small towns, as if they were a self-contained world on the social margins, an impression still deliberately fostered by some performers (Carmeli 1990). This social world as much as the actual performance became a source of fascination, generating publications and then films for popular consumption. Yoram Carmeli writes that circus literature became part of the performance as 'a vehicle for the reification of an illusionary real circus, a circus "outside" of social time and social relations' (1995–6: 214). The circus exemplified a cultural idea of mobility within geographical and social spaces. In an accompanying movement within imaginary spatial geographies, however, physical distinctions became obviated.

Traditional circus is the domain of bodies and physicalities that are out of the ordinary, and its hyperbole exploited ideas of extraordinariness. An exceptional athlete is potentially also freakish in surpassing physical norms, and contemporary bodybuilders might be termed 'freaks' because of overly developed musculature (Lindsay 1996: 356). Spatially, the circus ring presents animals, their trainers, and human body acts, and altogether for the opening and/or closing acts. Once the temporal spatial distinctions of acts and the visible specialized actions between performances are removed, body identity separations become elided, creating a chimeric circus body. Perhaps it is not surprising that an idea of freakish appearance and strangeness contained within the late nineteenth-century sideshow became absorbed into imagined representation as one amorphous circus that collapsed together very different acts and bodies. Furthermore, as twentieth-century ideals of superior physical prowess became the prerogative of competitive sports, abnormality was allocated to the circus. What probably developed in practice was not that actual circus became like sideshow, but the converse. Fred Bradna points out that in twentieth-century sideshow, the 'fat lady' had to be 'delightfully curvaceous', the strongman handsome, and the little person 'perfectly symmetrical' (1952: 236).

In some twentieth-century representations, however, weird and freakish identities that extend to unconventional sexualities and transgender identity coexist in a hybrid of circus and sideshow that also conflates performance and offstage life. The social distinctions of identity become bodily blurred. In the 1910s sideshow 'gaffed freaks' were fabricated yet popular, and the most marketable spectacles were the half-man-half-woman showing signs of disidentification in relation to social norms (Studlar 1996: 217–19 (Goffman)). A polymorphous circus recasts disciplined, superbly fit athletic bodies as physicalities and personalities that are sensationalized to appear misshapen in voyeuristic exchanges. This cultural idea of circus retains remnants of a nineteenth-century moral condemnation. The practice of circus, however, is ever performative as it opportunistically reinvents itself, echoing back cultural ideas through recent new circus.

The advent of the (live) new circus coincided with a social movement of mostly young people in 1970s Europe, North America and Australia who co-opted the term 'freak' to indicate rebellious political choices and social protest. Around this time, sideshow exhibitions of what Rosemarie Garland Thomson terms 'enfreakment' were being closed as public entertainments because they were socially unacceptable (1996b: 10).[16] By the mid-1970s there was only circus in some western countries. Hereafter, the new circus used circus skills to stage cultural ideas of a chimeric circus body that is also parodic of notions of freakery.

A short story set in a circus that is made into a film suggests how institutional live circus becomes overlaid with twentieth-century artistic representations of an idea of circus. The pattern of making a film from an earlier fictional representation is common, as indicated by the examples in Chapter 4. Ex-sideshow performer Tod Browning's prototypical film, *Freaks* (1932) is about a 'midget', Hans (Harry Earles), who falls in love with a full-sized aerialist, Cleopatra (Olga Baclanova), a femme fatale who intends to murder him for money. This is loosely based on the short story 'Spurs' by Tod Robbins (Adams 2001: 62). The moral of the film neatly inverts the superficial idea of a freak to make the outwardly beautiful Cleopatra's murderous behaviour monstrous, and therefore freakish. The film was initially banned and only became available in the 1960s. As a strong muscular woman, within gender norms, the aerialist Cleopatra is indicative of Mary Russo's female grotesque, and she is eventually punished and changed into chicken-woman (1994: 92). Russo explores subsequent cinematic depictions that generated more subtle and varied successors. This femme fatale, who is freakish because of her predatory acts of aggression, provides an artistic source for the aggro femme's parodic identity.

In early cinema the antithesis of an action hero was the suffering freak. Gaylyn Studlar describes how cinema utilized freak exhibition because it aroused curiosity, sexual interest and repulsion (1996: 222 (Gunning)). Browning had previously made successful films about sideshows starring the popular Lon Chaney, well known for acting Quasimodo in *The Hunchback of Notre Dame* (1923) and Erik in *The Phantom of the Opera* (1925). Studlar writes that 'Chaney's roles offered a revelation of the "exposed obscenity of the self" – as Other – as masculinity allowed to be failed and freakish' (1996: 210 (Fiedler)). Chaney's films depict physical monstrosity combined with emotional suffering.

Thomson explains that freaks were freaks of culture, who materially embodied deviance so that neutralized citizen bodies gained control over imagined fears through exclusionary strategies towards visible otherness including physical difference, gender ambiguity and racial difference (1996b: 10). Social surveillance accompanied spatial demarcation that allowed bodies displaying difference to be safely contained. At the same time, however, these encounters dissolve psychic boundaries around the norms of embodiment. Rachel Adams writes that freaks' performative identity is variable because they 'are creatures who lurk in the unsteady seams where corporeal matter meets fantasy, drama and promotional hype' (2001: 4, 6). Some new circus satirized culturally produced freakery, and fears of it, by physically transgressing orthodox ideas of bodily difference and spatial separation.

The chimeric circus in twentieth-century representation offers an imaginary space in which to locate socially deemed misfits and outcasts and violent behaviour. Successive European films after *Variety* depict circus as a bleak, tortured world of struggle and criminality. This idea of circus owes as much to a literary and cinematic tradition as it does to the working-class origins of performers. Traditional live circus may have been a difficult life, and the training brutal at times, but performers chose circus willingly because of economic opportunities and comparative social freedoms. Inspired by *Variety*, Ingmar Bergman uses circus life in *The Naked Night* (1953) as a backdrop for life as a sweaty, animalistic hell that can only be escaped through suicide (Cowie 1992: 115–20). The 1950s American films depict a converse heroic collective struggle against natural and human-made disasters. Yet even in these brightly cheerful circuses, death is melodramatically proclaimed as ever-present. Circus provides a cultural backdrop for narratives of life-and-death struggle.

Since live circus promotes its performances as defying death, it becomes a literal performance of liveness (Auslander 1999), one that is not only executed live but highlights this quality with its extremes of physical action. A realm of violence and death prevails in cinema's circus, whose inhabitants range from marginalized outcast to freak; the circus of the cultural imaginary is inhabited by a chimeric body. While live circus presents athletic bodies performing fast action which dispels stillness or deadness, some new circus shows, such as Cottle's *Circus of Horrors*, have become adept at an ironic and parodic presentation of symbols of deadness using fast acrobatic and aerial action.

The cultural fascination with circus reveals a social orientation to watching bodies doing physical action. It presupposes these processes outside circus. Hence new circus parodying a chimeric circus confronts an underlying cultural fear that the muscular body's live action might falter and stop in lived experience.

Chapter 6

Ecstasy and visceral flesh in motion

I watch aerialists with attention that jumps and flickers, but which shatters and splinters in the attempt to describe them. How to describe the physical action of aerialists – their reception by spectators? The question is not new or easily answered. For example, a response to Madame Sanyeah's act decides 'Sight is the only sense by which it can be realized, description not being within the bounds of language.'[1] The approach used in Chapters 1 to 5 is to undertake acts of translation between spectators' and performers' descriptions and images. In this process, the embodied reception of aerial performance is ever-present and, at times, even explicit.

This chapter offers a brief introductory outline of some theoretical ideas about spectators' sensory perceptions of muscular bodies. It proposes that aerial bodies are received bodily, and viscerally. A spectator will 'catch' the aerial body with his or her senses in mimicry of flying, within a mesh of reversible-body-to-body (or -bodies) phenomenology. In this visceral catching, motion and emotion converge. The premise is that ideas of the physicality, viscerality and tactility of bodies should not be misplaced as often happens when philosophers and theorists consider corporeality and the embodied subject-self in relation to the politics of social change. This aerial history has been exploring aspects of cultural identity delivered by a live performance genre in which bodies communicate visually and physically. The seeing of aerialists often seems to induce visceral reactions like those produced with tactile stimuli. Clearly performance reception involves sensory perception but this may not be fully explicable. At issue is the extent to which a spectator viscerally perceives the physicality of another body (or other bodies) in a process of oscillating identification and disidentification with its cultural identity.

Helen Stoddart claims that live circus defies 'literary embodiment' (2000: 6). It is not only the immediacy of physical presence that is lost with other forms of representation, but the way bodies in movement demand reciprocating bodily awareness from spectators during live performance. But because literature and film infuse aerial action with a wider range of emotions, there are compensatory visceral intercurrents for spectators.

Delight or anxiety?

The actions of aerialists can make spectators react with gasps, starts and averted looks. These are tangible, sensory reactions. Aerial action is a physical phenomenon for and of bodies and, like other circus performance, fosters bodily tension and release. If the immediacy of such reactions suggests that they are involuntary, the 'concreteness' of having fun coexists with the 'unruly perversities' of the body (Ferguson 1990: 68).

There is an assumption that aerial performance arouses less tangible responses of excitement, delight and even wonder. Descriptions of audience reactions to most performance are conjectural, and reviewers often describe spectators as all having the same reaction. In a further nineteenth-century example, 'The three sisters Martini are very clever on the flying trapeze, and their flying leap is witnessed with almost breathless attention.'[2] As outlined in Chapter 1, nineteenth-century descriptions accord strongly visceral reactions to seeing performance and to watching female performers. The most common expression of embodied reception would seem to be the holding of breath. It typifies tension in a spectator's body, but as a common phrase it might be summarizing a range of bodily reactions.

The sequencing of acts within circus and tricks within acts is structured to manipulate audience responses. A few knowledgeable circus writers helpfully describe their individual reactions, which are subjective and conveyed after the event as memories of visceral responses. Antony Hippisley Coxe describes watching the prolonged preparation for a cannon act culminating in a performer in a white coat sliding into a cannon barrel. He compares it to his remembered bodily sensations before returning to school, and living during the Second World War. Coxe explains, 'All this built up an almost unbearable feeling of tension. I experienced the same empty drag at the bottom of my stomach, the same constriction of the throat' (1980: 107).

These are bodily reactions of anxiety or dread from a very experienced circus-goer that connect the reception of circus to escalating experiences of social violence. Coxe acknowledges sudden constrictions localized in his stomach and throat in response to seeing a body in potential peril. In this example, a performing body is received with bodily sensations linked to prior experiences combining physiological and psychological activity.

Why would Coxe or any spectator willingly attend circus knowing the likelihood of experiencing such anxiety? Perhaps the immediacy of visceral reactions appeals irrespective of adverse ones. Coxe recalls disturbances experienced in conjunction with his own physical survival, so that visceral sensations become bodily reminders of the continuity of his aliveness. Here the spectator does not try to avoid anxiety by turning away. This raises a further complication unanswered here: in what ways, if at all, might a spectator become bodily, viscerally, desensitized?

Consideration of the significance and fluidity of spectators' sensory perception is most developed in cinema studies (Williams 1995; Gledhill and Williams 2000). Within psychoanalytic theory, this dimension might accord with the imaginary (pre-Oedipal) as unable to be represented in language (Russo 1994: 37). A contrary position is suggested by Steven Shaviro's argument that viewing film is a 'concrete' surface visceral encounter without interiority or psychic structure (1993: 31, 43). Visceral understanding, however, has been interpreted as sensitivity within the entrails that is a force like a psychic drive (Hillman 1996: 94 (Nietzsche)). Moreover, cinema's extreme sensory responses are often induced by presenting abject bodies and bodily substances, particularly blood (unlike traditional circus). Like circus, film deliberately manipulates subjective visceralities as it enacts larger cultural patterns. Interestingly, while traditional circus denies bodily abjection, some new circus promotes it.

Circus specialists make a distinction between aerial acts that require an appreciation of their artistry and those that cause more anxiety than enjoyment. For example, Ruth Manning-Sanders comments about the De Riaz Trio at the 1948 BMC who follow the trend of motorized aerial apparatus designed to look like planes and rockets after the Second World War, 'the girl alternatively whirls round in an aeroplane and gets out of it to perform on a trapeze, whilst, at the other end of the revolving apparatus, the two men do breath-taking stunts' (1952: 249). She extrapolates that the absence of a net causes 'such a strain of anxiety in the audience that all sense of artistry is lost' (ibid.). In disagreement with her is Bernard Mills, who describes this as his favourite act because it seems without danger. After years of catering for audiences, he dismisses any suggestion that they are ghoulish, and explains that an 'unscared audience' likes to be thrilled but not 'frightened' (Bernard Mills: 1954: 37). Clearly audience members react differently and gendered experience might partially explain these contrasting reactions, as would cultural identification or disidentification with a performer. Whether thrilled or frightened, a spectator is reacting bodily and viscerally to the visual stimuli. But this viscerality can be socially and psychically conditioned, and in the unruly turmoil of the carnivalesque (and circus), visceral body laughter triumphs over fear (Bakhtin 1968: 90). Bodily reactions might become differently qualified in subjective reflection and varied social experience.

Thus, while it is possible to claim a spectrum of jolts, gasps, contractions, and sighs in the perception of circus bodies, the extent of their arousal and interpretative significance for an individual spectator remains open-ended. The larger point is that the immediacy of visceral experience contributes to the reception of aerial performance, and therefore also invariably accompanies the perception of a body's cultural identity.

Cinema's aerial action

The actions of circus bodies in live performance and in cinema create images of motion. Unsurprisingly, early cinema (1895–1917) utilized acrobatic action as a corollary to the invention of motion picture technology, and Étienne-Jules Marey (1995/1891) investigated the progression of locomotion in evolution by photographing semi-dressed bodies leaping and jumping in order to document stages of motion. Athletes, acrobats, contortionists and dancers were used in Edison's mid-1890s films because they 'displayed intense physical motion' (Backer 2000: 95). Acrobatic acts and films were programmed together until the First World War; acrobat Pansy Chinery, formerly Alar the Human Arrow, worked in theatre shows that included short films.

In disagreeing with the assertion that a train's locomotion was metaphoric of the silent motion picture, Alison McMahan (2000) argues that aerodynamics are more apt. Perhaps both locomotion and aerodynamics provide useful concepts to explain how a technologically induced live experience of moving in and through space is brought to imagery of motion, and vice versa. Acknowledging Gorky's description of a train of shadows, Tom Gunning describes how the 'force of the cinematic apparatus' potentially induces excitement, thrills and terror through an 'illusion of motion' (1989: 34–5). Regardless of arguments about anxiety or delight, spectators bring sensory memories to seeing images in immediate sensory encounters. Prior kinaesthetic experience also makes an image of motion meaningful. It is clearly an individual's social experience of motion when, for example, a woman travelling alone might consider train travel unsafe for reasons to do with her gender, and a spectator's economic position might determine the extent of his or her familiarity with train or air travel motion. Each spectator brings his or her accumulated personal and social histories of body movement and motion to live and cinematic action, and these become absorbed into further live experiences of motion.

In considering early cinema as a disruptive 'technology of modernity', Mary Ann Doane points out that narratives of pain at least resist the rationalization of vision and its separation from body phenomena in the circumscribed avoidance of the spectator's body and its sensations (2002: 530, 534–5). In the structuring of film imagery for a gendered spectatorship, the dominant white (masculine) body's trauma is displaced onto either a superhuman body or a female spectacle (ibid.: 543). This expands on what Shaviro argues are the limits of theories about gendered identification that produce a phantasmic body rather than visceral affective 'lines of flight' (1993: 22 (Deleuze and Guattari)). Embodied visceral reactions need not be theoretically disconnected from other ways of understanding culturally constructed subjective responses (Williams 1995). A spectator's viscerality and bodily thrill cannot be detached from his or her cognitive, emotional and unconscious responses to culturally shaped artistic representation that is intended to stimulate them.

In drawing on Foucault's ideas of 'knowledge-pleasure' to consider pornography in early cinema, Linda Williams elaborates on Jean-Louis Comolli's 'machines of the visible', whereby optical apparatuses mediated the seeing of events and bodies contributing to the 'frenzy of the visible' (1999: 35–6). A short film, *The Trapeze Disrobing Act* (1903), provides an early example of a female body in eroticized aerial action replayed in cinematic motion imagery (Allen 1991: 267–70; Staiger 1995: 58–9). Cinema develops from 'the desire to place the clocked and measured bodies produced by the first machines into narratives that naturalize their movements' (Williams 1999: 36). The spectator will often respond to this culturally induced construction of natural movement from the 'gut' (ibid.: 5 (Kuhn)) because of a 'visceral appeal', but what appears to be an automatic response is mediated by images (ibid.). In responses to cinema across genres, Williams writes that 'viewers reincorporate a gaze that begins as an outward projection *from* their physical bodies and which returns *to* the body' (ibid.: 292, italics in original). Drawing on the psychoanalytical ideas of Carol Glover, and Jonathan Crary's 'carnal density', Williams finds that it is important to 'reconnect the organs of the eyes to the flesh' (ibid.). Visual pleasure arises from a criss-crossing of visceral and sensory patterns within eroticized perception.

A cinema spectator's bodily reactions from tensing to screaming, laughing to crying, happen in relation to constructed languages that initially spanned 'exhibitionism', 'surprise' and 'spectacle' like circus, and subsequently included 'voyeurism', 'suspense' and 'story' (Bean and Negra 2002b: 6). With the advent of films such as *Variety*, *Trapeze* and *The Greatest Show on Earth*, kinetic aerial action is framed within potent, offstage emotional interactions between characters that heighten tensions about risks and missed opportunities in story, suspense and voyeurism. The performing aerial body is transformed into a performer character with interiority embedded in a plot. Aerial action is powerfully replayed along with emotional struggle. While in live circus a socially recognized performing body is impersonal, in cinema and theatre spectators are also responding to a fictional personality's emotional responses. In the twentieth century's dominant acting form of lifelike realism, emotional phenomena are socially embodied (second-hand), and gendered rather than culturally neutral and universally true (Tait 2002; Shields 2002). Emotional languages unfold as and through embodied cultural spaces. An extension of these concepts about the social meaning of embodied emotions is that they are concurrently also related to sensory and visceral responses. While cinema contributes to the social habituation of bodily sensation, horror and porn are considered 'bad taste' fantasy because they 'incise' flesh (Shaviro 1993: 100). These engagements have a lower status because they are widely recognized as tangible visceral sensations, and in the cultural hierarchy of emotionally induced bodily responses, less tangible effects are more esteemed.

Like circus, bodies in action stunts for sensory effect are ubiquitous in cinema's imagery of motion, and more recently in game-based technologies, which often have unique motion aesthetics that can induce dizziness. Their reception presumes somatic knowledge as it generates it, and with progressive exaggeration. For example, the kinaesthetic understanding of driving a car using reflexive responses and spatial estimations in and out of conscious control is brought by most late twentieth-century spectators to watching images of car motion. Its social implications are found in, for example, a parent character driving or a male character driving rather than a female; its emotional effect might be derived from the moral significance of a car chase between good and bad characters. The social identity of bodies in action gives sensory motion imagery its meanings. Aaron Anderson refers to 'muscular sympathy or empathy' and 'memory' where movement evokes sensory responses including emotions (1998: 10). Scenarios of motion are culturally produced bodily experiences for targeted audiences, although enjoyment can vary across identity groupings. As outlined in earlier chapters, a body's kinetic action can also contribute to cultural identity. Towards the end of the twentieth century, there was a technological shift away from replicating the tempo of lived experience as naturalized action, while reinforcing male identity in relation to heightened action. As Richard Dyer explains about spectators in 1990s cinema, they prefer heightened sensations of speed action, and invariably as 'a masculine structure of feeling . . . in the body's contact with the world' (2000: 18). Motion imagery is viewed in combination with physiological and psychological remembering and with fantasizing. Sensory responses to motion might be difficult to quantify, measure and explain, but cannot be ignored.

The female aerialist in action has come to personify an attunement to love's longing. This is superbly illustrated by Wim Wenders's film *Wings of Desire* (1987), co-written with Peter Handke, in which a male angel, Damiel (Bruno Ganz), in an overcoat, loves a female aerialist who wears white (chicken) wings, and he chooses the metaphoric fall from grace into embodiment (Stoddart 2000: 181–7). Cesare Casarino writes that *Wings of Desire* represents a dying modernist circus with postmodern apocalyptic angels listening to fragmented thoughts about everyday experience, and, together with historical and geographical legacies, spectators are accorded their 'transcendental and omniscient vision' (1990: 179). The film articulates emotional longing through the male angel's desire for union with the female aerialist although this denies a same-sex bond between male angels (ibid.: 180).

Wenders repeatedly uses a male driver in his other films to show characters' movement as they unsuccessfully seek 'a consummation of the spatial and emotional dynamics' in his cinema's visualization of the 'interaction of motion and emotion' (Kolker and Beicken 1993: 59, 67). Emotions as sensations become inseparable from images of motion. In progression, *Wings of Desire* offers redemption only through 'a descent into physicality' (ibid.: 140). The film's poetic and spiritual images belong to western humanism but as an 'inverse resurrection' (ibid.: 152). The character Marion (Solveig Dommartin), the French aerialist, is an object of romantic passion, a cliché of male voyeurism (ibid.: 156). Perversely, then, the aerialist is a safe woman (Russo 1994: 29 (Modleski)). But the female aerialist has a more intriguing significance since the angel spectator first sees her on trapeze. The aerial action becomes inseparably also one of emotion in motion; it functions as an 'action-image' (Deleuze 1986) for the lover's observing sensory body. The aerial body's subsequent spinning on a web suggests an increasing momentum in the motion of the lover's emotional experience. The angel lover longs for a visceral tactile (human) body to consummate the promise of aerial transcendence.

Depiction by aerial action of emotional and spiritual transcendence remains the province of socially defined bodies. In Patricia Rozema's film *When Night is Falling* (1995), twin female aerialists (Karyne and Sarah Steben) perform on trapeze interjected with imagery of two women characters making love and the doubling of the female aerialist functions as a motif for a lesbian union. A circus performer, Petra (Rachael Crawford), seduces Camille (Pascale Bussières) away from an impending marriage and her lecturing work in a religious college. Camille's crisis of faith arising from her defence of homosexuality is set against an implied sexual freedom from life in new circus. In turn, its arduous lifestyle makes a female manager lose faith with circus and depart. Imagery of aerialists and gliders metaphorically represent the bodily sensations of the two female lovers, and when Camille falls to the ground in the snow in the emotional crisis of their separation, she develops hypothermia or physiological stasis. A body's heightened sensory experience is like the motion imagery of aerial action. In these films, love's action is accorded aerial imagery to suggest bodily sensations, and to enhance its visceral impact for spectators.

Catching body phenomenologies

The performance history of aerialists over 140 years is one of imitating the physical actions of other aerialists, and repeatedly pushing beyond the established limits of aerial athleticism. This unfolds as a history in which bodies performing action contribute to changing perceptions of physicality. Physical and social spaces converge as bodies become reshaped along with subjective perceptions of them. As Jane Desmond points out about the study of dance, movement can illuminate thinking about embodiment, identity and self by melding 'materiality and representation' to interpret 'kinesthetic subjectivity' (1997b: 2). A performer's moved action is encountered kinaesthetically, as well as subjectively by a spectator.

An aerialist imitates his or her previous (rehearsed) action as well as that of other seen bodies. Action is re-membered as it is performed and a performer's activation of somatic memory implicates this potential in a spectator. Spectators might be attracted to athletic movement that is physically familiar, whether it is sport or dance or aerial movement. Conversely, they might be bodily drawn to watch unfamiliar extremes. Comments by performers and spectators imply that a body in action can create sensory spaces that momentarily enter 'opaque zones' (Merleau-Ponty 1995: 148). These presume moments of wordless sensory exchange. Aerial performance produces bodies moving in and out of mindful reflective spaces.

A spectator's capacity to see aerial action might be finely tuned by his or her prior movement experience of moving and seeing other moving bodies. Merleau-Ponty gives the example of how a body learns to dance, exceeding the more basic movements of walking or running and necessarily accomplishing it physically rather than with an 'intellectual synthesis' (1996: 142). For much of the twentieth century, Eurocentric actor training focused on the physical retraining of an actor's body to facilitate changeable external movement (Hodge 2000), and arguably thereby inducing 'kinesthetic subjectivity' in the reception of meaning from texts. But the ways in which a spectator body sees theatre are contingent on ideological influences (Dolan 1988). The physiological and psychological perception of kinaesthetic motion is also a cultural transaction.

The specificity of lived experience disrupts generalizations about a process of phenomenological body-to-body (or -bodies) encounters. Merleau-Ponty presumes that 'the gestures of the masculine body' (1996: 156) are socially and sexually normative in unravelling his ideas of an originating bodily experience in lived worlds, and these are thoroughly criticized for their universalizing singularity (Grosz 1994: 106). The movement and action of a lived body is socially structured as it is experienced within variable subjective habituation that encompasses representation. Reinterpretations of Laura Mulvey's well-established theory of the gaze in cinema, and ideas of subject–object relations, confirm multiple fluid positions of cultural identification in relation to narrativized imagery and fetishistic visual spectacles (Neale 1983: 5 (Ellis); Williams 1995). Gilles Deleuze writes that while Merleau-Ponty made phenomenology and cinema confrontational (1986: 57), he perceived 'the spirit of the cinema' through finding a 'sensory-motor link' to behaviour (ibid.: 155). Deleuze draws on Merleau-Ponty to explain two aspects of his argument that a different order of subjectivity was arising around the time of early cinema, one in which the spaces of consciousness and movement in a 'dynamic sublime' pass into each other (ibid.: 53). Deleuze finds that matter is '*movement-image*', and 'image is movement' that expands into 'action-images, affection-images, perception-images' through cinema (ibid.: 59–60, italics in original). 'The action-image inspires a cinema of behaviour (behaviourism), since behaviour is an action which passes from one situation to another' (ibid.: 155). Deleuze expands on his idea of 'affect-image' as close-ups of the face (ibid.: 109), and points out that the film actor as a character is not stationary but active on a small scale (ibid.: 155).

Vivian Sobchack draws on Merleau-Ponty's idea of 'experience by experience' to explain fluid embodied subjective and intrasubjective consciousness within the sensuous and sensible perception of cinema (1992: 3). With regard to social behaviour, Nick Crossley (1994) re-evaluates Merleau-Ponty in relation to Foucault and delineates political phenomenology. More specifically, Stanton Garner writes on phenomenological intersubjectivity in theatre as a 'phenomenal space, governed by the body' (1994: 3), and Amelia Jones describes the open motion of a fleshed body-self in reception in the visual arts (1998: 11 (Merleau-Ponty and Butler)). Accordingly, Merleau-Ponty's ideas are applicable to the reception of circus performance, even when it is not representing a spectrum of emotional subjectivity through close-ups of faces and other modes. Instead, live circus offers 'action-images' of bodies through sensory visceral encounters within an unfolding orientation to kinaesthetic motion, with additional emotional effects from music.

In his statement that the body catches movement (Merleau-Ponty 1996: 143), Merleau-Ponty outlines physical processes for acquiring movement that consist of imitation, reflexive responses, and spatial estimations which appear to be happening simultaneously in a body but not dominating its mental faculties. Catching provides a relevant concept to this discussion as a spectator sees a flyer caught or a soloist catches the trapeze bar as he or she drops. Merleau-Ponty's idea of catching is not a literal touching but perceptual attunement and engagement of a whole body that is orientated to others through its pre-existing history of movement, its motility, and this catching is underpinned by sensory perception, by sight in particular. This suggests a consciousness capable of dispersal within, and outwards from, the body in motion. Irigaray's understanding of touch to include sight is a useful corollary for how the senses are not isolated processes but flow together (Grosz 1994: 104).

Cultural anthropology that finds the senses are the 'shapers' and 'bearers' of culture questions the dominance of sight – brain imaging claims sight predominates. A clash of cultures might arise from a different ordering, with, for example, the dominance of taste over sight (Howes 1991: 17). As dancer, Cynthia Jean Cohen Bull writes, 'I experience kinesthetic, visual, tactile, and auditory sensations and my *sensible* dance experience includes and implies *intelligible* choreographic and social meanings' (1997: 269, italics in original). In linking sensory perception to bodies in movement, Bull distinguishes the primacy of seeing in ballet, touching in contemporary dance-making, and hearing in Ghanaian dance, as perception combines cognitive, emotional and kinaesthetic knowledge (ibid.: 282). Moving bodies reproduce cultural kinetic sensory patterning rather than pure motion.

Sensory catching might manifest as awareness of a bodily sensation, which can be generalized as holding the breath or be localized in the stomach or the throat. In this way, motion seen live might be absorbed into interior awareness, and continue to be dynamic even when it is not externally reproduced. The retention of movement in the imagination implicates circulating interconnections in kinaesthetic knowledge, dependent on other moving bodies and experience that need to be seen (or felt) in the first instance.

A lived body in action moves in body schemata that are also culturally habituated by gender, ethnic and sexual identity and these impact on how it viscerally responds to other bodies. What is uncertain is where and how this embodied perception of a lived body's action becomes limited by the social setting of inner and outer action and orientations. Using an example from aerial performance history, multiple somersaults were most feasible as backward movement, but there was a cultural identity blockage by the mid-twentieth century, in that male bodies were expected to attempt this backward action.

Historically, a female aerialist who imitated male action, and thereby also developed a muscular body, upset the accustomed cultural seeing of bodies. A resulting visceral disturbance of seen identity might be considered a disruption of an ideological process (Tait 2000). In the nineteenth century seeing femininity made the aerial action more visible. Conversely, by the mid-twentieth century a feminized body that was not expected to do difficult tricks made its athleticism harder to see.

Merleau-Ponty's ideas raise a relatively unexplored precept that if the perceptual world is constantly interpreted through a body-in-the-world, then counteracting its subjective kinaesthetic positioning might require body-to-body (or -bodies) visceral interventions. To effect a change in patterns of social relationships between bodies might require unfolding bodily disruptions of kinetic cultural orientations. Challenges to embodied dominance might need sensory and visceral as well as ideological reconfiguration. A visceral encounter with an ambiguous body identity bends pre-existing patterns of body-to-body (or -bodies) phenomenological exchanges and is at least potentially disruptive of hierarchical patterning. Thus, a lived body might momentarily catch a surprising cultural identity.

Pleasurable flesh, ecstatic motion

Coxe describes the beauty of watching an aerial body in action that shows moving muscles, the 'aesthetic pleasure' of the 'lithe grace' (1980: 150–1). His pleasure is derived from the muscular action and he states that a stationary body is boring (ibid.: 65). This may or may not be inclusive of Freud's idea of pleasure allied to sexual desire and release, but it almost certainly involves bodily tension, which may or may not implicate perversity. Coxe finds pleasure in action extremes. Modern circus was developing as notions of happiness and fun shifted more towards pleasure and excitement under early capitalism (Ferguson 1990: 137, 214). Fast bodies can be pleasurable to watch.

In Merleau-Ponty's ideas of fleshed worlds in which observing sensory bodies perceive the world through and as fleshed experience, primary visibility cannot happen without a secondary visibility of 'lines of force and dimensions, the massive flesh without a rarefied flesh, the momentary body without a glorified body' (1995: 148). In drawing on these ideas, an aerial body in action is seen through the bodily fleshing of 'a glorified body' and viscerally with 'the momentary body', but reversibly, so that the observing body becomes glorified momentarily in aerial motion. The visible is inhabited by the invisible, and experienced bodily and expressly, and potentially operates in a 'dialectic of love' (ibid.: 149).

From the nineteenth century the American three-ring circus presented a spectacle of numerous active bodies across a visual field. It required scopic responses that scanned multiple trajectories of fast action. As Janet Davis outlines, however, spectators became disorientated in an emotional response of 'passive bedazzlement' (quoted in 2002: 25), through perceptual and sensory stimulus overload. A spectator may need a selective perspective within a visual field, such as the camera provides for filmed spectacle or selective identity habituation provides within social experience. Otherwise sensory responses may shift away from enjoyment and pleasure.

The spectator's sensory attunement needs to be caught by a muscular performing body in what Merleau-Ponty terms the 'difficult point, that is, the bond between the flesh and the idea, between the visible and the interior armature' (1995: 149). The flesh has visibility, but elliptically to thought and to the 'aesthesiological' body (ibid.: 152). Motion is fleshed through a sensory identity-catching.

How is a performer's experience implicated in this pleasurable sensory catching? Writing about Ernie and Charles Clarke and from his own flying experience, Irving Pond claims that 'accomplishment of a rhythm in the three dimensions of space induce[s] a joy akin to ecstasy' (1937: 135). Lisa Hofsess writes of the somatic enjoyment of feeling the air around her with a density like water, and seeking the motionlessness or 'stillness' at the height of the trapeze's pendulum swing (1987–8: 45). This requires 'kinesthetic perception', timing that is compensated somatically rather than mentally, and time itself that seems to expand (ibid.: 45–6).[3] These examples reveal an aerialist's sensory enjoyment and raise the proposition that something akin to visceral delight might be performable.

The imperceptibility of an aerial performer's pains and muscle strains, however, confirm that bodily sensation is not easily communicated to others. A smile using the facial muscles can be understood, as can, conversely, a grimace. A performer's enjoyment might not need spectators, unless an ecstatic feeling comes also from the presence of spectators (or recognition of their presence). As indicated, aerial performers repeatedly describe how they mentally focus their thoughts on instructions and/or imagine the physical action as they perform. An aerialist is focused on bodily doing and specifying the action.

In analysing early twentieth-century dance, Susan Manning argues that a performer's claim to depict ecstasy largely depends on how it is recognized within the wider culture – in her examples, through association with the iconography of religious ecstasy (1993: 62–8). Ecstasy is embodied in social languages and spectators might expect to find aerial action beautiful because it is widely known to represent a sublime (feminine) aesthetic within culture. But accounts of responses to the visible performance of heightened dynamism confirm a visceral effect to aerial aesthetics. They manifest social ideas of motion as do other types of extreme fast athletic action in arousing bodily sensations. Is an awareness that the performance is sublime action therefore induced by bodily viscera? Viewing pleasures or anxieties arise from the fleshed motion of flying action that evokes a body momentarily freed of everyday limitations, its muscular solidity carried away by invisible 'lines of force'. This suggests kinetic pleasure from a fleshed perceptual awareness that defies the weight of a lived body and the density of its habitual identity patterning.

Bodies have culturally variable histories of muscular movement towards others (bodies) within unfolding patterns of visible and invisible fleshed motion. The immediacy and heightened effect of fleshed visceral reactions to performance functionally provides a reminder of the experiences of a lived body. Body-to-body (or -bodies) phenomenologies within live aerial action are metonymical of liveness that is culturally fleshed. Hence the pleasure of watching motion is in part always indicative of an awareness of the body's unfolding dynamic liveness.

Aerial motion and emotion produce sensory encounters; a spectator fleshes culturally identifiable motion, emotionally. The action of muscular power creates buoyant and light motion, which corresponds with reversible body phenomenologies in the exaltation and transcendence with and of sensory experience. The aerial body mimics the sensory motion of and within lived bodies in performances of delight, joy, exhilaration and elation. Aerial bodies in action seem ecstatic in their fleshed liveness.

Glossary

For photographs and guidance for beginners on safe practices see Burgess (1977). For videos see Van Loo Productions, *Secrets of the Circus Revealed*, 3 and 4 (2002).

Aerial apparatus

Aerial ring or **cerceau** is a large metal ring often suspended from a swivel, on which the aerialist performs spinning and flexible moves.

Ascent or **descent rope** see Web.

Bungee is a cord of elasticized strands.

Catch trap or **bar** is a catcher's trapeze.

Cloud swing or ***corde volante*** is a rope suspended on swivels at both ends.

Cradle is a rectangular frame, swinging for a catcher or fixed for a weight-bearer, to hang his or her knees over with feet braced.

Double trapeze is either a wide bar or two trapezes or a duo.

Duo is used in *Circus Bodies* for two performers in an act.

Fly bar is the flyer's solid trapeze bar hung from steel cables.

Iron jaw (teeth or dental) is a leather mouthpiece gripped by the teeth with a hook or an extension at the other end.

Lunge or **longe** is one safety line or more attached to a flyer's belt, which passes through a pulley system down to a person on the ground, who can arrest a fall.

Lyre is harp-shaped and similar to an aerial ring.

Mechanic see Lunge.

Net is rigged underneath flying troupes.

Pedestal is a small mid-air platform on which the flyers stand to launch themselves. A **raise** is an additional bar, which gives extra height.

Rig is the framework or truss from which a system of cables or ropes and apparatuses or rigging is suspended.

Rings or **Roman rings** are two rings hanging from vertical ropes, originally used in gymnastics.

Rope or ***corde lisse*** is a vertically hanging rope or descent rope. Tight-rope/ -wire and slack-rope/-wire have both ends strung between fixed supports.

Russian swing is a ground-based swinging platform that propels a performer standing on one end high into the air through the pushing of another performer or performers at the other end.

Safety line runs from the aerialist to the apparatus (see Lunge), and was first widely used in eastern Europe from the 1960s.

Static or **fixed trapeze bar** is hollow, allowing moves where the bar flips up.

Strap or **leather strap** (usually two) is a hanging vertical apparatus predominantly used by male performers, wrapped around their arms.

Swinging trapeze bar is solid with heavy weights and cabled ropes.

Tissu or **silk** is a long vertical length of fabric, doubled, in which the aerialist wraps and drops.

Trapeze is a horizontal steel (formerly wood) bar, with two vertical ropes at each end padded at the joints (elbows), and suspended from a low or high height. It is used as static apparatus for solo poses, also for balancing and swinging or flying.

Trapeze Washington or **balance trapeze** has movable joints allowing the aerialist to balance and add props, e.g. a chair or a metal plate for headstands.

Web or **Spanish web** is a vertical hanging rope (often cotton fibre) on a swivel with a loop for hand (wrist) or foot suspension at the top. An aerialist hangs spinning and another performer on the ground spins the base of the web.

Movements

Angel is an ankle and wrist hold with torso horizontal.

Balling up or **tucking up** is curling up the body.

Bearer holds another's weight.

Bird's-nest position is a back arch under the trapeze with feet flexed on top of the hands and chest forwards.

Casting is catchers (casters) passing a flyer between them either standing braced on a platform or a fixed or swinging cradle or swinging on a catch trap.

Cross-over or **pass** is a flyer leaving the platform on the fly bar, releasing it, and passing to the catcher – it can mean the flying return action.

Cut-away is a flyer changing or varying the grip with a catcher, usually swapping between feet and hand holds.

Double-double is a flyer executing a double somersault with a double twist.

Double pass is a cross-over or pass done by two flyers simultaneously.

Fliflus is a flyer's half twisting lay-out followed by a backward tuck to a catcher (or second bar).

Flip-flap or **flic-flac** is a backflip, usually a backward handspring.

Flying return act (see Cross-over) is a flyer letting go of the swinging fly bar and passing with tricks to be caught by a swinging catcher. Swinging together, the catcher releases the flyer, who passes back with tricks to catch the fly bar and return to the starting platform. The catcher swings in an upside-down position slightly below the arc of the fly bar. Accomplished flyers add somersaults, twists and pirouettes.

Hand-to-hand or **hand-to-feet** are the grips used by flyers and catchers.

Hand-to-hand climb is climbing a rope without using the legs.

Hocks is hanging with the knees over the trapeze.

Lay-out is the flyer's body fully extended in a 360-degree rotation.

Pass see Cross-over.

Pike is the legs raised horizontally.

Pirouettes are a full rotation of the extended vertical straight body on a vertical axis.

Planche pass involves the flyer bringing the feet straight under the bar, extending the legs vertically, holding the hips close to the bar, then releasing at the front of the swing to the catcher.

Plange on a web in a hand loop involves the whole body rotating around the shoulder joint ('dislocations').

Skin the cat is a hang with arms backwards on the trapeze bar.

Somersaults are executed by flyers mid-air, tucking up the knees to the chest; single, double, triple and quadruple. Somersaults can be followed by twists or pirouettes before and after catching. The easier backward somersault is executed in the direction of travel with knees tucked up and chest thrown back.

Straight pass see Cross-over.

Twister is a turn in two directions at the same time (Pond 1937: 135).

Twists (see Pirouette) involve the body rotating without tucking up but not completely straight.

Vault or **shootover** on trapeze is the arms holding body weight up to go over the bar.

Vaulting is leaping up (over an object).

Notes

Introduction: aerial bodies

1 The circus parade took place on 19 July 2003, in Peru, Indiana, USA, for the town's annual circus festival. The 2003 (USA) Circus Historical Society Conference was being held in conjunction with the festival. Betty Hutton's trapeze is in Peru's Circus Hall of Fame museum.

2 Circus historians claim a long history in Europe for separate circus skills performed at fairs by itinerant performers, and some may have Chinese origins. There are medieval drawings of performers jumping through hoops and hanging by the knees from poles, stilt-walkers and seventeenth-century rope-walkers (funambules) on a courtyard rig raised on crossed poles at either end (Croft-Cooke and Cotes 1976: 28–31). Writers in ancient Rome describe circus-like spectacles (Bouissac 1976a: 12).

1 Graceful manliness, unfeminine maidens and erotic gods

1 See Gossard (1994: 9–10; *The Illustrated London News*, 23 October 1852). Frenchman Julio Buislay may have pioneered leaping to ropes in North America and to a hand-held trapeze (ibid.: 80) – Alfredo Codona is a descendant through his mother, Hortense. Also see Frost (1881: 144).

2 Léotard was born on 3 August 1838 and died on 16 August 1870 from smallpox (Lartigue 1980: 24, 92). His Paris debut in 1859 was delayed due to typhoid (ibid.: 35).

3 See *Le Monde illustré*, 4–5 November 1859: 332, 231.

4 'Les Amoureuses de Léotard', *Figaro* (Paris), 21 June 1860: 3–5.

5 *The Era*, 17 December 1871: 15.

6 *The Era*, 25 December 1870: 15.

7 *The Era*, 17 December 1871: 15.

8 *The Illustrated London News*, 10 October 1868: 338.

9 *The Era*, 17 December 1871: 15; 15 July 1871: 16.

10 Advertisement for a diorama of the Sepoy Rebellion in India and the reappearance of Léotard, 22 September 1861 (Alhambra box, JJBL). The Sepoy war (1857–8) was the first sustained struggle against British forces.

11 *The New York Clipper*, 7 November 1868: 246.

12 'Clipper's Circus Record for 1874'. *Clipper*, 18 April 1874: 1. In comparison, a variety couple in the USA earned around $40 weekly, a carpenter $12 and an actor $5–7 (Gilbert 1968: 19).

13 'Sensational Gymnastics and Acrobatism', *Pencil*, 21 October 1876 (box 3, JJBL).

14 *The Era*, 4 February 1872: 14.

15 *Clipper*, 4 May 1867: 31.

16 'Woman as an Acrobat', *Clipper*, 30 January 1869: 338.

17 *Clipper*, 28 August 1869: 168, drawing; Older's Grand Museum and Circus, 30 August 1870 (newspaper advertisements folder 1866–72, CW). The 1869 drawing is published again in the 1871 Older's poster bill (Fox and Parkinson 1969: 72).

18 *The Era*, 25 June 1871: 12; 18 February 1872: 14. Advertisement, 23 March 1869 (newspaper advertisement folder 1866–72, CW).

19 *Clipper*, 3 December 1870: 275 (quoted reviews).

20 Ibid.

21 *Clipper*, 29 May 1869: 63; 8 October 1892: 491.

22 *Clipper*, 5 June 1869: 70. However, Zuleila is first described as a dancer (Odell 1936–8: volume VIII, 509). Munby describes a respectable-looking Zuleilah (Lizzie Foster) starting in 1868 inspired by Pereira, and leaping between trapezes, doing balance poses and being tossed about by a partner like a puppet from a wrist or ankle hold and climbing ropes in 'monkeyfashion' (1972: 254).

23 *Clipper*, 24 April 1869: 22.

24 *Clipper*, 10 April 1869: 6.

25 *Clipper*, 26 June 1869: 94; *Clipper*, 25 January 1873: 343.

26 Slout names Maude Sanyeah as Phoebe Frost, 1841?–25 June 1910 (1998a: 267). A name variation, Senyah, is described as the name Haynes reversed (Frost 1881: 180).

27 *Clipper*, 31 July 1869, 135; 28 August 1869: 167; 15 October 1870: 224.

28 *Clipper*, 1 October 1870, 207. Ada debuted at Tammany Hall and later went on to perform in the horse drama *Mazeppa* and the scandalous mime *The Female Bathers* (1875) (Odell 1936–8: volume IX, 568, 605).

29 *Clipper*, 17 December 1870: 291.

30 *The New York Daily Tribune*, 7 January 1869: 4.

31 *The Illustrated London News*, 21 March 1868: 274; 28 March 1868: 314.

32 *Clipper*, 4 January 1873: 319.

33 Advertisements for Blooms in North America: *Clipper*, 19 April 1879: 32, with a drawing of a woman holding a trapeze; 3 May 1879: 48, lists silk including flesh-coloured, lisle, cotton including superfine, and worsted hose and tights.

34 Andrew Ducrow had used Grecian-like poses in equestrian action at Astley's around 1830 (Frost 1881: 65).

35 *The Illustrated London News*, 11 April 1868: 359; 18 April 1868: 394.

36 *The Illustrated London News*, 25 April 1868: 402. Also see Frost (1881: 180).

37 *The London Entr'arte*, 19 March 1870: 2.

38 *Clipper*, 18 January 1873: 335.

39 Azella worked with Nestor and they were caught by Gonza in 1877. In 1878 Azella was performing at The Oxford, London (*The Daily Telegraph*, 1 January 1878: 1; 9 February 1878: 1), and again in 1879 with Gonza and Lunardi – group members changed (programme for the week ending 14 June 1879, Oxford box, JJBL). Azella had imitators: an Azzella appeared in Australia in a programme that included female gymnast Zulu (*The Argus* (Melbourne), 11 November 1876: 12). Azella had an accident in August 1879 at Hengler's Circus when Gonza failed to catch her, but she recovered (Turner 1995–2000: volume I, 8).

40 *Clipper*, 7 March 1874: 387; *The Argus* (Melbourne), 3 March 1877: 12.

41 *Clipper*, 24 April 1869: 22.

42 *Clipper*, 16 October 1869: 223.

43 *The New York Daily Tribune*, 15 April 1869: 5; *The New York Daily Tribune*, 12 April 1869: 4; photograph in Odell (1936–8: volume IX).

44 Coles Bros Courier 1877 (NYPL); Turner 1995–2000: volume I, 79; Slout 1998a: 169. Maggie was also the 'Winged Mercury of Flying Rings' with the P. T. Barnum Greatest Show on Earth and Great London Circus programme which included

Zazel (circa 1881, NYPL). Mercury was a mythic persona adopted by equestrians for a standing, balance pose.

45 Thomas (1833–68), George (1835–1926), William (1839–1923), Alfred (1842–86), Edward (1845–1931), adopted Frederick (1848–86), and adopted Bob Hanlon (died 1907) (McKinven 1998: x). See programmes 14 May 1861–June 1861, Alhambra box (JJBL).

46 *Clipper*, 21 December 1861: 286; 28 December 1861: 295. Women attended, and some spectators received complimentary tickets; 5 November 1881: 538.

47 *The New York Daily Tribune*, 8 November 1869: 8.

48 Ibid.

49 *Clipper*, 19 December 1885: 625, 627.

50 For example, see London's Aquarium programmes in the week ending 14 January 1888 (JJBL); 'Twenty Years in the Circus', *The Era*, 1 June 1895: 16; 'Bristol Amusements. A Chat with the Flying Dillons', *The Bristol Magpie*, 20 January 1898: 16; and Gossard about the Fishers and LaVans (1994: 134–9).

51 Aerial file (MM).

52 *The Music Hall and Theatre Review* XX (499), 9 September 1898: 171.

53 'People's Palace', *The Bristol Magpie*, 31 March 1898: 8.

54 *The Penny Illustrated Paper*, 16 March 1878: 166–7. Charles Reade's most popular novel was *It Is Never too Late to Mend*, and he wrote over 30 plays. Reade's 'The Coming Man' describes the evolution of society matched to a growing and aging human body, and is published as a letter to the editor in *The Daily Telegraph*, 21 February 1878: 3. 'The Coming Man' was a widely used nineteenth-century term that originated in religious ideas by the Richard Brothers in 1790 (*The Literary World* 4 (7), 1 December 1873: 97).

55 Silbon family file (CW).

56 'Circusiana', *Hobbies: The Magazine for Collectors*, July 1950: 24.

57 'Memories of Edythe Siegrist', *Sarasota Herald-Tribune*, 1948, aerialist's scrapbook (CW).

58 The 1926 RBBBC route book (NYPL).

59 *The Sydney Mail*, 26 April 1905: 1056.

60 For example, Alexandra Palace programme, 8 September 1877, 'Great Circus'. High Bars by 'Dezmon and Maraz, after which Maraz, the Aerial Diver will descend in a rapid eagle-like swoop from the roof to the Great Central Hall to the floor, one hundred feet below. Daring acrobats have been known to dive 30 or 40 feet, but such a feat as that of Maraz's has never been hitherto dreamed of as within man's power. Pluck, presence of mind, and science combine to command applause. The extreme peril of the feat to any but such an accomplished gymnast as Maraz, would inspire with terror rather than pleasure' (HFNF).

61 For example, see the Canterbury Theatre of Varieties programme, 26 July 1879 (HFNF). For an example of rope-climbing used in a theatre production see *Zip* (Odell 1936–8: volume X, 388).

62 'The Danseuse', *Chambers' Edinburgh Journal* (2) 13 January 1844: 32.

2 Unnatural acts, female strongmen

1 'The Coming Man', *The Literary World*, 4 (7), 1 December 1873: 97–8, quoted.

2 For example, *The Era*, 1 July 1893: 22, advertisement for Zulima, the female Sampson. Desbonnet (1911) lists a number of male and female partnerships as well as solo strongwomen.

3 *The Sketch*, 6 February 1895: 85.

4 *The Sydney Morning Herald*, 20 April 1885: 2.

5 Desbonnet states that Lala worked with Cirque Rancy in 1887, where he saw her in a pantomime and he was jealous of her biceps (1911: 351). For a Paris programme listing, see juggler Paul Cinquevalli and Madame's Scrapbook, from 1885–9, 1891–January 1901 (TM).

6 *Clipper*, 28 June 1890: 246; 13 September 1890: 431; 20 September 1890: 447. See Slout for a list of circuses (1998a: 151).

7 For Dare, see *The Daily Chronicle*, 14 January 1879: 1. For Jutau, see Oxford programme ending 10 January 1880 (Oxford Theatre Box, MM).

8 Lala performing at Cirque Fernando, Paris, *Le Figaro*, 11 December 1878: 6; 24 December 1878: 3, 'Miss Lala, La Vénus noire, L'affût vivant' is advertised performing until February, *Le Figaro*, 11 February 1879: 3.

9 'The Playgoer', *The Penny Illustrated Paper*, 15 March 1879: 163.

10 *The Morning Advertiser*, 13 March 1879: 2. *The Daily Chronicle*, 11 March 1879: 6. *The Morning Post*, 12 March 1879: 3. For poster, see Frueh *et al.* (2000: 59). See London's Aquarium programmes (JJBL): 10 March 1879, Centre Stage Grand Hall, 9.40, Lala 'in her famous Cannon Feat', 10.30, M. Blondin The Hero of Niagara Falls; 17 March 1879, billing includes Lala 'and the Kaira Troupe'; 26 April 1879, 2 February 1880, Lala back with Kaira Troupe; 26 February 1880 has claims to be the last appearance, although Kaira Troupe was still there on 6 March 1880.

11 Exhibition, 'Picturing the Modern Amazon', New Museum of Contemporary Art, New York, March–April 2000. This showed a Lala poster from the Bibliothèque nationale de France, Paris, and photos from the collection of Sandow's biographer, David Chapman. Contemporary bodybuilders trace precedents to historical examples of female muscularity (Frueh *et al.* 2000: 59–60, note 5).

12 Steve Gossard's private collection.

13 *The Morning Advertiser*, 13 March 1879: 2.

14 *The Daily Chronicle*, 11 March 1879: 6.

15 *The Morning Post*, 12 March 1879: 3.

16 P. T. Barnum Courier 1873. Circulation 1,000,000 (NYPL).

17 *The Era*, 16 March 1879: 4.

18 Ibid.

19 'Our Representative Man', *Punch*, 26 October 1878: 184–5.

20 J. E. Warner's Co., 25 July 1872 (newspaper advertisements 1866–72 folder, CW). J. E. Warner's Co., 28 August 1873 (newspaper advertisements 1873–5 folder, CW).

21 'The Crusade Against Dangerous Performances', *The Penny Illustrated Paper*, 13 March 1880: 163. 'Our Representative Man', *Punch*, 26 October 1878: 184.

22 For two other posters see Broido (1980).

23 There are contradictory newspaper reports that name two Hall brothers, George and Thomas, as Dare's husband. *Clipper*, 29 November 1884: 581; this account of her 1884 accident names George as her husband and says he toured as George Dare. *The Daily Telegraph*, 30 May 1879, 5; this account of the court case names Thomas. Also see court case in *The Era*, 16 March 1879: 4.

24 'Career of Leona Dare', *Spokane Spokesman Review*, 18 June 1922, no pagination (*Billboard*, 3 June 1922, 106) (CW). In this account, Dare married Thomas Hall on 1 July 1871, ceased performing at 40, and died in 1922. Henry Thétard's disdainful account of her life states that she married and divorced an Austrian banker, and later married an Austrian railway man (1947, volume II: 158). Steve Gossard suggests Signor Saltarino's 'Artisten-Lexikon' and Joseph Halperson's (1926) *Das Buch vom Zirkus* for scarce biographical information.

25 'An Acrobat's Nervousness', *The New York Times*, 23 November 1884: 7; *Clipper*, 29 November 1884: 592.

26 *Clipper*, 18 October 1890: 501.

27 *Clipper*, 29 April 1876: 39; Cooper Bailey and Co's International Circus with Jutau trapezist and George Brown trapezist and a rival iron jaw act by Madame Frances de Covona; *Clipper*, 11 March 1876: 399, Jutau and partner George Brown 'trapeze performers are to join Howe's Circus which starts from St Louis'. Also Howe's 1876 Route book. *Clipper*, 15 July 1876: 12, Howe's collapsed financially, but soon touring again it would appear as Howe Cushing and London's.

28 'Advertiser', *The Era Almanack* 1880, no pagination.

29 The 1883 *Barnum and London Courier* (newspaper advertisements 1875–9 folder, CW). Week commencing 30 April 1883, Jutau and Brown: 'High Trapeze and Mid-air Evolutions and her Sensational Slide Down a 300ft Wire Suspension by Her Teeth'.

30 Advertisements in *Clipper*, 1 May 1886: 111; 28 June 1890: 246; 13 September 1890: 431; 20 September 1890: 447. There is a death notice for Mary Tancoast, Jutau's twin sister, in 1889, in *Clipper*, 20 April 1889: 97. The Jutau Sisters working as Human Butterflies with Coop and Lent Circus 1916 may be related.

31 See Durant and Durant (1957: 170, poster); Speaight (1980: 76, drawing); and Verney (1978: 222, poster). The Guy Little Collection (TM) has seven studio photographs of Zazel.

32 See Munby (1972: 389) and London's Royal Aquarium Programmes (JJBL). Programme, 2 April 1877, lists Zazel's appearance with the cannon trick. Programmes for 1877 list the act as Farini's greatest invention, and on 15 October 1877 one specifies that she dives 97 feet 6 inches, before being fired 70 feet from a cannon, to 'The Zazel Waltz' by M. Chas Dubois. The programme announcements stop on 8 February 1879 until 1882.

33 *The Illustrated Sporting and Dramatic News*, 26 May 1877: 223.

34 Ringling Bros World's Greatest Show Season of 1909. Official Programme (NYPL).

35 The act lasts three seconds, during which Hugo Zacchini learnt to guide his body six feet to the right or left, and shorten the 145-foot trajectory by 9 feet (Bradna 1933: 86).

36 *Clipper*, 6 December 1879: 291.

37 *The Illustrated Sporting and Dramatic News*, 18 July 1877: 447. Also front-page drawing of Zazel's head and shoulders.

38 *The Penny Illustrated Paper*, 13 March 1880: 163; Peacock (1996: 261–2, 299).

39 *The Morning Advertiser*, 2 February 1880: 3.

40 *The Music Hall and Theatre Review*, XX (491) 5 August 1898: 84, 88.

41 London's Aquarium programme, week ending 14 November 1885 (JJBL).

42 Letter, 30 July (circa 1967, based on her age cited in the letter – a reply to a published letter) (PC).

43 F. F. 'Poole's Twentieth Century Novelty. A Chat with Mr Zedora', *The Bristol Magpie*, 24 January 1901: 14.

44 In North America in 1909, Ringling Brothers programme (NYPL). The Tybell Sisters at Adam Forepaugh's in 1910 (Loxton 1997: 73). Flying Human Butterflies were in the New York Hippodrome Season programme 1914–15 (NYPL). In 1921, RBBBC still had the Sisters Silbon as the Human Birds of the Air, but by 1923 they had morphed into butterflies. These acts remained in RBBBC until the 1930s, and Coles Brothers through to the late 1940s.

45 Coles Brothers programme 1949 (NYPL). Cross-dressed Barbette worked in Erford's Whirling Butterfly Sensations (Steegmuller 1986b: 525).

46 *The Truth* (Sydney), 23 May 1897: 2.

47 *Clipper*, 12 September 1896: 448, advertising that 'people stand up and cheer for five minutes'.

48 'Theatre Royal', *The Truth* (Sydney), 2 May 1897: 2.

49 'The Triple', *The Truth* (Sydney), 23 May 1897: 2.
50 'From Cradle to Trapeze', *The New York World*, 6 September 1896, 16.
51 *The Sketch*, 13 February 1895: 146
52 Ibid.
53 (CW and NY). One Ringling poster of this era shows two women flyers mid-air moving towards two female catchers hanging off trapezes, against a bird-like backdrop of sea and coastline (Toll 1976: 69).
54 Circus Boxes (MM).
55 *Adam Forepaugh's Annual Courier* 1881 (ML).

3 Cross-dressing and female muscular drag

1 *The Billboard*, 9 December 1922: 73. Herbert cancelled his 1923 contract with Sells-Floto.
2 See 1881 poster for William Cameron Coup's United Monster Show 1878–82 railroad show (NY).
3 Holburn Royal Amphitheatre and Circus programme, London, 22 July 1871. Part II: Lulu (JJBL). The tricks are described in detail.
4 'As she appeared before their royal highnesses, the Prince and Princess of Wales', 20 February 1871, Royal Amphitheatre (aerialist file, MM).
5 *Clipper*, 22 October 1870: 232; 5 November 1870: 248; 26 November 1870: 267, description of act. A Monsieur De Lave, wire-walker, appears on a poster (Peacock 1996: 50).
6 'Woman as Acrobat', *Clipper*, 30 January 1869: 338. *The Daily Telegraph*, 30 May 1879: 5 – Zoe is also listed as one of Dare's stage names.
7 *Clipper*, 17 May 1879: 63. Sam Kingsley's obituary.
8 Bob Valentino appeared in female costume in 1906 (Aerialists' Scrapbook, volume one, CW). Jack Oliver appeared in a tutu with parasol as a wire-walker (Siegrist-Silbon Scrapbook, CW).
9 *Magazine of Wonders* (microfilm, NYPL).
10 'High-flyers at the Aquarium. The Queen of the Air', *The Sketch*, 13 February 1895: 146. Antonio spoke five languages and wrote in three. *The Music Hall and Theatre Review* XXV (633) 5 April 1901: 215. By 1901 Antonio was working with Fitzgerald's, touring Australia and New Zealand in the Flying Dunbar trio.
11 BMC programme 20 December 1926–22 January 1927 (NYPL).
12 Barbette, also spelt Babette in early BMC programmes, was born Vander (Van der) Clyde at Round Rock, Texas, either in 1899 or December 1904, and died on 5 August 1973 (*The New York Times*, 10 August 1973: 34). Vander went solo and was picked up by the William Morris agency which sent him to Europe in 1921. He performed in London, Paris, Berlin, Hamburg, Copenhagen, Warsaw, Madrid, Barcelona and other places, travelling with 28 trunks and a maid (Steegmuller 1986: 526–7).
13 *The Sydney Morning Herald*, 11 March 1972: 7.
14 Allegedly he was found with a young male in his dressing room at the London Palladium, by producer Val Parnell (Castle 1982: 196–70 (Dolin)). He is also reported to have died of an overdose of tablets on 5 August 1973 (Newley 1981: 5).
15 Sverre Braathen's letters to Luisita Leers, 2 April 1947; 21 May 1949 (BCML).
16 *The Sydney Morning Herald*, 11 March 1972: 7.
17 *The Billboard*, 14 April 1928: 85, 1.
18 RBBBC programme 1930 (microfilm, NYPL). *The White Tops* XXVI (3) 1953: 13. Leers was in Madrid when the Spanish Press called her Luisita. She was born in Wiesbaden, her parental home was Braunschweig, and she also worked in Warsaw. She seems to have had an accident in Valencia.

19 Letter, 3 May 1933 (BCML). Leers corresponded regularly with lawyer Sverre Braathen and his partner, Faye Braathen, a medical centre administrator.
20 Letters, 12 October 1933; 19 December 1933 (BCML).
21 *Sunday Standard-Times*, New Bedford, MA, 2 July 1933: 4.
22 Letter, 3 May 1933, mistakes in original (BCML).
23 Letter, 3 May 1933 (BCML).
24 'House Reviews', *Variety*, 20 March 1935: 16.
25 'House Reviews', *Variety*, 4 December 1935: 14.
26 *Sunday Standard-Times*, New Bedford, MA, 2 July 1933: 4. There is a typed transcript of this article in Braathen's manuscript collection (BCML).
27 Ibid.
28 Letter, 27 September 1936, mistakes in original (BCML).
29 *Sunday Standard-Times*, New Bedford, MA, 2 July 1933: 4.
30 St Leon 1993: 161, 163 and 165 (photographs); Manning-Sanders (1952: 249).
31 Occasionally performers do just slip, for example, from a heel hang (Gaona 1984: 69). Fritzi Bartoni fell doing a one-heel catch, but her 'remarkable physical condition' assisted her recovery (Hallowell 1939: 3).
32 Lillian's biography, if not a full description of her act, is included in most comprehensive circus histories, e.g. Kirk (1972: 49–52).
33 Manuscript Collection, Box 2. 'Circus Talk', volume 1 (BCML).
34 Letter, 23 August 1932 (BCML).
35 Letter, 24 January 1947 (BCML).
36 'R. R. Packing 'Em at Garden', *The Billboard*, 23 April 1932: 30.
37 Letter, 20 April 1934 (BCML).
38 Letter, 24 January 1947, mistakes in original (BCML).
39 *Courier*, Curtis-Gregg Circus 1934: 1 (CW).
40 Letter, 6 November 1946 (BCML). Sverre Braathen writes that Eriksons, who are known to Leers, are performing at RBBBC presented as Swedes although they are from Germany, because they were interned in Sweden during the war (Letter, 6 December 1946, BCML).
41 By April she describes how important the food parcels had become supplementing her monthly food ration (Letter, 31 April 1948, BCML).
42 Leers married Geerhard Glage on 30 August 1952.
43 Letter, 7 April 1934 (BCML).
44 Letter, 23 September 1936 (BCML).

4 Gender competition, camp spectacles and impossible machismo

1 For information on approximately 50 flying troupes working in the first half of the twentieth century see Sturtevant (1932); Couderc (1964a, 1964b, 1964c, 1965); Thétard (1947: volume II, 138–47); Coxe (1980: 156–8); Gossard (1986, 1989a, 1989b, 1994); Adrian (1988). A and M Veress Entertainment currently represent 30 flying troupes and acts using a range of apparatuses, and also see the Internet.
2 *The London Entr'acte*, 19 February 1870: 6. See Thétard for photograph (1947: volume II, 157).
3 See, for example, British Film Institute's Film Index International for about 20 films.
4 For information on Alexander, see Couderc (1964b: 16–17) and Gossard (1994: 160–2). Steve Gossard established that Norma Fox did the aerial work for this film (email, 20 March 2004).
5 The Clarkes remained a feature act for the major circuses in the USA until the 1940s. Ernie was a technically brilliant aerialist and also did a double somersault

with a full pirouette, which is more difficult than a double somersault with a twist action (Couderc 1964a: 16–17).

6 Gossard explains that a Russian catch bar was described as a 'girl's catch bar' (email, 10 June 2004).

7 There were a few female aerialists carrying on the tradition; the Cutanos in Europe with one man and six women seemed to have female catchers, and there was an all-female group, the Five Varias (Coxe 1980: 161).

8 Author's interview, 18 July 2003.

9 Information courtesy of Tim Tegge, who has an extensive Alfredo Codona archive. Alfredo's work on *Variety* is not credited, and he also performed stunts, and with Vera Bruce, in *Tarzan and His Mate* and *Polly of the Circus* (1932), and as himself in *Swing High* (1932) and *Circus Clown* (1934). Alfredo and Vera probably initially did the stunt work for *Tarzan, the Ape-Man* (1932), doubling for Johnny Weissmuller and Maureen O'Sullivan.

10 *Variety* was remade as a talkie called *Salto Mortale* (1931) (also called *Trapeze*), with a further remake in 1935.

11 See, for example, *High Jump* (1958) about an ex-trapezist jewel thief.

12 See Culhane (1990: 195 (Codona's letter)); Beal (1938: 245–55); Cosmopolite (1937–8).

13 See Beal (1938: 114–17). Vera was from a circus family, and was a rider like her mother, Anne. Born in Singapore, Vera lived in an Australian convent until 16, worked in vaudeville, and on a large web of female performers in a 'spider and fly' act at New York Hippodrome, and then with the famous Australian May Wirth's RBBBC riding act before joining the Codonas after 1928 to replace Clara, apparently at Leitzel's suggestion. For information on Vera Bruce's wedding to Alfred Codona in San Antonio, see Wilding (1932: 32). It seems that Vera was asking for over $30,000 in marriage settlement at a time when neither she nor Alfredo was earning a top performer's wage.

14 A photograph for BMC at Olympia programme, 22 December to 25 January 1932–3 (NYPL).

15 Mickey King died on 4 January 2004. Steve Gossard's private collection has interviews and documentation about her career. Also see Beal (1938: 105–7).

16 'Truth is Stranger', *The Sawdust Ring* 3 (7) July–September 1935: 39. Arthur and Antoinette also did 'the double, the double full, the double cutaway, the double with the half twist, fliflus, pirouettes back to the bar' (Culhane 1978: 30). Antoinette left flying with a shoulder injury and for motherhood in 1943, but returned to performing around 1949. Arthur became general manager at RBBBC (Albrecht 1989: 93). Combined personal and professional partnerships are everywhere in aerial and circus work, which does become complicated if relationships end. Antoinette was intermittently aerial director for RBBBC even after her marriage breakup in the 1950s, and Arthur's appointment of his personal partner, Margaret Smith, as aerial director in 1958 (ibid.: 275).

17 *The Billboard*, 2 January 1937: 38, training all-girl flyers. See Gossard about Valentinos (1994: 142); and author's conversation with Steve Gossard, 19 July 2003, about Jane Melzer. Also see *The Billboard*, 4 May 1935: 39; Eileen Harold of Flying Harolds doing a two-and-a-half somersault with a pirouette and a half on the return.

18 Author's interview with Nellie's daughter, Lorraine Maynard, 20 November 2000.

19 RBBBC Programme 1963, photographs of La Toria with well-developed upper-body muscles posing in a one-piece costume, and on web and rings, do not match the accompanying description of a 'beauteous little miss' in the 'Debutantes Ball' (NYPL).

20 One fashion photographic session is framed at the circus and shows a woman on a rope in a sequined bikini (*Harper's Bazaar*, December 1951, no pagination).
21 The aerial work might be attributed to Sally Marlowe (Wapshott 1990: 279), but she was not an aerialist, and Willie Krause also doubled for Lollobrigida on the pedestal (email, Steve Gossard, 8 April 2004).
22 *Health and Strength: The National Physical Fitness Journal* 79 (26), 28 December 1950: 1, and posed cover photograph. Anderson caught Harold Voise with the Flying Harolds, and other flyers with the Concellos, Behees and Artonies. Also see Durant and Durant (1957: 266–9 (photographs)).
23 Clayton replaced Alfredo, and Rose replaced Vera Bruce in the Codonas. The Behees included Ralph Swisher, and toured with Wirth's in 1950.
24 The troupe was Lalo, Raoul, Eduardo and Irma. Ordinary leapers might do an angel, fliflus, 'pike-forward, crab or bird's nest, shoot over dive, cutaway-to-stick, seat jump, passing leap. Principal also does doubles (double full-twister, double to the hocks, double cut-aways) and two-and-a-half' (Ballantine 1955: 8). Also see Couderc (1964c: 17).
25 In the mid-1970s Terry worked in the Flying Terrells with her husband Ron Lemus, Eva Dunlevy and Judy McCardell (née Cavaretta), and also in the Flying Medallions with Barry Mitchell, Maureen Mitchell (née Cavaretta) and Jimmy and Judy Cavaretta (Terry Cavaretta's letter to Steve Gossard, Gossard's private collection). Tragically, Ron Lemus died in an aeroplane accident in 1976, and this changed the composition of the groups. As the Flying Cavarettas, the siblings Kandy, Jimmy, Maureen, Marleen and Terry worked together until 1991, when they retired from Circus Circus. Terry and Jimmy did a double trapeze act at Folies Bergère in Las Vegas, and also worked at the Tropicana. Terry is married to renowned juggler Rejean St Jules and became a mother at 48.
26 *Circus World Championships* 1977 programme: 2.
27 *Guinness Book of Records* 1976, compiler Norris McWhirter, Middlesex: Guinness, 230–1 (action photograph); ibid. 1978: 232 (action photographs). Also see Speaight (1980: 180); and Loxton 1997: 69 (action photograph)).
28 *Southern Sawdust* (49), November 1966: 14. They worked at Ruby Brothers Circus.
29 *Circus World Championships* 1977 programme: 2.
30 Letter, Terry Cavaretta to Steve Gossard, Gossard's private collection.
31 The 1978 World Championship was won by the Flying Oslers, originally from South Africa, with a perfect score of 100, and bare-chested flyer Freddy Weppenaar doing the triple. The 1979 Championship was won by the Mexican Flying Jimenez, and competitors included the Flying Volares from Circus Circus in Reno, USA, with Cathy Fletcher who did triples, and Lisa Hartog and Eva Dunleavy as flyers to their catcher and trainer Billy Woods.
32 Author's conversation with Terry Cavaretta, 10 August 2003.
33 This follows a pattern evident in an empirical study of representational imagery of sportspeople that finds women more highly sexualized in comparison to men doing action (MacClancy 1996: 15 (Dobson)).
34 In 1980 Juan of the Flying Farias, who could do the triple at the age of 9, died in Tucson doing his routine three-and-a-half when his safety harness line got caught and he crashed outside the net. With sad irony, Miguel finally mastered the quadruple in Tucson. Gino with the Farfans broke his neck hitting the catch-bar and the catcher's knee. Then 29-year-old Marguerite Vazquez fell on 20 February 1982 and broke her neck, when a wire of the suspension apparatus, plaited into her hair, failed (Culhane 1990: 318–19). Marguerite Vazquez's two daughters continue performing the act (Loxton 1997: 74). Also for a photograph of female performers in the Farfans, see Meyer (1978: xii).

35 *The Progressive Woman*, January–March 1996: 8–9.
36 Two flyers stood on the platform; first one performer flew to the lower of two catchers who threw him or her to the second upper catcher 10 feet above the first, and who returned the flyer as the second flyer completed the same movements so they passed each other. (North Korean troupes also performed group routines but with casting action during the 1990s.)
37 *The Philadelphia Daily News*, 2 June 1995: 86.
38 Author's interview, 18 July 2003.

5 Androgyny to queer violence: Cirque du Soleil, Archaos and Circus Oz

1 Archaos programme, Sixteenth Biennial Adelaide Festival, March 1990.
2 Interview with Stephanie Barnaud for the author, 22 April 2001.
3 All-female aerial groups in new circus during the 1990s included England's Skinning the Cat and France's Cirque de Barbarie.
4 Viewed by the author, 11 November 1993, Brooklyn Academy of Music.
5 HorsLesMurs, Paris, has information and industry publications like *Arts de la piste*, that list new circus groups in France and elsewhere in Europe.
6 Author's interview with Willy Ramsay, 18 June 2003.
7 The author first viewed *Saltimbanco*®, 17 October 1993, in Washington, DC – the then President Clinton took his daughter, Chelsea, to that show. The author viewed *Mystère*®, 16 August 1995, Las Vegas; *Dralion*™, 31 July 1999, Toronto; *Quidam*®, 5 January 2000, London; *Alegría*®, 18 March 2001, Melbourne; *Varekai*™, 25 July 2003, Chicago; *O*®, 9 August 2003, Las Vegas. The artistic teams and performers' names are listed in programmes.
8 Christie, her sister, trapezist Anna, and their brother, acrobat Brendan, attended Australia's Flying Fruit Fly circus school, and have all worked with Cirque as well as leading Australian new circuses and physical theatres.
9 'The Westernization of the East Goes North', *Spectacle: Quarterly Journal of Circus Arts* 2 (4) 1999: 20–2.
10 Tank acts were presented at London's Royal Aquarium (Munro 1971: 12), and at the Casino de Paris in 1923 (Damase 1962: 106).
11 The author viewed the following shows: 10 September 1998, Melbourne; 17 June 1999, Melbourne; 29 June 2001, Melbourne; 21 June 2003, Melbourne.
12 A sport associated with older people in which heavy, black balls are rolled on grass.
13 Author's interview, 5 May 2000, and Circus Amok shows viewed by video.
14 Author's interview, 23 May 2000, and viewing of productions on video.
15 Some entrepreneurs worked across both entertainment fields, most notably nineteenth-century America's P. T. Barnum moving from dime museum to circus, and in the mid-twentieth century in England, Billy Smart moved from fairground into circus after the Second World War.
16 Consequently, professional performers were denied employment. In a gesture of postmodern nostalgia, theatricalized sideshows with performed freakery returned in the 1990s. RBBBC was again employing little people in 2000.

6 Ecstasy and visceral flesh in motion

1 *Clipper*, 29 May 1869: 63.
2 *The Bristol Magpie*, 26 January 1899: 8.
3 In her qualitative research on people attracted to performing aerial tricks, Hofsess finds that so-called 'risk-takers' are actually searching for mastery and control (1986: 16).

References

Adams, Rachel. (2001) *Sideshow U.S.A. Freaks and the American Cultural Imagination*, Chicago: University of Chicago Press.

Adrian. (1973) *En Piste, les acrobates*, Paris: Bourg-la-Reine.

—— (1988). *Ils donnent des ailes au cirque*, Paris: Paul Adrian.

Albrecht, Ernest J. (1989) *A Ringling by Any Other Name: The Story of John Ringling North and His Circus*, Metuchen, NJ: Scarecrow Press.

—— (1995) *The New American Circus*, Gainesville, FL.: University Press of Florida.

Allen, Robert C. (1991) *Horrible Prettiness*, Chapel Hill: University of North Carolina Press.

Altick, Richard D. (1978) *The Shows of London*, Cambridge, MA: The Belknap Press.

Anderson, Aaron. (1998) 'Kinesthesia in Martial Arts Films: Action in Motion', *Jump Cut*, (42): 1–11, 83.

Archer, William. (1896) *The Theatrical World of 1895*, London: Walter Scott.

Armitstead, Claire. (1995) 'Let's Twist Again', *The Guardian*, 17 January: T10.

Aston, Elaine. (1988) 'Male Impersonation in the Music Hall: The Case of Vesta Tilley', *New Theatre Quarterly*, IV (15): 247–57.

Atkinson, Paul. (1987) 'The Feminist Physique: Physical Education and the Medicalization of Women's Education', in J. J. Mangan and Roberta J. Park (eds), *From Fair Sex to Feminism*, London: Frank Cass: 38–57.

Auguet, Roland. (1974) *Histoire et légende du cirque*, Paris: Flammarion.

Auslander, Philip. (1999) *Liveness*, London: Routledge.

Backer, Noèmia. (2000) 'Reconfiguring Annabella's *Serpentine* and *Butterfly* Dance Films in Early Cinema History', in Simon Popple and Vanessa Toulmin (eds), *Visual Delights*, Trowbridge: Flick Books: 93–104.

Baker, Aaron. (2003) *Contesting Identities: Sports in American Film*, Urbana/Chicago: University of Illinois Press.

Baker, Roger. (1994) *Drag*, NY: New York UP.

Bakhtin, Mikhail. (1968) *Rabelais and His World*, translated by Helene Iswolsky, Cambridge, MA: The MIT Press.

Ballantine, Bill. (1955) 'Sawdust and Spangles', *Sarasota Herald-Tribune*, 7 February: 8.

Balsamo, Anne. (1996) *Technologies of the Gendered Body*, Durham: Duke UP.

Banner, Lois W. (1983) *American Beauty*, NY: Alfred A. Knopf.

Barnes, Djuna. (1961) *Nightwood*, NY: New Directions.

Barnes-McLain, Noreen. (1998) 'Bohemian on Horseback: Adah Isaacs Menken', in Robert A. Schanke and Kim Marra (eds), *Passing Performances*, Ann Arbor: University of Michigan Press: 63–79.

Beal, George B. (1938) *Through the Back Door of the Circus*, Springfield: McLoughlin.

Bean, Jennifer M. (2002) 'Technologies of Early Stardom and the Extraordinary Body', in Bean and Negra (eds), (2002a): 404–43.

Bean, Jennifer M. and Negra, Diane (eds). (2002a) *A Feminist Reader in Early Cinema*, Durham: Duke UP.

—— (2002b) 'Introduction', in Bean and Negra (2002a): 1–26.

Beaumont, Mary. (1899) *Two New Women and Other Stories*, London: James Clarke.

Bederman, Gail. (1995) *Manliness and Civilization*, Chicago: University of Chicago Press.

Behee, Bob. (1947) 'From My Point of View', *Health and Strength*, December: 11.

Blondin. (1862) *His Life and Performances*, edited by Linaeus Banks, London: Routledge, Warne and Routledge.

Boa, Elizabeth. (1987) *The Sexual Circus*, Oxford: Basil Blackwell.

Boscagli, Maurizia. (1996) *Eye on the Flesh*, Boulder: Westview Press.

Bouissac, Paul. (1976a) *Circus and Culture*, Bloomington: Indiana UP.

—— (1976b) 'Circus Performances as Texts: A Matter of Poetic Competence', *Poetics*, 5: 101–18.

Bradley, Marion Zimmer. (1979) *The Catch Trap*, NY: Ballantine Books.

Bradna, Fred, as told to Earl Chapin May. (1933) 'Circus Dare-devils', *Popular Science Monthly*, 123 (2): 23–4, 86.

Bradna, Fred, as told to Hartzell Spence. (1952) *The Big Top: My Forty Years with the Greatest Show on Earth*, NY: Simon and Schuster.

Bratton, J. S. (1992) 'Irrational Dress', in Viv Gardner and Susan Rutherford (eds), *The New Woman and Her Sisters*, Hertfordshire: Harvester Wheatsheaf: 77–91.

Broido, Lucy. (1980) *The Posters of Jules Chéret*, NY: Dover Publications.

Bull, Cynthia Jean Cohen. (1997) 'Sense, Meaning, and Perception in Three Dance Cultures', in Jane C. Desmond (ed.) (1997a): 269–87.

Burgess, Hovey. (1977) *Circus Techniques*, NY: Thomas Y. Cromwell.

Burleigh, Bertha Bennet. (1937) *Circus*, London: Collins.

Burt, Ramsay. (1995) *The Male Dancer*, London: Routledge.

—— (1998) *Alien Bodies*, London: Routledge.

Busby, Roy. (1976) *British Music Hall*, London: Paul Elek.

Butler, Judith. (1990) *Gender Trouble*, NY: Routledge.

Butler, Roland. (1943) 'The Circus of 1943', RBBBC route book, no pagination (NYPL).

Callen, Anthea. (1995) *The Spectacular Body*, New Haven: Yale UP.

Cannon, Judy with Mark St Leon. (1997) *Take A Drum and Beat It: The Astonishing Ashtons 1848–1990s*, Sydney: Tytherleigh Press.

Captain, Gwendolyn. (1991) 'Enter Ladies and Gentlemen of Colour: Gender, Sport, and the Ideal of African American Manhood and Womanhood During the Late Nineteenth and Early Twentieth Centuries', *Journal of Sport History*, 18 (1): 81–102.

Carmeli, Yoram S. (1990) 'Performing the "Real" and "Impossible" in the British Travelling Circus', *Semiotica*, 80 (3/4): 193–220.

—— (1991) 'Performance and Family in the World of British Circus,' *Semiotica*, 85 (3/4): 275–89.

—— (1994) 'Text, Traces, and the Reification of Totality: The Case of Popular Circus Literature', *New Literary History*, 25 (1): 175–205.

—— (1995–6) 'The Invention of Circus and Bourgeois Hegemony: A Glance at British Circus Books', *Journal of Popular Culture*, 29 (1): 213–21.

—— (1996) 'Marginal Body and Bourgeois Cosmology: The British Acrobat in Reference to Sport', *International Journal of Comparative Sociology*, 37 (3–4): 252–73.

——(1997) 'The Sight of Cruelty: The Case of Circus Animal Acts', *Visual Anthropology*, 10: 1–15.

Casarino, Cesare. (1990) 'Fragments on *Wings of Desire* (or, fragmentary representation as historical necessity)', *Social Text* (24): 167–81.

Castle, Charles. (1982) *The Folies Bergère*, London: Methuen.

Catto, Max. (1950) *The Killing Frost*, London: William Heinemann.

Charney, Leo and Schwartz, Vanessa. (1995) 'Introduction', in Leo Charney and Vanessa Schwartz (eds), *Cinema and the Invention of Modern Life*, Berkeley: University of California Press: 1–12.

Chisholm, Ann. (2002) 'Acrobats, Contortionists, and Cute Children: The Promise and Perversity of US Women's Gymnastics', *Signs*, 27 (2): 415–50.

Christopher, James. (1996) 'Chaos Theory', *Time Out*, 15–22 May: 20–1.

Church, Michael. (1996) 'The Rules of Enchantment', *The Independent*, 5 January: 8–9.

Clausen, Connie. (1961) *I Love You Honey, But the Season's Over*, New York: Holt, Rinehart and Winston.

Cleto, Fabio. (1999) 'Introduction', in Fabio Cleto (ed.), *Camp: Queer Aesthetics and the Performing Subject*, Ann Arbor: University of Michigan Press: 1–42.

Codona, Alfredo, as told to Courtney Ryley Cooper. (1930) 'Split Seconds', *The Saturday Evening Post*, 6 December: 12–13, 75–6, 79.

Cohan, Steven. (1997) *Masked Men: Masculinity and the Movies in the Fifties*, Bloomington: Indiana UP.

Collins, Glenn. (1982) 'A Quadruple for the Flying Miguel Vazquez', *The New York Times*, 13 July: C11.

—— (1990) 'Daring the Impossible', *The New York Times Magazine*, 30 December: 10–15, 27, 29, 32, 35.

—— (1994) 'New Yorker's Job: Snagging Hurtling Bodies', *The New York Times*, 22 March: C15, C18.

Conover, Richard E. (1959) 'The Great Forepaugh Show: America's Largest Circus from 1864 to 1894', unpublished pamphlet (TM).

Cooper, Courtney, R. (1931) *Circus Day*, NY: Farrar and Rinehart.

Cosmopolite. (1937–8) 'Alfredo Codona and the Art of the Aerial Acrobat', *The Sawdust Ring*, 15 (Winter): 84–6.

Couderc, Pierre. (1964a) 'Truth or Fiction, Legend or Fact', *Bandwagon*, 8 (2) March–April: 16–19, 24.

—— (1964b) 'Truth or Fiction, Legend or Fact', *Bandwagon*, 8 (3) May–June: 15–18.

—— (1964c) 'Truth or Fiction, Legend or Fact', *Bandwagon*, 8 (4) September–October: 16–18.

—— (1965) 'Fiction or Fact, Truth or Legend', *Bandwagon*, 9 (5) July–August: 24–8.

Cowie, Peter. (1992) *Ingmar Bergman: A Critical Biography*, London: André Deutsch.

Coxe, Antony Hippisley. (1950) 'Death in the Sawdust Ring', *Leader Magazine*, 14 January: 16–17, 38.

—— (1980) *A Seat at the Circus*, Hamden, CN: Archon Books.

—— (undated) 'The Clarkes', Part II, unpublished manuscript for L'Union des historiens du cirque (box 11, TS).

Croft-Cooke, Rupert and Cotes, Peter. (1976) *Circus*, Paris: Albin Michel.

Crossley, Nick. (1994) *The Politics of Subjectivity*, Aldershot: Avebury.

Crowson, Lydia. (1976) 'Cocteau and "Le Numéro Barbette"', *Modern Drama*, 19: 79–87.

Culhane, John. (1978) 'Trapeze: The Quest for the "Impossible" Quadruple Somersault', *The New York Times Magazine*, 19 March: 22–6, 30, 32, 34, 36, 85–6, 88–94.

—— (1990) *The American Circus: An Illustrated History*, NY: Henry Holt.

Daley, Caroline. (2003) *Leisure & Pleasure: Reshaping & Revealing the New Zealand Body 1900–1960*, Auckland: Auckland UP.

Dalle Vacche, Angela. (2002) 'Femininity in Flight: Androgyny and Gynandry in Early Silent Italian Cinema', in Bean and Negra (eds) (2002a): 444–75.

Damase, Jacques. (1962) *Les Folies du Music-Hall: A History of the Music-Hall in Paris from 1914 to the Present Day*, London: Spring Books.

Davis, Janet M. (2002) *The Circus Age*, Chapel Hill: University of North Carolina Press.

Davis, Jim and Emeljanow, Victor. (2001) *Reflecting the Audience: London Theatregoing 1840–1880*, Iowa City: University of Iowa Press.

Davis, Tracy. (1990) 'Sex in Public Places: The Zaeo Aquarium Scandal and the Victorian Moral Majority', *Theatre History Studies* 10: 1–13.

—— (1991) *Actresses as Working Women*, London: Routledge.

Day, Helen. (1992) 'Female Daredevils', in Viv Gardner and Susan Rutherford (eds), *The New Woman and Her Sisters*, Hertfordshire: Harvester Wheatsheaf: 137–57.

de Jongh, Nicolas. (1990) 'French Circus Banned', *The Guardian*, 21 July: 2.

Deleuze, Gilles. (1986) *Cinema 1: The Movement-Image*, translated by Hugh Tomlinson and Barbara Habberjam, Minneapolis: University of Minnesota Press.

de Marly, Diana. (1982) *Costume on the Stage 1600–1940*, London: B. T. Batsford.

Desbonnet. (1911) *Les Rois de la force*, Paris: Libraire Athlétique.

Desmond, Jane C. (ed.). (1997a) *Meaning in Motion*, Durham: Duke UP.

—— (1997b) 'Introduction', in Desmond (ed.) (1997a): 1–25.

—— (1997c) 'Embodying Difference: Issues in Dance and Cultural Studies', in Desmond (ed.) (1997a): 29–54.

Devenney, Robert. (1947) 'Aerial Performers', *Muscle Power*, December: 12–13, 34.

Dijkstra, Bram. (1986) *Idols of Perversity*, NY: Oxford UP.

Disher, Willson M. (1942) *Fairs, Circuses and Music Halls*, London: William Collins.

Doane, Mary Ann. (2002) 'Technology's Body: Cinematic Vision in Modernity', in Bean and Negra (eds), (2002a): 530–51.

Dolan, Jill. (1988) *The Feminist Spectator as Critic*, Ann Arbor: UMI Research Press.

Dolin, Anton. (1938) *Ballet Go Round*, London: Michael Joseph.

Durant, John and Durant, Alice. (1957) *Pictorial History of the American Circus*, South Brunswick, NY: A. S. Barnes.

Dyer, Richard. (1982) 'Don't Look Now – the Male Pin-Up', *Screen*, 23 (3–4): 61–73.

—— (1992) *Only Entertainment*, London: Routledge.

—— (2000) 'Action!', in José Arroyo (ed.), *Action/Spectacle Cinema*, London: BFI Publishing.

Elias, Norbert and Dunning, Eric. (1993) *Quest for Excitement: Sport and Leisure in the Civilizing Process*, Oxford: Blackwell.

Essoe, Gabe. (1972) *Tarzan of the Movies*, Secaucus, NJ: The Citadel Press.

Faber, Marion. (1979) *Angels of Daring: Tightrope Walker and Acrobat in Nietzsche, Kafka, Rilke and Thomas Mann*, Stuttgart: Akademischer Verlag Hans-Dieter Heinz.

Fargo, Franklin. (1926) 'The Man Who Tried 9,000 Times', *Liberty*, 7 August: 47–9.

Fenner, Mildred Sandison and Fenner, Wolcott. (1970) *Circus Lure and Legend*, Englewood Cliffs, NJ: Prentice-Hall.

Ferguson, Harvie. (1990) *The Science of Pleasure*, London: Routledge.

Fields, Sidney. (1963) 'Only Human', *The New York Mirror*, 21 April: 42.

Fitzroy, David. (1996) *Charles Clarke and the Clarkonians*, April, pamphlet (TM).

Fletcher, Sheila. (1987) 'The Making and Breaking of a Female Tradition: Women's Physical Education in England, 1880–1980', in J. A. Mangan and Roberta J. Park (eds), *From Fair Sex to Feminism*, London: Frank Cass: 145–60.

Fogarty, Jim. (2000) *The Wonder of Wirths*, Sydney: JB Books.

Foster, Frank. (1948) *Pink Coats, Spangles and Sawdust*, London: Stanley Paul.

Foster, Susan Leigh. (1997) 'Dancing Bodies', in Desmond (ed.) (1997a): 235–57.

Foucault, Michel. (1979) *Discipline and Punish*, translated by Alan Sheridan. NY: Vintage Books.

—— (1980) *Power/Knowledge: Selected Interviews and Other Writings 1972–1977*, edited by Colin Gordon, Brighton: The Harvester Press.

Fox, Charles Philip and Parkinson, Tom. (1969) *The Circus in America*, Waukesha, WI: Country Beautiful.

Franko, Mark. (1992) 'Where He Danced: Cocteau's Barbette and Ohno's Water Lilies', *PLMA* 107 (3): 594–607.

Frega, Donnalee. (2001) *Women of Illusion*, NY: Palgrave.

Freud, Sigmund. (1986) [1919] 'The Uncanny' , *An Infantile Neurosis and Other Works, Complete Psychological Works*, Volume XVII, edited by James Strachey and Alan Tyson, London: Hogarth Press: 217–53.

Frost, Thomas. (1881) *Circus Life and Circus Celebrities*, London: Chatto and Windus.

Frueh, Joanna, Fierstein, Laurie, and Stein, Judith. (2000) *Picturing the Modern Amazon*, NY: Rizzoli International Publications.

Gaines, Jane. (1990) 'Introduction', in Jane Gaines and Charlotte Herzog (eds), *Fabrications: Costume and the Female Body*, NY: Routledge: 1–27.

Gallagher, Jim. (1982) 'Flying High: The Magic of Miguel Vazquez', *Chicago Tribune Magazine*, 5 December: 20, 22–4, 26, 32, 34, 36, 38, 40.

Gänzl, Kurt. (2002) *Lydia Thompson: Queen of Burlesque*, NY: Routledge.

Gaona, Tito, with Harry L. Graham. (1984) *Born to Fly*, Los Angeles: Wild Rose.

Garb, Tamar. (1998) *Bodies of Modernity*, London: Thames and Hudson.

Gardner, Viv. (2000) 'The Invisible Spectatrice: Gender, Geography and Theatrical Space', in Maggie Gale and Viv Gardner (eds), *Women, Theatre and Performance*, Manchester: Manchester UP: 25–45.

Garner, Stanton B. (1994) *Bodied Spaces*, Ithaca: Cornell UP.

Gay, Peter. (1984) *The Bourgeois Experience*, volume I, Oxford: Oxford UP.

—— (1993) *The Cultivation of Hatred*, NY: W. W. Norton.

Gibbs-Smith, Charles Harvard. (1985) *Aviation: An Historical Survey*, London: Her Majesty's Stationery Office.

Gilbert, Douglas. (1968) *American Vaudeville*, NY: Dover Publications.

Gledhill, Christine and Williams, Linda (eds). (2000) *Reinventing Film Studies*, London: Arnold.

Goodall, Jane. (2002) *Performance and Evolution in the Age of Darwin*, London: Routledge.

Gossard, Steve. (1986) 'Flying Wards', *Bandwagon*, 30 (6) November–December: 5–20.

—— (1989a) 'The Flying Thrillers', *Bandwagon*, 33 (4) July–August: 16–25.

—— (1989b) 'Walt Graybeal's Bloomington', *Bandwagon*, 33 (6) November–December: 35–41.

—— (1990) 'Frank Gardner and the Great Leapers,' *Bandwagon*, 34 (4) July–August: 12–25.

—— (1994) *A Reckless Era of Aerial Performance, the Evolution of the Trapeze*. Manuscript Publication (obtained c/- ML).

—— (2003) 'A Conversation With Mickey King', *Bandwagon*, 47 (2) March–April: 27–30.

Gossard, Steve and Valentine, Cherie. (1987) 'The Valentine Family of Flyers', *Bandwagon*, 31 (6) November–December: 30–47.

Graves, Charles. (1935) *The Price of Pleasure*, London: Ivor Nicholson and Watson.

Greenwood, Isaac J. (1898) *The Circus: Its Origins and Growth Prior to 1835*, NY: The Dunlop Society.

Grosz, Elizabeth. (1994) *Volatile Bodies*, Sydney: Allen and Unwin.

Gundle, Stephen. (2002) 'Hollywood Glamour and Mass Consumption in Postwar Italy', in Rudy Koshar (ed.), *Histories of Leisure*, Oxford: Berg: 337–59.

Gunning, Tom. (1989) 'An Aesthetic of Astonishment', *Art & Text* 34 (Spring): 31–45.

—— (1995) 'Tracing the Individual Body: Photography, Detectives, and Early Cinema', in Leo Charney and Vanessa Schwartz (eds), *Cinema and the Invention of Modern Life*, Berkeley: University of California Press: 15–45.

Haber, Honi Fern. (1996) 'Foucault Pumped: Body Politics and the Muscled Woman', in Susan J. Hekman (ed.), *Feminist Interpretations of Michel Foucault*, Pennsylvania: The Pennsylvania State UP: 137–56.

Halberstam, Judith. (1998) *Female Masculinity*, Durham, NC: Duke UP.

Hallowell, Henry C. (1939) 'A Lovely Artiste Who Wouldn't Give Up', *The White Tops*, 12 (10–11): 1.

Handelman, Don. (1991) 'Symbolic Types, the Body and Circus', *Semiotica*, 85 (3/4): 205–25.

Hanlon-Lees. (1879/1995) *Mémoires et pantomimes des Frères Hanlon-Lees*, Paris: Reverchon et Vollet.

Hardcastle, Valerie Gray. (1999) *The Myth of Pain*, Cambridge, MA: The MIT Press.

Hargreaves, Jennifer A. (1985) '"Playing Like Gentlemen While Behaving Like Ladies": Contradictory Features of the Formative Years of Women's Sport', *The British Journal of Sports History*, 2 (1): 40–52.

—— (1986) 'Where's the Virtue? Where's the Grace? A Discussion of the Social Production of Gender Relations in and through Sport', *Theory, Culture and Society*, 3 (1): 109–21.

Hart, Clive. (1985) *The Prehistory of Flight*, Berkeley: University of California Press.

Hewitt, John. (2000) 'Poster nasties: censorship and the Victorian theatre poster', in Simon Popple and Vanessa Toulmin (eds), *Visual Delights*, Trowbridge: Flick Books: 154–69.

Higham, Charles. (1973) *Cecil B. DeMille*, NY: Da Capo Press.

Hillman, David Asaf. (1996) 'Hamlet, Nietzsche, and Visceral Knowledge', in Michael O'Donovan-Anderson (ed.), *The Incorporated Self*, Lanham, MD: Rowman and Little-field Publishers: 93–110.

—— (1997) 'Visceral Knowledge', in David Hillman and Carla Mazzio (eds), *The Body in Parts*, NY: Routledge: 81–105.

Hobsbawm, Eric. (1983) 'Introduction: Inventing Traditions', in Eric Hobsbawm and Terence Ranger (eds), *The Invention of Tradition*, Cambridge: Cambridge UP: 1–14.

Hodge, Alison. (2000) *Twentieth Century Actor Training*, London: Routledge.

Hofsess, Lisa. (1986) 'Those Daring Young Men (and Women) on the Flying Trapeze: Impetuous Folly or Calculated Mastery?', *The Association for the Anthropological Study of Play Newsletter*, 12 (2): 14–17.

—— (1987–8) 'A Somatic View of Flying', *Somatics Magazine. Journal of the Bodily Arts and Sciences*, 6 (3): 43–7.

Holland, Charlie. (1998) *Strange Feats and Clever Turns*, London: Holland and Palmer.

Holland, Wendy. (1999) 'Reimagining Aboriginality in the Circus Space', *Journal of Popular Culture* 33 (1): 91–104.

Hollingshead, John. (1895) *My Lifetime*, volume I, London: Sampson Low, Marston.

Holmlund, Chris. (1997) 'Visible Difference and Flex Appeal: The Body, Sex, Sexuality, and Race in the "Pumping Iron 'Films'"', in Aaron Baker and Todd Boyd (eds), *Out of Bounds*, Bloomington: Indiana UP: 145–60.

Howes, David (ed.). (1991) *The Varieties of Sensory Experience*, Toronto: University of Toronto Press.

Hubler, Richard. (1967) *The Cristianis*, London: Jarrolds.

Hunt, Leon. (1993) 'What are Big Boys Made Of? *Spartacus, El Cid* and the Male Epic', in Kirkham and Thumim (eds) (1993a): 65–83.

Ian, Marcia. (1995) 'How Do You Wear the Body? Bodybuilding and the Sublimity of Drag', in Monica Dorenkamp and Richard Henke (eds), *Negotiating Lesbian and Gay Subjects*, NY: Routledge.

Jackson, Arnold. (1937) 'Under the Big Top', *Los Angeles Times Sunday Magazine*, 7 March: 4–5.

Jamieson, David and Davidson, Sandy. (1980) *The Love of Circus*, London: Octopus Books.

Jann, Rosemary. (1996) 'Darwin and the Anthropologists', in Andrew Miller and James Eli Adams (eds), *Sexualities in Victorian Britain*, Bloomington: Indiana UP.

Jeffords, Susan. (1994) *Hard Bodies*, New Brunswick, NJ: Rutgers UP.

Johnson, William. (1974) 'The World's Greatest: The Sensational Tito Gaona', *Sports Illustrated*, 8 April: 100–4, 107–8, 110, 112.

Jones, Amelia. (1998) *Body Art/Performing the Subject*, Minneapolis: University of Minnesota Press.

Kelley, Francis Beverly. (1931) 'The Land of Sawdust and Spangles', *The National Geographic Magazine* LX (October): 463–516.

Kelly, Veronica. (1996) 'Female and Juvenile Meanings in Late Nineteenth-Century Australian Popular Theatre', in Ken Stewart (ed.), *The 1890s*, Brisbane: University of Queensland Press: 109–27.

Kenward, Edith. (1902) 'Notes From Paris', *Music Hall and Theatre Review*, 21 November: 339.

Kibler, Alison M. (1999) *Rank Ladies*, Chapel Hill: University of North Carolina Press.

Kirk, Rhina. (1972) *Circus Heroes and Heroines*, USA: Hammond.

Kirkham, Pat and Thumim, Janet (eds). (1993a) *You Tarzan: Masculinity, Movies and Men*, London: Lawrence and Wishart.

—— (1993b) 'You Tarzan', in Kirkham and Thumim (eds) (1993a): 11–26.

—— (eds). (1995a) *Me Jane: Masculinity, Movies and Women*, NY: St Martin's Press.

—— (1995b) 'Me Jane', in Kirkham and Thumim (eds) (1995a): 11–35.

Kober, A. H. (1928) *Circus Nights and Circus Days*, translated by C. W. Sykes, London: Sampson Low, Marston.

Kolker, Robert Phillip and Beicken, Peter. (1993) *The Films of Wim Wenders*, Cambridge: Cambridge UP.

Koritz, Amy. (1995) *Gendering Bodies/Performing Art*, Ann Arbor: University of Michigan Press.

Kuhn, Annette. (1988) 'The Body and Cinema: Some Problems for Feminism', in Susan Sheridan (ed.), *Grafts*, London: Verso: 11–23.

Kwint, Marius. (2002) 'The Circus and Nature in Late Georgian England', in Rudy Koshar (ed.), *Histories of Leisure*, Oxford: Berg: 45–60.

Lancaster, Jane. (1994) '"I could easily have been an acrobat": Charlotte Perkins Gilman and the Providence Ladies' Sanitary Gymnasium 1881–1884', *ATQ*, 8 (1): 33–52.

Landay, Lori. (2002) 'The Flapper Film: Comedy, Dance and Jazz Age Kinaesthetics', in Bean and Negra (eds) (2002a): 221–48.

Lartigue, Pierre. (1980) *La Course aux trapèzes*, Toulouse: Presse de la Société.

Laurie, Joe. (1953) *Vaudeville*, NY: Henry Holt.

Leitzel, Lillian, as told to Paul Brown. (1932) 'Circus Women', *Circus Scrap Book* (11): 30–42 (ML).

Léotard. (1860) *Mémoires de Léotard*, Paris: Simon Bacon et Cie.

Le Roux, Hugues and Garnier, Jules (illustrator). (1890) *Acrobats and Mountebanks*, translated by A. P. Morton, London: Chapman and Hall.

Leslie, Peter. (1973) *A Hard Act to Follow: A Music Hall Review*, NY: Paddington Press.

Liebovitz, David. (1946) *The Canvas Sky*, NY: Harcourt, Brace and Co.

Lindsay, Cecile. (1996) 'Bodybuilding: A Postmodern Freak Show', in Thomson (ed.) (1996a): 356–67.

Little, Judy. (1991) 'Humoring the Sentence: Women's Dialogic Comedy', in June Sochen (ed.), *Women's Comic Visions*, Detroit: Wayne State UP: 19–32.

Little, W. Kenneth. (1991) 'The Rhetoric of Romance and the Simulation of Tradition in Circus Clown Performance', *Semiotica*, 85 (3/4): 227–55.

—— (1995–6) 'Surveilling Cirque Archaos: Transgression and the Spaces of Power in Popular Entertainment', *Journal of Popular Culture*, 29 (1): 15–27.

Low, Ernest W. (1895) 'Acrobats: And How They are Trained', *Strand Magazine*: 730–5.

Loxton, Howard. (1997) *The Golden Age of the Circus*, NY: Smithmark.

MacClancy, Jeremy. (1996) 'Sport, Identity and Ethnicity', in Jeremy MacClancy, *Sport, Identity and Ethnicity*, Oxford: Berg: 1–20.

McCrone, Kathleen E. (1988) *Sport and the Physical Emancipation of English Women 1870–1914*, London: Routledge.

McGill, Stewart. (1999) 'Archaos Joins the Undead in the UK', *International Spectacle*, 2 (3): 34–5.

MacGregor-Morris, Pamela. (1960) *Sawdust and Spotlight*, London: H. F. and G. Witherby.

McKinven, John A. (1998) *The Hanlon Brothers*, Glenwood, IL.: David Meyer Magic Books.

—— (2000) *Stage Flying*, Glenwood, IL.: David Meyer Magic Books.

McMahan, Alison. (2000) 'The quest for motion: moving pictures and flight', in Simon Popple and Vanessa Toulmin (eds), *Visual Delights*, Trowbridge: Flick Books: 181–93.

McMullen, Roy. (1985) *Degas: His Life, Times and Work*, London: Secker and Warburg.

McWhirter, Ross and McWhirter, Norris. (1972–1983) *Guiness Book of Records*, editions 19–31, Middlesex: Guiness Books.

Maguire, Joe. (1986) 'Images of Manliness and Competing Ways of Living in Late Victorian and Edwardian Britain', *The British Journal of Sports History*, 3 (3): 265–87.

Maleval, Martine. (2002) 'An Epic of New Circus', translated by Jane Mullett, *Australasian Drama Studies* (41): 63–76.

Mander, Raymond and Mitchenson, Joe. (1974) *British Music Hall*, London: Gentry Books.

Mangan, J. A. (1996) '"Muscular, Militaristic and Manly": The British Middle-Class Hero as Moral Messenger', *International Journal of the History of Sport*, 13 (1) March: 28–47.

Mankowitz, Wolf. (1982) *Mazeppa*, NY: Stein and Day.

Manning, Susan A. (1993) *Ecstasy and the Demon*, Berkeley: University of California Press.

Manning-Sanders, Ruth. (1952) *The English Circus*, London: Werner Laurie.

Man Ray. (1980) *Le Numéro Barbette*, Paris: Jacques Damase.

Marey, Étienne-Jules. (1995/1891) 'La Chronophotographie', in Laurent Mannoni, Donata Pesenti Campagnoni and David Robinson (eds), *Light and Movement*, Gemona, Italy: Le Giornate del Cinema Muto.

May, Earl Chapin. (1963) *The Circus From Rome to Ringling*, NY: Dover Publications.

Merleau-Ponty, Maurice. (1995) *The Visible and the Invisible*, translated by Alphonso Lingis, Evanston: Northwestern UP.

—— (1996) *Phenomenology of Perception*, translated by Colin Smith, London: Routledge.

Meyer, Charles R. (1978) *How to Be an Acrobat*, NY: David McKay.

Miller, Toby. (2001) *Sportsex*, Philadelphia: Temple UP.

Mills, Bernard. (1933) 'Heroines of the Circus', *Bristol Evening World*, 17 January: 8.

—— (1954) 'The Greatest Act I Ever Saw', *The Tatler and Bystander*, 18 November: 37.

Mills, Bertram. (1933) 'Women's Courage in Circus Ring', *The Yorkshire Weekly Post Illustrated*, 30 December: 7.

Moffett, Cleveland. (1901a) *Music Hall and Theatre Review*, XXV (633) 5 April: 213 (*New York Herald*).

—— (1901b; 2nd edn, 1926) *Careers of Danger and Daring*, NY: D. Appleton-Century.

Moore, F. Michael. (1994) *Drag! Male and Female Impersonators on Stage, Screen and Television*, Jefferson, NC: McFarland Publishers.

Morris, Ron. (1976) *Wallenda. A Biography of Karl Wallenda*, Chatham, NY: Sagarin Press.

Morton, Walt. (1993) 'Tracking the Sign of Tarzan: Trans-Media Representation of a Pop-Culture Icon', in Kirkham and Thumim (eds) (1993a): 106–25.

Moss, Robert F. (1987) *The Films of Carol Reed*, London: Macmillan.

Mosse, George L. (1985) *Nationalism and Sexuality*, NY: Howard Fertig.

Mrozek, Donald, J. (1983) *Sport and American Mentality, 1880–1910*, Knoxville: University of Tennessee Press.

Mullett, Jane. (forthcoming) 'Circus Alternatives: The Development of "New Circus" in Australia, Canada, the USA and France', dissertation, La Trobe University.

Munby, Arthur J. (1972) *Man of Two Worlds: The Life and Diaries of Arthur J. Munby 1828–1910*, edited by Derek Hudson, London: John Murray.

Munro, John M. (1971) *The Royal Aquarium: Failure of a Victorian Compromise*, Beirut: American University of Beirut.

Neale, Steve. (1983) 'Masculinity as Spectacle', *Screen*, 24 (6): 2–16.

Newley, Patrick. (1981) 'The Amazing Barbette', *Call Boy*, Winter: 5.

Newsinger, John. (1987) 'Reader, He Rescued Her: Women in Tarzan Stories', *Foundation: The Review of Science Fiction*, 39 (Spring): 41–9.

Noble, Clyde V. (1950) 'Bloomington, Illinois, The Home of the Man on the Flying Trapeze', *The White Tops*, 23 (9–10): 5–6, 12–13.

Odell, George C. (1936–8) *Annals of the New York Stage*, volume VIII 1865–70; volume IX 1870–5; volume X 1875–9; NY: Columbia UP.

O'Shea, John Augustus. (1892) *Roundabout Recollections*, volume I, London: Ward and Downey.

Park, Roberta J. (1987) 'Sport, Gender and Society in a Transatlantic Victorian Perspective', in J. A. Mangan and Roberta J. Park (eds), *From Fair Sex to Feminism*, London: Frank Cass: 58–93.

Peacock, Shane. (1996) *The Great Farini*, Toronto: Penguin Books.

Peiss, Kathy. (1986) *Cheap Amusements: Working Women and Leisure in Turn-of-the-Century New York*, Philadelphia: Temple UP.

Petit, Philippe. (1991) *Funambule*, Paris: Albin Michel.

Pfisterer, Susan and Pickett, Carolyn. (1999) *Playing with Ideas*, Sydney: Currency.

Phelan, Peggy. (1993) *Unmarked*, London: Routledge.

Pilcher, Velona. (1930) 'A Star Turn', *Theatre Arts Monthly*, XIV (12) December: 1033–6.

Pollock, Griselda. (1995) 'Empire, Identity and Place: Masculinities in *Greystoke: The Legend of Tarzan*', in Kirkham and Thumim (eds) (1995): 128–47.

Pond, Irving K. (1937) *Big Top Rhythms*, Chicago: Willett, Clark.

Porter, Amy. (1946) 'The Daring Old Man', *Collier's*, 13 July; 16, 26.

Powell, Kerry. (1997) *Women and Victorian Theatre*, Cambridge: Cambridge UP.

Presner, Todd Samuel. (2003) '"Clear Heads, Solid Stomachs, and Hard Muscles": Max Nordau and the Aesthetics of Jewish Regeneration', *Modernism/Modernity*, 10 (2): 269–96.

Rendle, T. McDonald. (1919) *Swings and Roundabouts*, London: Chapman and Hall.

Reynolds, Ruth. (1946) 'Death Stalked the Circus Lovers', *National Police Gazette*, May: 6, 14.

Ritter, Naomi. (1989a) 'Art and Androgyny: The Aerialist', in *Studies in Twentieth Century Literature*, 13 (2): 173–93.

—— (1989b) *Art as Spectacle*, Columbia: University of Missouri Press.

Rosenberg, George J. (1962) 'Daring Dames', *The New York Mirror*, 1 April: 8, 9.

Rotundo, E. Anthony. (1993) *American Manhood*, NY: Basic Books.

Rubinstein, Ruth P. (1995) *Dress Codes*, Boulder: Westview Press.

Russell, Charles and Depping, Guillaume. (1871) *Wonders of Bodily Strength and Skill in All Ages and Countries*, translated and enlarged from the French by Charles Russell, NY: Charles Scribner.

Russo, Mary. (1994) *The Female Grotesque*, NY: Routledge.

St Leon, Mark. (1983) *Spangles and Sawdust: The Circus in Australia*, Melbourne: Greenhouse Publications.

—— (1993) *The Wizard of the Wire: The Story of Con Colleano*, Canberra: Aboriginal Studies Press.

—— (1999) 'Yankee Circus to the Fabled Land: The Australian–American Circus Connection', *Journal of Popular Culture*, 33 (1): 77–89.

Scarry, Elaine. (1985) *The Body in Pain: The Making and Unmaking of the World*, NY: Oxford University Press.

Scott, W. S. (1948) *Bygone Pleasures of London*, London: Marsland Publications.

Seeling, Charlotte. (2000) *Fashion*, Cologne: Könemann.

Senelick, Laurence. (1993) 'Boys and Girls Together', in Lesley Ferris (ed.), *Crossing the Stage*, London: Routledge: 80–95.

—— (2000) *The Changing Room*, London: Routledge.

Shapiro, Dean. (1989) *Blondin*, St Catherines, Ontario: Vanwell Publishing.

Shaviro, Steven. (1993) *The Cinematic Body*, Minneapolis: University of Minnesota Press.

Shields, Stephanie A. (2002) *Speaking From the Heart: Gender and the Social Meaning of Emotion*, Cambridge: CUP.

Singer, Ben. (1995) 'Modernity, Hyperstimulus, and the Rise of Popular Sensationalism', in Leo Charney and Vanessa Schwartz (eds), *Cinema and the Invention of Modern Life*, Berkeley: University of California Press: 72–99.

Slout, William L. (1998a) *Olympians of the Sawdust Circle*, San Bernardino, CA.: The Borgo Press.

—— (1998b) 'The Recycling of the Dan Rice Paris Pavilion Circus', *Bandwagon* 42 (4) July–August: 13–21.

Smith-Rosenberg, Carroll. (1985) *Disorderly Conduct*, NY: Oxford UP.

Sobchack, Vivian. (1992) *The Address of the Eye: A Phenomenology of Film Experience*, Princeton: Princeton UP.

Speaight, George. (1980) *A History of the Circus*, London: The Tantivy Press.

Spencer, Charles. (1990) 'Bring on the Performing Elephants', *The Daily Telegraph*, 2 August 1990: 14.

S. R. (1891) *The Life of Zaeo. Diva Dell' Aria and the Story of the Vigilance Persecution*, London: Universal Press Agency.

Staiger, Janet. (1995) *Bad Women*, Minneapolis: University of Minnesota Press.

Steedman, Carolyn. (1995) *Strange Dislocations*, London: Virago Press.

Steegmuller, Francis. (1986a) *Cocteau*, Boston: Nonpareil Books.

—— (1986b) 'A Visit to Barbette, 1966', in Steegmuller (1986a) 523–9.

Stewart, Paul. (1999) 'Birthday Bash, A Hometown Treat', *The Sunday Herald-Sun*, 20 June: O84.

Stocking, George W. (1987) *Victorian Anthropology*, NY: The Free Press.

Stoddart, Helen. (2000) *Rings of Desire: Circus History and Representation*, Manchester: Manchester UP.

Stokes, John. (1989) *In the Nineties*, NY: Harvester Wheatsheaf.

Stoller, Paul. (1989) *The Taste of Ethnographic Things*, Philadelphia: University of Pennsylvania Press.

Strong, A. A. (1898) *Dramatic and Musical Law*, London: The Era Publishing Office.

Studlar, Gaylyn. (1996) *This Mad Masquerade*, NY: Columbia University Press.

Sturtevant, C. G. (1932) 'The Flying Act and Its Techniques', *The White Tops*, 6 (1) May: 4.

—— (1938) 'The Clarke Family', *The White Tops*, 12 (2–3) December–January: 3–5, 12.

Sussman, Mark. (1998) 'A Queer Circus: Amok in New York', in Jan Cohen-Cruz (ed.), *Radical Street Performance*, London: Routledge.

Tait, Peta. (1994) *Converging Realities: Feminism in Australian Theatre*, Sydney: Currency Press.

—— (1996a) 'Feminine Free Fall: A Fantasy of Freedom', *Theatre Journal*, 48 (1): 27–34.

—— (1996b) 'Devouring Lesbian Bodies: Aerial Desire in Club Swing's *Appetite*', *Theatre-Forum* (9): 4–11.

—— (2000) 'Fleshed, Muscular Phenomenologies Across Sexed and Queer Circus Bodies', in Peta Tait (ed.), *Body Show/s: Australian Viewings of Live Performance*, Amsterdam: Rodopi: 60–78.

—— (2001) 'Queer Circus Bodies in Rock 'n' Roll Circus' *The Dark* and Club Swing's *Razor Baby*', in Marc Maufort and Franca Bellarsi (eds), *Siting the Other: Re-visions of Marginality in Australian and English-Canadian Drama*, Brussels: Peter Lang: 115–25.

—— (2002) *Performing Emotions: Gender, Bodies, Spaces, in Chekhov's Drama and Stanislavski's Theatre*, Aldershot: Ashgate, 2002.

—— (2003a) '"The Australian Marvels": Wire-walkers Ella Zuila and George Loyal, and Geographies of Aerial Gender Body Identity', in Elizabeth Schafer and Susan Bradley Smith (eds), *Playing Australia*, Amsterdam: Rodopi: 80–92.

—— (2003b) 'Unnatural Bodies from Violent and Queer Acts in Australian Physical Theatre', *Australasian Drama Studies* (41): 3–14.

—— (2004) 'Circus Oz Larrikinism: Good Gender Sport?' *Contemporary Theatre Review*, 14 (3): 77–85.

—— (2005) 'Viewing Deadly Targets for Feminine Identity: Alar, the Human Arrow', in Simon Popple and Vanessa Toulman (eds), *Visual Delights 2: Audience and Reception*, London: John Libbey Publishing.

Tasker, Yvonne. (1993) *Spectacular Bodies*, London: Comedia, Routledge.

Taylor, Rogan P. (1985) *The Death and Resurrection Show*, London: Blond.

Thétard, Henry. (1947) *La Merveilleuse Histoire du cirque*, volumes I and II Paris: Prisma.

Thomas, Tony and Terry, Jim, with Berkeley, Busby. (1973) *The Busby Berkeley Book*, London: Thames and Hudson.

Thomson, Helen, (2002) 'Circus Oz Still Takes Breath Away', *The Age* (Melbourne), 22 June: 18.

Thomson, Rosemarie Garland (ed.). (1996a) *Freakery*, NY: NY UP.

—— (1996b) 'Introduction: From Wonder to Error – A Genealogy of Freak Discourse in Modernity', in Thomson (ed.) (1996a): 1–19.

Todd, Jan. (1998) *Physical Culture and the Body Beautiful*, Georgia: Mercer UP.

Toepfer, Karl. (1999) 'Twisted Bodies', *Drama Review*, 43 (1): 104–36.

Toll, Robert C. (1976) *On With the Show*, NY: Oxford UP.

Toole-Stott, Raymond. (1935) 'That Daring Young Girl on the Flying Trapeze', *Sawdust Ring*, January–March: 8–10.

—— (1958–71) *Circus and Allied Arts, A World Bibliography 1500–1970*, volumes I–IV, Derby: Harpur and Sons. Volume V in manuscript publication.

Towsen, John H. (1976) *Clowns*, NY: Hawthorn Books.

Troy, Nancy J. (2003) *Couture Culture*, Cambridge, MA: MIT Press.

Tucker, Herbert F. (1996) 'When the Soul Had Hips . . .', in Andrew Miller and James Eli Adams (eds), *Sexualities in Victorian Britain*, Bloomington: Indiana UP: 157–86.

Turner, John. (1995–2000) *Victorian Arena: The Performers. A Dictionary of British Circus Biography*, volumes I and II, Formby: Lingdales Press.

Ueberhorst, Horst. (1979) 'Jahn's Historical Significance', *Canadian Journal of History of Sport and Physical Education*, 10 (1): 7–14.

Valdez, Sarah. (2000) 'Daredevil Drama', *Art in America*, 88 (2): 51.

Verney, Peter. (1978) *Here Comes the Circus*, NY: Paddington Press.

Vesque, Marthe and Vesque, Juliette. (1977) *Le Cirque en images*, Paris: G. P. Maisonneuve et Larose.

Wapshott, Nicholas. (1990) *The Man Between: A Biography of Carol Reed*, London: Chatto and Windus.

Waring, Peter. (1948) 'Circus Novelties', *Leader Magazine*, 25 December: 15–17.

Weber, Bruce. (1998) 'Holding their Breath as the Curtain Rises', *The New York Times*, 15 October: 1–2.

Whannel, Garry. (1993) 'No Room For Uncertainty: Gridiron Masculinity in *North Dallas Forty*', in Kirkham and Thumim (eds) (1993a): 200–11.

Whissel, Kristen. (2002) 'The Gender of Empire: American Modernity, Masculinity and Edison's War Actualities', in Bean and Negra (eds) (2002a): 140–65.

Whiteley, Henry, with Allen Alexander. (1981) *Memories of Circus, Variety, etc., As I Knew It*, edited by George Speaight, London: The Society for Theatre Research.

Wilding, Harry. (1932) 'Circusdom', *The World's Fair*, 19 November: 32.

Wilkinson, Peter. (1990) 'Clowns from Hell', *Special Report: Personalities*, May–July, Knoxville: Whittle Communications: 48, 51.

Williams, Linda (ed.). (1995) *Viewing Positions: Ways of Seeing Film*, New Brunswick, NJ: Rutgers UP.

—— (1999) *Hard Core: Power, Pleasure, and the 'Frenzy of the Visible'*, Berkeley: University of California Press.

Williams, Simon J. and Bendelow, Gillian. (1998) *The Lived Body*, London: Routledge.

Wills, Gary. (1997) *John Wayne's America*, NY: Simon and Schuster.

Wilmeth, Don B. (1982) *Variety Entertainment and Outdoor Amusements*, Westport: Greenwood Press.

Wilson, Ame. (2002) 'Cirque du Soleil Reimagines the Circus', dissertation, University of Oregon.

Winter, Marian Hannah. (1964) *The Theatre of Marvels*, translated by Charles Meldon, NY: Benjamin Blom.

Yount, Sylvia (ed.). (1999) *Maxfield Parrish 1870–1966*, NY: Harry N. Abrams.

Index

Made in the USA
Las Vegas, NV
05 March 2022

45097737R00111